The New Gourmet Light

Praise for previous editions:

"Greer Underwood wrote *Gourmet Light* not as a weight-loss manual
but as a collection of techniques and recipes aimed at *prevention*
of weight gain for lovers of fine food."
—*Woman's Day*

"[The recipes] call for French cooking techniques but are 'lightened'
with special cooking methods that cut in half the calorie content of
traditional gourmet meals."
—*Tufts University Diet & Nutrition Letter*

"At last—a book that shows how to take a basic recipe and cut down its calories
by reducing fattening ingredients without totally changing its taste."
—*ALA Booklist*

"For lots more tips and recipes on cooking leaner, we like
Greer Underwood's *Gourmet Light*."
—*Mademoiselle*

"A guide to cutting the calories without cutting the good taste. . . .
The food is lighter, but definitely not short on taste."
—*Richmond* (VA) *Times-Dispatch*

*Winner of the Duncan Hines / IACP 1985 Best Cookbook of the Year award
in the special diet catagory*

THE NEW GOURMET LIGHT

Low-fat Recipes for the Health-Conscious Cook

THIRD EDITION

BY GREER UNDERWOOD

ILLUSTRATED BY FRANK WESTERBERG

The Globe Pequot Press

OLD SAYBROOK, CONNECTICUT

Nutrition analysis by Nutrition and Diet Services, Portland, Oregon
Cover and text design by Nancy Freeborn
Cover photo by Zeva Oelbaum

Library of Congress Cataloging-in-Publication Data

Underwood, Greer.
      The new gourmet light: low-fat recipes for the health-conscious
   cook /by Greer Underwood ; illustrated by Frank Westerberg.—3rd
   ed.
            p. cm.
      Includes index.
      ISBN 0-7627-0322-9
      1. Reducing diets—recipes.   I. Title.
   RM222.2.U543   1998
   641.5'635—dc21   98-30910
                                                         CIP

Manufactured in the United States of America
Third Edition/First Printing

Contents

Acknowledgments

This book is hardly the work of a single person, despite the credit on the cover. The know-how of a lot of people is bound between the covers; were it not for them, the book would be fraught with inconsistencies. Tidier minds than mine have labored over this collection of recipes to ensure that titles are the same throughout, directions are clear, and countless other ambiguities have been clarified. Since I couldn't achieve this by myself, it amazes me that other people were able to see into my brain, decipher what I meant, and know how to say it so that the reader could understand it as well. My thanks to Roberta Winston and Liz Taylor who put long, hard hours into combing these pages for such snags and tangles. Thanks, too, to those who cooked many of these recipes and offered suggestions for revision. To Connie Chapin, Jay Sadlon, Bernice Hawkins, and Denise Yocum—thanks for the cooking and tasting.

INTRODUCTION

The Health-Conscious Cook

These are exercise-crazed yet food-happy times. Never have so many Americans panted and pumped their way to visions of physical perfection. And never have so many been interested in food and its paraphernalia—an irony peculiar to this athletic-shoe era. The culinary consciousness of the last two decades, like the national obsession with exercise, continues to grow. The challenge of the times is to enjoy the one without compromising the other.

Fitness is more than physical; it's a healthy psyche as well as a strong body. It's a vitality of body and spirit that can't be nurtured on an inadequate diet. One too rich in calories and fats or too poor in nutrients defeats all that hard work. As eaters one and all, we have our homework to do. The basics of nutrition are as foreign to most of us as the intricacies of a silicon chip. While we wouldn't try to build a computer without knowing how one works, we often try to build our bodies on a similar lack of knowledge. Of the three classifications of food—proteins, carbohydrates, and fats—which do you think nutritionists recommend should make up the bulk of our daily diet? And the second? Most experts agree that carbohydrates should account for more than half (60 to 65 percent), fats for a bit less than a third (25 to 30 percent), and proteins the remaining 10 to 15 percent.

You may think your daily fat intake is decidedly below that 30 percent figure. Yet in this century, according to the Food and Nutrition Board of the National Academy of Sciences, fat intake has risen from 32 to 42 percent of our daily intake, probably due to the excessive use of fats, oils, and, to some degree, meat. We have one of the highest fat-content diets in the world. Fat lurks in most everything we eat, from avocados to zwieback, making a 100 percent fat-free diet as impossible as it is unhealthful. With our burgeoning culinary curiosity and fat intake, it makes sense to cut calorie corners where we can—without diluting our pleasure or endangering our health.

Voicing a concern about calories, fats, and vitamins was once the province of health food faddists, the type who would forage for wild nuts and berries rather than eat anything a machine had touched. Today the cook who is unconcerned with overprocessed foodstuffs, nutritionally empty foods, and fats is the rarity. Many are finding it difficult to indulge their love of fine food and maintain a healthy respect for the body. This book will point the way.

Thinking Thin

Is your life a revolving cycle of Spartan restraint followed by hedonistic indulgence? Do you diet successfully for a week or two, denying all pleasures, then binge on goodies? Is a hot fudge sundae your idea of a reward for losing weight?

If you answered yes to all the above, you're probably still looking for a way to lose weight. Yo-yo dieting, the starvation-binge route, is ineffective because the body's metabolic rate slows during times of calorie restriction. As you eat less, the body adjusts to function on fewer calories. Unfortunately, as you resume more normal eating habits, the body continues to prepare for times of "starvation" and the pounds start packing back on. Now you're eating a fairly normal diet but actually gaining weight, instead of just maintaining. Nobody ever said life was fair. But there is a bright side: If you learn to cook and eat in the most healthy way possible, you can enjoy delicious foods without ever being hungry and manage to maintain your ideal weight.

The most successful dieters are those who don't. Don't binge diet, that is. They enjoy good food, in moderation, every day. They are aware of calorie counts in common foods. They know there is no such thing as a skinny food, that only water is calorie-free. And they are active people, not necessarily marathon runners, but people who stand when they can sit, walk instead of ride, climb stairs, and shun elevators. Successful dieters know, perhaps intuitively, that taking fat off via exercise and semistarvation is much harder than eating less of it to begin with.

Consider this: A 120-pound person running an eight-minute mile expends about 82 calories per mile; a 160-pounder will use about 110 calories. That's the equivalent of an apple for the lighter runner or a glass of low-fat milk for the heavier one. Nutritionists estimate that a pound of fat represents about 3,500 calories your body didn't use. Assuming you can exercise off 100 calories for every mile run, it would take eleven or twelve days to lose a pound of fat running 3 miles every day. Disheartening, isn't it? In light of these figures (and your own), thinking thin must be a mode of life.

What The New Gourmet Light Is

To be a winner at the weight-loss game means educating yourself about the basics of metabolism and nutrition. It means learning how to eat to satisfy your hunger and learning how to cook to satisfy your appetite. This is a cookbook, an everyday guide to good, healthful eating habits. Many of you don't need to lose a pound, but you are looking for ways to eat well and maintain your happy weight state.

The New Gourmet Light is for those who enjoy fine food but keep a health-conscious eye peeled. This is a cookbook for people who exercise not only for the sport of it but also because it feels good. This is also a cookbook for people who plan to exercise but can never quite fit it in, people who are looking for viable ways to trim extra calories and fat from their daily meals. This is for those who like to keep abreast of food trends, from peas tendrils to foie gras, and for people who relish a meal not only for what it is but also for what it is not.

Herein the reader will find information on nutrition, metabolism, and the role of fats, proteins, and carbohydrates. You'll find out what equipment makes low-cal eating easier and where to find hard-to-come-by ingredients. There are tips on cooking techniques, and short soliloquies or Nutrabytes on nutritional concerns. Because not everyone is a seasoned cook, the recipes are thorough and detailed. If you already know your way around the kitchen, this book will teach you how to reduce calories in many of the dishes you now prepare, as well as give you some new and delicious ideas. When the fundamentals of *The New Gourmet Light* cooking become as natural to you as boiling water, you'll be able to pare calories from many of your favorite dishes.

This is not meant to be the only cookbook you'll ever need, for there are decidedly occasions when a no-stops, full-calorie-ahead dinner is in order. This is a way of cooking for everyday sort of use that you can live with happily, for a lifetime. Learn to cut a few superfluous calories from your daily "bread" and those strident days of dieting may become a thing of the past.

What It Is Not

This is not a diet manual. No promise here of pounds lost in two easy weeks.

It's tempting when writing a reduced-calorie cookbook to imply that all manner of foods can be prepared in such a way as to render them skinny. Not so. You'll find a chocolate cake, but not a chocolate mousse. You'll enjoy Pork Cutlet in Cider Cream Sauce, but without unhealthy amounts of saturated fats. Many dishes can be rewritten to remove excessive calories; those that cannot simply aren't here. The aim was not to make do but to do well, and if that couldn't be done the recipe wasn't included. Indulge in Sole and Crab Peppers, Chilled Tomato Soup with Basil-Walnut Cream, or Turkey Cutlets with Cranberry-Curaçao Sauce, and finish with a Hot Apple Tart. Here are the techniques of good cooking without excessive use of highly fatty, cholesterol-choked foods.

How It Came to Be

Historically, in the food world the French reigned. When they did away with flour as a thickener, turning instead to reduction sauces with their mounds of butter, we followed. When they churned vegetables into smooth purees, so did we. When they undercooked all manner of meat, not just beef, nothing remotely gray, only pink, touched our forks too. The French, by way of the inimitable Julia Child, taught us what good food was and how to cook it.

This was the early 1980s, long before calorie-controlled cooking was in vogue. I was teaching full-fat French recipes, but at home I was cooking and eating low-calorie, low-fat foods. Occasionally I'd sneak into a class a skinny recipe that was enthusiastically welcomed by my students, who asked for more. Eventually I concentrated solely on developing this style of cooking, which for its time was definitely out of the mainstream. Understandably, finding a publisher proved difficult, until my proposal landed on the desk of a like-minded editor at Globe Pequot Press, one who enjoyed great food but didn't want lots of calories too. The then small publisher took a chance on this quirky idea from an unknown and published what would become the award-winning *Gourmet Light.* Unlike many in this genre, we are proud that the book—truly a pioneer in this now saturated field—remains viable some thirteen years after its initial publication.

Since that time, American chefs have claimed the culinary crown, conjuring up innovative combinations of flavors and dishes that dazzle with nearly architectural perfection. Food today is flippant and trendy. Yesterday's sun-dried tomatoes are replaced by today's baby arugala. East meets West and ethnic differences in foods meld wonderfully. Nutrition information changes too: Is butter better or should we go with the stuff in the tub? Just what are phytochemicals? All this, of course, leads to this third and most extensive update of the original, hence the name *The New Gourmet Light*. More than 50 percent of the recipes are new, all have been streamlined to reduce preparation and cooking time. The spirit of the book remains unchanged, but specifics, such as new nutritional information, have been revised to reflect the latest theories and food trends. Enjoy!

CHAPTER 1

THE PRIMER

The Primer

The Primer is perhaps the most important chapter in this book, for here are the fundamentals of *The New Gourmet Light* cooking. Once you've mastered them, paring calories and fat from most any recipe will become automatic. Nothing here is tricky or requires culinary expertise; anyone who can separate an egg can cook—deliciously—the thin way. Success rests on your resolve to think thin, always looking for ways to cheat a dish of excessive calories but not at the expense of flavor.

This Primer will teach you how to cut down on the overuse of butter, fats, and oils. You'll discover how some readily available kitchen equipment can make you a winner at the calorie game. And you can have some fun testing your calorie and fat IQ.

So hone those knives, and fill your kitchen with appetizing aromas fat only in flavor!

Getting Started

Not convinced? Think the only way to watch your weight is to go on a celery and water regime for a few days? Perhaps the following tallies will give you pause. The same meal, one prepared the traditional way and one *The New Gourmet Light* way. Both are good, but which would you choose?

The Traditional Meal

Caesar Salad	369 calories
Chicken Pot Pie	550 calories
Apple Pie	404 calories
TOTAL	1323 calories

The New Gourmet Light Meal

Caesar Salad	106 calories
Old-Fashioned Chicken Pot Pie	366 calories
Hot Apple Tart	159 calories
TOTAL	631 calories

Cooking *The New Gourmet Light* way is no more difficult than any other. It takes only the resolve to want to change a few habits, the knowledge of what to change, and a nodding acquaintance with calorie and fat counts. Why not test your calorie IQ right now with the quiz below? And then on to the stove!

Check Your Calorie and Fat IQ

You can't play the game until you know how to score. Calorie and fat awareness is the key to weight control. While it's not necessary to carry a pocket calorie guide, it is sensible to have a working knowledge of some basic calorie and fat facts. Check your nutritional IQ here.

TRUE or FALSE

1. Following a low-fat diet is the best way to lose weight.

2. At a fast-food restaurant, you'd be better off with a regular hamburger than a garden salad (without meat and cheese) and a packet of ranch dressing.

3. Margarine is better for you than butter.

4. Baked goods, snack foods, and breads that boast "No Cholesterol" and "100% Vegetable Oil" can still be high in unhealthy fats and contribute to blood cholesterol levels.

5. Even though all the visible fat is trimmed from a T-bone steak, about half its calories will still be in the form of fat.

6. Low-fat and reduced-fat foods are always lower in calories than the full-fat version.

7. A tablespoon of honey has more nutrients and is lower in calories than a tablespoon of sugar.

CIRCLE THE FOOD LOWER IN CALORIES

8. A Pepperidge Farm Sandwich Bun with Sesame Seeds or a 9-inch sandwich wrap.

9. A tablespoon of vegetable oil, margarine, or butter.

10. A glazed Dunkin' Donuts doughnut or a plain Dunkin' Donuts bagel.

11. A McDonald's Grilled Chicken Deluxe sandwich or a McDonald's hamburger.

12. A half-cup serving of chocolate pudding, a cup of New England–style clam chowder, or 1 cup of fruited yogurt.

THE ANSWERS

1. False. While it's true that you'll lose weight if you eat fewer calories than you need—the 1990s diet of choice—the low-fat diet may not be the best way. The scales don't lie. One out of three adult Americans is overweight. That's an *increase* over the late 1970s, when just one out of four of us was too heavy. Further, the National Center for Health Statistics projects that the number of overweight adults is rising. John B. Allred, a nutrition professor at Ohio State University, feels that this gain might be the result of overindulgence in the very foods designed to get and keep us skinny—the low-fat goodies. Yes, high-fat foods do have more calories than foods high in proteins or carbohydrates do. But not all low-fat foods are low-calorie. And if sugars are added to compensate for lackluster flavor, the calorie count mounts. It is not that low-fat foods or fat replacers have no place in a weight-loss or weight-maintenance program. They do! But the label "Reduced Fat" shouldn't be a license to overeat. Diets— whether they're low-fat, low-carbohydrate, grapefruit diet or whatever—achieve

temporary weight loss. Only changing poor eating habits forever will make that loss permanent.

2. True. A McDonald's regular hamburger has 260 calories and 9 grams of fat, 3½ of them saturated. A garden salad with a packet of ranch dressing has about the same number of calories, and 21 grams of fat, 3 of them the bad, "sat" fat. And that's without croutons or bacon bits.

3. True if there's no trans-fat, false if there is. Trans-fat is created when margarine is chemically altered so it will look more like butter at room-temperature-solid. This process makes the fat in margarine act like saturated fat, the "bad" kind that clogs arteries, even though it isn't saturated. So you get the negative nutritional profile of butter but without the excellent flavor. As of this writing, legislation is pending requiring amounts of trans-fat to be included in nutritional labeling.

4. True. If the products are made with a highly saturated fat (for example, an oil that is hydrogenated, such as trans-fat, or a tropical oil, such as coconut), they may lead to higher blood cholesterol levels.

5. True. About 20 percent of the calories in a T-bone steak are in the form of protein; the remaining 80 percent are mostly fat. Even when the steak is very well trimmed, about half the calories will be in the form of fat.

6. False. Some reduced-fat or fat-free foods have the same amount of calories as the regular versions; some even have more. Here are some examples:

CALORIES OF REGULAR AND REDUCED FAT FOODS COMPARED

	Regular Kind	Reduced Fat or Fat-Free Kind
Drake's Yodel (1 yodel)	140	145
Campbell's Vegetable Soup (½ cup)	80	90
Jif Peanut Butter (2 tablespoons)	190	190

Total calories do count. Read labels to check for both total fat grams and total calories.

7. False. A tablespoon of honey has 61 calories; a tablespoon of sugar has 46. Honey does supply a very small amount of potassium.

8. Don't assume that thin bread is lower in calories and fat than thick bread. A puffy Pepperidge Farm Sandwich Bun with Sesame Seeds has 160 calories and 3½ grams of fat; a skinny 9-inch sandwich wrap has 200 calories and 4½ grams of fat. Flatbreads such as lavash, pita, tortillas, and sandwich wraps are made without yeast and thus are dense and often just as fattening as, if not more so than, regular breads.

9. All the same, approximately 100 calories and 12 to 14 grams of fat per tablespoon.

10. This is a good-news/bad-news answer. Surprisingly, the glazed, raised Dunkin' Donuts doughnut has half the calories (160) of the bagel's hefty 330 calories but it also packs in 7 grams of fat, 2 of them saturated. The plain bagel (125 grams)—no butter or cream cheese—weighs in with only 1 gram of unsaturated fat. A little container of their cream cheese (2 tablespoons) adds 10 grams of fat, more than half of them saturated. The "lite" variety adds 5 grams of fat, with 3 of them unsaturated.

11. The McDonald's burger has 260 calories and 9 grams of fat; the chicken sandwich has 440 calories and 20 grams of fat.

12. The pudding has 247 calories and 9 grams of fat; the chowder has 271 calories and 14 grams of fat; the fruited yogurt has 260 calories and 7 grams of fat.

11 to 12 correct ....highest honors
8 to 10 correct ....honor roll
5 to 7 correct ....passing grade
0 to 4 correct ....it's study time

This is not to suggest that those interested in losing pounds or maintaining their weight should opt for a doughnut instead of a bagel, or pudding instead of chowder; its intent is to point out some commonly held misconceptions and myths. Chicken and fish are not automatically low in calories; how they're prepared is essential. Butter is not more fattening than margarine, honey isn't much better for you than sugar, and a well-dressed salad may wreak havoc with your daily fat tally. A paperback calorie and fat-gram guide is good reading for anyone interested in weight control.

Here are the cornerstones of *The New Gourmet Light* cooking. Digest them and say good-bye to diets forever.

THE FUNDAMENTALS OF THE NEW GOURMET LIGHT COOKING

1. "Sautéing" in stocks, broths, and wine instead of fats and oils

When a recipe calls for butter and/or oil for the sautéing of onions, garlic, shallots, and so on, substitute stock, broth, or wine or a combination for calorie- and fat-free cooking. Add enough liquid to cover the bottom of the pan by about ⅛ inch; bring to a boil; add food to be "sautéed"; cover or not, as you prefer; and reduce heat to medium. Stir frequently, adding more liquid if it evaporates before the food is cooked. Train yourself to think of oil as a flavoring, not as a cooking medium.

2. Reducing and replacing oil in salad dressings

When a skinny bowl of greens is lavished with 2 tablespoons of regular dressing, the result is a caloric avalanche of at least 200 calories and 12 to 14 grams of fat. If you eat but five salads a week, it will take only 3½ weeks for that dressing to be a pound of fat. Why not reduce or even eliminate much of the oil used in dressings with a skinny alternative? The unlikely but excellent surrogate is chicken stock (the kind you make yourself) or canned beef consommé. Why homemade? Why the consommé and not just canned broth? Both the canned consommé and your homemade stock contain enough gelatin—one occurring naturally as the collagen in the bones melts, the other added—to somewhat duplicate the natural viscosity of oil. Another very acceptable alternative is enriched commercial broth; instructions can be found on page 292. Stock-based salad dressings are light, flavorful, and nutritious, without the "tinny," chemical taste so prevalent in commercial bottled dressings.

3. Retaining the natural moisture in foods

Select the cooking method that best retains the natural moisture in fresh foods, reducing, even eliminating, the need for fats, oils, and rich sauces. Here are suggestions, in no particular order of importance.

a. *Parchment paper*, aluminum foil, and waxed paper. By encasing the food in an envelope, evaporation is greatly reduced and the food stews in its own juices, creating a natural sauce. Lettuce, cabbage leaves, and cornhusks may also be used.

b. *Salt-encased cooking.* This very old method of cooking is excellent for roasting large pieces of meat, fish, or poultry to juicy perfection. The food is encased in a paste of coarse salt and water, forming an inedible crust that is cracked open and discarded after roasting. Oddly, the salt doesn't permeate the food; because of the salt the moisture in the food isn't lost.

c. *Poaching.* The term means to immerse a food in a simmering liquid. Poaching is generally reserved for poultry, but lamb and even beef can be deliciously poached. For oven poaching the food is placed in a film of liquid, covered with aluminum foil or waxed paper, and roasted; it's excellent for chicken breasts (see Curried Chicken Breasts with Shiitakes and Asparagus, page 183).

d. *Steaming.* Using either a cake rack, Chinese bamboo steamer, or metal basket with folding sides, the steaming of fish, poultry, and vegetables is often used in *The New Gourmet Light* cooking.

e. *Grilling.* This signature style of American cooking is ideal for our purposes, for foods pick up the added flavor of the smoke and cook with a minimum of added fats.

f. *Microwaving.* Ideal for today's fat-conscious cooking style, microwaving allows foods to be cooked with little to no fat and with maximum retention of vitamins and minerals.

Note: The recipes in this book were tested in a 900-watt microwave oven. Because cooking times vary considerably depending on wattage, oven size, and the temperature of the food when you begin cooking, you may need to adjust the suggested cooking times.

4. Thickening with cornstarch or arrowroot instead of flour

While restaurant kitchens and dedicated cooks thicken sauces by reduction (that is, boiling down), it is occasionally necessary to thicken a soup, stew, or sauce by means of a starch—either flour, arrowroot, or cornstarch. Note these measures for the *same* thickening ability:

> 3 teaspoons flour (1 tablespoon) ......50 calories
> 2 teaspoons cornstarch ....20 calories
> 1 teaspoon arrowroot ....15 calories

Arrowroot and cornstarch (you may also use potato starch) give a shiny, translucent quality to a sauce, while flour gives a more opaque look. Both arrowroot and cornstarch must be dissolved in a little cold water before using; if heated too long or brought to a boil, a sauce thickened with arrowroot or cornstarch may liquefy, a process called hydrolyzing. To avoid this problem, always keep foods with these starches added to them on moderate heat.

5. Equipment for reduced-calorie and fat-free cooking

The cook who wants to incorporate *The New Gourmet Light* way into his or her cooking style might like to investigate the following:

a. *Cooking sprays.* There are several nonstick sprays on the market that grease a pan while adding only minimal calories. Better yet, look in cookware stores for a stainless steel dispenser that lets you spray your own oils without the chemical propellants of the canned sprays. You can infuse the oil with ½ teaspoon lemon extract or with roasted garlic or herbs for added flavor. See Shopping Sources, page 306.

b. *Teflon and other nonstick pans.* Although it is sometimes difficult to brown foods in these pots and pans, they do allow high-heat searing and cooking without sticking. Buy the best you can afford.

c. *Degreaser.* This looks like a measuring cup with the spout coming off the bottom and is an excellent device for separating fats from soups, broths, and sauces.

d. *Parchment paper.* Parchment and waxed papers allow food to cook without losing precious juices to evaporation.

e. *Chinese bamboo steamer.* This inexpensive and useful contraption allows you to cook a whole meal in one pot (see Fillets of Fish Martini, page 220).

f. *Immersion blender, also called a hand-held blender.* This gadget is an electric whisk that can be used right in a pot on the stove or counter; it also comes with a handy, small chopper that is great for onions, peppers, and the like, without getting the big food processor dirty. Sauces blend and thicken much more quickly when made with an immersion blender than when whisked by hand.

g. *Grill.* Indoor or outdoor grills allow for fat-free cooking with maximum flavor.

6. Focus on food

This may seem like contradictory advice in a book dedicated to thinness. Yet it's my belief that those who eat mindlessly—grabbing a quick sandwich, munching a snack food at 4:00 P.M., drinking a soda or lemonade on the fly—are more often the ones with a few pounds to lose, compared with people who always think about what they eat. The calorie meter runs twenty-four hours a day. Every time you eat, make it yummy and make it count; after all, your body does count. Make time for a bowl of cereal with 1 percent milk instead of grabbing a reduced-fat muffin at the coffee shop before work; order two or even three sides of veggies instead of a Caesar salad; opt for a banana instead of cookies or crackers for a 3:00 P.M. snack. Once home, don't "throw food on the table"—plan for it, shop for it, and prepare it with great taste and calories in mind. Present it as something worthy of attention, something you've created. Cooking is a pragmatic art, one that pays off in a healthy, trim, and sound body. What better focus to have?

A Note About Nutrition Analysis

The nutrition information that appears with each recipe shows you at a glance how light and healthy the dish is. It tells the number of calories in the dish as well as the amount of protein, total fat, cholesterol, carbohydrates, sodium, and fiber. The saturated fat is broken out so you can see how much of the total fat content is made up of the unhealthy kind.

When a choice of ingredients is given in a recipe, the analysis has been based on the choice that's the lowest in calories, fat, and sodium. Optional ingredients are not included in the nutrition analysis.

Recipes that call for beef broth have been analyzed using *The New Gourmet Light* beef stock unless the recipe specifically calls for a canned product. Similarly, the analysis for recipes that call for rice wine vinegar or Chinese cooking wine is based on a reduced-sugar and reduced-sodium product. Skim milk was used for the analysis of all recipes that call for milk.

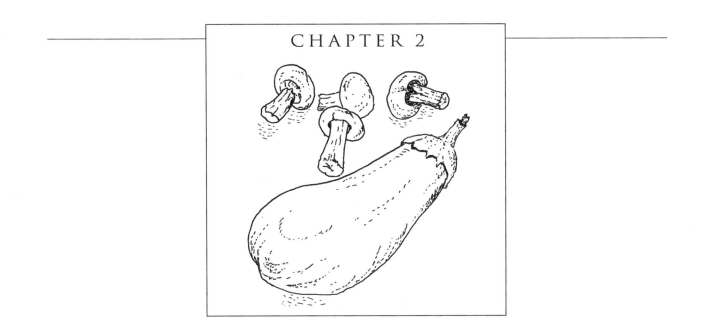

SMALL
PLATES

THE RECIPES

SMALL PLATES

The recipes in Small Plates defy category. More than just hors d'oeuvres, there are recipes here that would be appropriate for breakfast, or lunch—like the Puffy Egg White Omelet—or a light dinner—such as the Portabello, Eggplant, and Red Pepper Roll-ups. Your Basic(ally) Delicious Marinated Mushrooms are an excellent cocktail snack or a fine accompaniment to grilled fish. Asian Scallop and Shrimp Flatcakes are great served with Tuna Spring Rolls. Be inventive and enjoy individually or in a combination of two or more.

CRUDITÉS AND SKINNY DIPS

Raw vegetables cut into bite-size pieces (crudités) have been a popular nibble for years. Obviously, they're just right for *The New Gourmet Light* cooking too, if the accompanying dip is on the slender side.

When choosing vegetables for a crudité basket, keep color and texture in mind. Mushrooms, a soft vegetable, need the crunch of a celery stick, for example, and radishes can be offset with cherry tomatoes. Choose any vegetable that can be eaten raw. Happily, most vegetables can be prepared in advance and held as long as two days in ice water, which keeps them crisp. Those that resemble flower buds, such as cauliflower and broccoli, are great timesavers, requiring no more preparation than the snap of a stalk.

Because most baskets are too deep for the vegetables to look attractive in, a false bottom will create the illusion of bounty. Layer crumpled-up waxed paper in the bottom, and cover with a cloth napkin. Position the dip in a bowl—perhaps one made from a vegetable—in the center, and arrange prepared vegetables around it.

Another pretty presentation is to choose a rectangular tray. Arrange the vegetables in "ribbons" that run diagonally, a mirror image on either end of the tray, with small bowls of different dips (also on the diagonal) in the center.

Basil-Walnut Cream

My good friend Lissa paid this the highest compliment: "This tastes like calories!" Terrific with crudités or spread on sun-ripened tomatoes.

6 ounces fat-free cream cheese

2 ounces reduced-fat Havarti cheese, garden vegetable variety preferred

1/2 cup snipped fresh basil leaves

1 shallot

2 tablespoons Parmesan-Reggiano cheese

1 tablespoon balsamic vinegar

1 teaspoon fresh thyme leaves

1/2 teaspoon horseradish mustard or to taste

a dash seasoned salt

2 tablespoons chopped walnuts

1. Combine all ingredients except the walnuts in the bowl of a food processor and process until smooth. Thin, if desired, with chicken broth or skim milk. Add walnuts and pulse machine just to mix. Will keep refrigerated up to 5 days.

Yield: 1 cup

Calories per tablespoon: 30

Protein per tablespoon: 3 g

Fat per tablespoon: 1 g

Saturated fat per tablespoon: 1 g

Cholesterol per tablespoon: 5 mg

Carbohydrates per tablespoon: 1 g

Sodium per tablespoon: 109 mg

Fiber per tablespoon: trace

CURRIED CREAM DIP

Raw vegetables are the perfect nibble for cocktails or anytime, but typical fat-laden dips are anything but. If you eat but 2 tablespoons of an ordinary dip, you may be padding your fat-gram tally with as much as 22 grams, more than a third of an average person's daily allotment. Offer this dip next time. Your friends won't ask if it's low-fat, only if there's any more.

¹/₂ small onion, cut into chunks

1 clove garlic

¹/₂ cup yogurt cheese (see page 305)

¹/₄ cup nonfat sour cream

5 tablespoons low-fat mayonnaise

1 tablespoon honey

1 tablespoon curry powder

2 teaspoons prepared horseradish

2 teaspoons white wine vinegar

1 teaspoon sugar

¹/₂ teaspoon seasoned salt

freshly ground pepper to taste

3 tablespoons golden raisins

Yield: 1½ cups

Calories per tablespoon: 18

Protein per tablespoon: 0.5 g

Fat per tablespoon: 0.4 g

Saturated fat per tablespoon: trace

Cholesterol per tablespoon: 1 mg

Carbohydrates per tablespoon: 3 g

Sodium per tablespoon: 38 mg

1. Process the onion and garlic together in the bowl of a food processor until minced. Add all remaining ingredients except the raisins. Process until well combined. Taste and correct seasonings, if necessary. Add raisins and process briefly just until they are mixed in. Mixture will keep in the refrigerator up to 3 days.

BLUE CHEESE AND HERB DIP

Substituting tarragon for the rosemary will produce an equally delicious dip. In the unlikely event of leftovers, try a spoonful or so on a baked potato. Keeps in the fridge about 5 days.

> *4 ounces fat-free cream cheese*
> *¼ cup fresh minced parsley*
> *2 tablespoons fresh basil leaves*
> *2 teaspoons fresh rosemary or tarragon leaves*
> *1 clove garlic*
> *1 teaspoon fresh thyme leaves*
> *2 teaspoons Worcestershire sauce*
> *few drops lemon juice*
> *1½ ounces blue cheese*

Yield: 1 cup
Calories per tablespoon: 15
Protein per tablespoon: 2 g
Fat per tablespoon: 0.7 g
Saturated fat per tablespoon: trace
Cholesterol per tablespoon: 3 mg
Carbohydrates per tablespoon: 0.8 g
Sodium per tablespoon: 74 mg

1. Combine all ingredients except the blue cheese in the bowl of a food processor and process until smooth. Stir in the blue cheese. Refrigerate.

ROQUEFORT SKINNY DIP

If any of this is left over, it will make a great partner for a romaine lettuce salad.

> *2 ounces Roquefort or blue cheese*
> *2 ounces nonfat sour cream*
> *2 tablespoons fat-free cream cheese*
> *¼ teaspoon paprika*
> *½ teaspoon sugar*
> *freshly ground pepper to taste*

Yield: 10 tablespoons
Calories per tablespoon: 30
Protein per tablespoon: 2 g
Fat per tablespoon: 2 g
Saturated fat per tablespoon: 1 g
Cholesterol per tablespoon: 5 mg
Carbohydrates per tablespoon: 2 g
Sodium per tablespoon: 119 mg

1. Combine all ingredients in a food processor or blender and mix well.

PUFFY EGG WHITE OMELET

A really good egg white omelet needs external flavor boosts, because if truth be told, an egg white is a flavorless thing. It is an excellent-quality protein source, nearly fat-free, cheap, and easy—there's a lot going for it, except the taste. So look to fresh herbs, sauces, and the like to give this versatile, any-time-of-day entree the boost it craves. This recipe is for a basic omelet flavored with the Pesto and Red Pepper Butter recipes in this book. Following is also a recipe for Cheesy Dill Sauce. Or you can omit sauces entirely, adding instead some sliced mushrooms, minced arugula, and/or cilantro and a sparse grating of a reduced-fat or strong cheese such as a Parmesan-Reggiano when the omelet is folded.

Yield: 1 serving

Calories per serving: 87

Protein per serving: 12 g

Fat per serving: 3 g

Saturated fat per serving: trace

Cholesterol per serving: 63 mg

Carbohydrates per serving: 2 g

Sodium per serving: 166 mg

Per omelet

1 egg white, whipped to soft peaks

2 egg whites and 1 teaspoon egg yolk, whisked till foamy

1 teaspoon fresh minced herbs, such as parsley, basil, thyme and/or tarragon, in a combination to suit your taste, or ½ teaspoon dried herbs

salt and pepper to taste

1 teaspoon white sesame seeds

2 teaspoons Pesto (page 301; optional)

2 teaspoons Red Pepper Butter (page 124; optional)

1 teaspoon minced fresh parsley or herbs, for garnish (optional)

1. Fold the whipped egg white into the remaining eggs. Season with herbs, salt, and pepper.

2. Spray an 8-inch skillet with olive oil and place on high heat. Sprinkle the pan with the sesame seeds. When the skillet is hot, add the egg mixture. When the bottom sets, add the Pesto and 1 teaspoon of the Red Pepper Butter, stirring to blend without disturbing the bottom. Adjust heat to medium-high to prevent burning. Cover, preferably with a glass cover so you can see the cooking.

3. When the bottom is set and the omelet has cooked about 2 to 3 minutes, flip one half of the omelet over the other half. Smear the top with the remaining teaspoon Red Pepper Butter. Cook, covered, about 4 minutes more, adjusting the heat to cook the eggs without burning them. The omelet will swell and emit wisps of steam when it is done. Garnish with minced parsley or herbs, if desired.

Serves 1

CHEESY DILL SAUCE

In lieu of the Pesto and Red Pepper Butter, try this simple sauce, folding a tablespoon or so on top of the omelet before folding. This is also lovely thinned a little more with a bit of wine as a sauce for pasta, or serve it as is as a dip for carrots at cocktail time.

Yield: 6 to 7 tablespoons
Calories per tablespoon: 19
Protein per tablespoon: 1 g
Fat per tablespoon: 1 g
Saturated fat per tablespoon: trace
Cholesterol per tablespoon: 4 mg
Carbohydrates per tablespoon: 0.9 g
Sodium per tablespoon: 23 mg

3 tablespoons part-skim ricotta cheese

1 tablespoon light cream cheese, flavored (such as roasted garlic) or plain

1 tablespoon yogurt cheese (page 305) or plain yogurt

1 tablespoon skim milk (a bit less if using regular yogurt)

2 teaspoons minced fresh dill or 1 teaspoon dried dill

a few drops lemon juice

1. Combine all ingredients in a food processor or in the bowl of an immersion blender. Will keep refrigerated up to 3 days.

Makes 6 to 7 tablespoons

PORTABELLA, EGGPLANT, AND RED PEPPER ROLL-UPS

Equally yummy—and, oddly enough, no more caloric in a toasted crusty roll with some of the soft insides removed than in a wrap—these are terrific with the Lemon Broccoli Soup on page 62.

Yield: 3 servings

Calories per serving: 339

Protein per serving: 13 g

Fat per serving: 11 g

Saturated fat per serving: 1 g

Cholesterol per serving: 1 mg

Carbohydrates per serving: 51 g

Sodium per serving: 922 mg

Fiber per serving: 6 g

4 tablespoons canned beef consommé or beef stock

1 tablespoon olive oil

1 tablespoon balsamic vinegar

1 teaspoon grainy, stone-ground mustard, such as Pommery

1 tablespoon minced fresh oregano or 1 teaspoon dried oregano

1 teaspoon fresh thyme leaves (stripped from about 6 sprigs) or ½ teaspoon dried thyme

½ teaspoon salt

pepper to taste

1 clove garlic, minced

1 portabella mushroom cap, thinly sliced

6 ounces regular mushrooms, quartered

1 red bell pepper, seeded and sliced lengthwise

½ (cut crosswise) medium, unpeeled eggplant, cut into ½-inch-wide spears, then cut in half crosswise again

½ large white sweet onion, peeled and thinly sliced

3 flavored sandwich wraps (such as spinach or garden vegetable, if available) or lavash or flour tortillas, heated according to package instructions

2 tablespoons fat-free feta cheese, crumbled

alfalfa or similar-style sprouts

1. Make a dressing by combining in a food processor or jar with a tight-fitting cover the consommé or stock, olive oil, vinegar, mustard, oregano, thyme, salt, and pepper. Set aside.

2. Spray a 12-inch skillet with olive oil. Add the garlic, mushroom cap slices, and quartered mushrooms and sauté, adjusting heat to keep them from burning. When they're browned but not quite cooked through, add the red pepper, eggplant, and onion. Stir-fry about 8 to 10 minutes over medium to medium-high heat, until vegetables are softened and browned. Spray with olive oil if necessary, to prevent burning.

3. Add the dressing and toss to combine over medium-low heat. Remove from heat. The mixture can be held up to 2 hours at room temperature; reheat before continuing.

4. Divide the mixture among the wraps as illustrated on the package (or simply in a centered column). Sprinkle with the feta and sprouts. Wrap. Slice in half and serve, standing half of each sandwich on its flat end.

Serves 3

WHOLE WHEAT VEGETABLE TORTILLAS

Speed your prep time by picking up prechopped vegetables from the super-market salad bar. Be sure to check the label when purchasing tortillas; buy those made without lard, which is high in saturated fat.

Yield: 4 servings

Calories per serving: 195

Protein per serving: 10 g

Fat per serving: 6 g

Saturated fat per serving: 2 g

Cholesterol per serving: 10 mg

Carbohydrates per serving: 30 mg

Sodium per serving: 533 mg

Fiber per serving: 4 g

1 stalk broccoli, flowerets only, chopped

2 small carrots, thinly sliced

½ green pepper, thinly sliced

½ zucchini, thinly sliced

1 cup thinly sliced mushrooms

4 tablespoons chopped Spanish onion

½ teaspoon seasoned or regular salt

½ teaspoon dried oregano

4 whole wheat (soft flour) taco-size tortillas

1 medium tomato, chopped

2 scallions, chopped

2 ounces reduced-fat Cheddar cheese, shredded

Blackened Tomato Salsa (page 304) to pass at the table

1. Combine the broccoli, carrots, green pepper, zucchini, mushrooms, onion, salt, and oregano in a 4-cup glass measure or other microwave-safe container. Add 3 tablespoons water, cover with plastic wrap, and microwave at high (100 percent power) for 5 minutes or until vegetables are tender but crisp. Drain.

2. Spray a 12-inch nonstick skillet with olive oil. Lay the tortillas, two at a time, in the skillet.

3. Cover one half of each tortilla with the mixed vegetables. Divide the tomatoes, scallions, and cheese among them. Fold the top half of the tortilla over the filling. Sauté at medium-high heat until one side is lightly browned, about 4 minutes. Flip and cook on the other side until lightly browned, about 3 minutes. Pass salsa at the table.

EGGPLANT CLUB SANDWICHES

A veggie sandwich of substance and flavor. While not needed, a puddle of Red Pepper Butter (page 124) under the sandwich is a very fine addition. *Note:* Leftover rosemary skewers are great for grilling shrimp.

Yield: 4 servings

Calories per serving: 218

Protein per serving: 11 g

Fat per serving: 12 g

Saturated fat per serving: 4 g

Cholesterol per serving: 13 mg

Carbohydrates per serving: 21 g

Sodium per serving: 300 mg

Fiber per serving: 5 g

1 large eggplant, sliced lengthwise into ½-inch-thick steaks

1 tablespoon olive oil

2 tablespoons rice wine vinegar

1 cup plus 2 tablespoons chicken broth

1 bunch (about 3 ounces) fresh rosemary skewers

¼ cup Balsamic–Walnut Oil Vinaigrette (page 75) or bottled balsamic vinegar and oil low-fat dressing

1 cup loosely packed fresh basil leaves, minced

1 clove garlic, peeled

½ teaspoon sugar

1 tablespoon Parmesan-Reggiano cheese, grated (optional)

1 teaspoon Asian sesame oil

2 large portabella mushroom caps, stems removed

2 medium tomatoes, thinly sliced

3 ounces skim-milk mozzarella, thinly sliced

fresh basil leaves for garnish (optional)

1. Place eggplant slices on toweling and sprinkle liberally with salt. Let rest 10 minutes while continuing with recipe. Turn eggplant over and salt underside. After another 10 minutes, rinse thoroughly and pat dry.

2. Combine the olive oil, 1 tablespoon of the rice wine vinegar (reserve other tablespoon for Step 3), ¾ cup broth (reserve the rest), and rosemary needles from two of the skewers (reserve remaining skewers) in an 8-inch skillet. Boil for about 8 minutes or until mixture is reduced to about 4 tablespoons liquid, plus the herbs. Add vinaigrette. Set this rosemary marinade aside.

3. Combine the basil, garlic, sugar, cheese, sesame oil, and remaining rice wine vinegar and chicken broth in a food processor and puree. Set this basil drizzle aside.

4. Place remaining rosemary skewers on a low-heat grill (I place them on the upper racks of my gas grill, with the heat at medium-low, adjusting the heat down as needed). Place the eggplant and mushroom caps, gill side up, over the rosemary. Lavish with half the rosemary marinade, close the cover, and grill at medium-low heat.

5. Turn eggplant and mushrooms after 6 to 7 minutes, when grill marks have formed and vegetables are somewhat softened. Brush with remaining marinade. Grill another 5 or 6 minutes. Vegetables should retain some spring when pressed; they should not be mushy or the sandwich will fall apart.

6. Drizzle a third of the basil mixture over *half* of the largest eggplant slices. Divide the tomatoes and cheese over these (one layer thick only; reserve any extras for another purpose). Drizzle with another third of the basil mixture. Spray with olive oil if the veggies seem dry.

7. Close the cover and grill over lowest heat about 8 to 10 minutes, until cheese melts. Raise the cover and drizzle with remaining basil mixture.

8. Remove veggies to a serving platter. Slice mushrooms diagonally in ½-inch slices. Divide mushrooms over the cheese-and-tomato-topped eggplant; cover with remaining eggplant slices. Pour off the accumulated juices, if desired. Slice sandwiches in half on the diagonal, securing them with rosemary skewers, if necessary. Garnish with basil leaves, if desired.

Serves 4

Nutrabyte

Think of bread as the starch of a main meal, not a side dish.

Tuna Spring Rolls

Think of this deliciously light small plate as a starting point for many variations. These spring rolls, which can be steamed or sautéed, can be a cocktail snack or, when served with sticky Japanese rice, an entree. If made without the tuna, they can be an elegantly different vegetable side dish and need no further cooking. For a different filling see Rice Stick Noodle Salad with Sesame Shrimp, page 170. Even the wrappers have various names. Known as rice roll wrappers, rice paper rounds, or spring roll skins, they are very inexpensive, keep indefinitely, and are available in Asian food stores or by mail order (see Shopping Sources, page 306).

Preparation can be completed a few hours in advance, but if cooking is needed, do so just before serving. A 4-millimeter Cuisinart shredding disk produces perfectly shredded vegetables for these rolls.

Yield: 12 rolls

Calories per roll: 69

Protein per roll: 5 g

Fat per roll: 1 g

Saturated fat per roll: trace

Cholesterol per roll: 5 mg

Carbohydrates per roll: 11 g

Sodium per roll: 233 mg

Fiber per roll: 1 g

For the Filling

6 ounces tuna steaks, skin removed, minced, or crabmeat or shrimp (optional)

2 cups bean sprouts

3 to 4 ounces shiitake mushrooms, stemmed and thinly sliced

1 red pepper, seeded and shredded

1 large carrot, shredded (about 1 cup, packed)

4 scallions, with about 3 inches of green stalk, shredded

2 tablespoons reduced-sodium soy sauce

1 tablespoon plus 1 teaspoon fresh minced cilantro

1 tablespoon grated ginger root (no need to peel)

2 tablespoons white sesame seeds, toasted (see page 38)

2 teaspoons hoisin sauce (available in the Asian section of the supermarket)

¼ teaspoon powdered wasabi (available in the Asian section of the supermarket), stirred into the juice of ½ lime (about 2 tablespoons)

zest of a lime, for garnish (optional)

a few sprigs cilantro for garnish (optional)

For the Wrappers

12 to 14 rice paper rounds

For the Soy-Lime Dipping Sauce

juice of ½ lime
6 tablespoons reduced-sodium soy sauce
3 tablespoons water
1 clove garlic, minced
1 teaspoon grated fresh ginger root
1 teaspoon sugar
2 scallions, minced
zest of 1 lime and/or cilantro (optional)

Yield of sauce: ¾ cup
Calories per tablespoon: 7
Protein per tablespoon: 1 g
Fat per tablespoon: trace
Saturated fat per tablespoon: trace
Cholesterol per tablespoon: 0
Carbohydrates per tablespoon: 2 g
Sodium per tablespoon: 300 mg
Fiber per tablespoon: trace

To Prepare the Sauce

1. Place all ingredients in a screw-top jar and shake to combine.

To Prepare the Filling

1. In a medium bowl combine the tuna (if desired), bean sprouts, mush-rooms, pepper, carrot, scallions, soy sauce, cilantro, ginger root, 2 teaspoons of the sesame seeds (reserve remaining seeds), hoisin, and wasabi stirred into the lime juice. Mix well.

To Prepare the Rolls

1. Half-fill a large skillet with hot tap water. Place on a turned-off burner (add heat if the water cools off too much). Lay a thick towel on the counter. Dip a rice paper round into the hot water (you should be able to put your fingers in the water). Press the edges to submerge them. In about 5 seconds flip the wrapper and submerge the edges again. Lift from the bath after about 10 to 15 seconds in all, or when pliable but not so soft that the wrapper rips. Spread on the towel. Turn to absorb excess water.

2. Scoop ⅓ cup of the filling (use a dry measure for ease), squeeze out and

reserve juice, and place in a column in the center of the wrapper. Fold one half of the wrapper over the filling and roll tightly, bringing both wrapper "poles" to the center and tucking in all edges as you wrap. Dip the top of the roll in the reserved sesame seeds. Place seam-side down. Repeat.

3. If no fish or cooked shellfish is used, the rolls can be served without cooking, or sliced in half on the diagonal (they may be held refrigerated up to 3 hours). If fish is used, the rolls may be sautéed or steamed. To sauté, spray a nonstick pan with olive oil. Sauté the rolls about 6 minutes, turning once or twice. To steam, spray a bamboo steamer with olive oil. Place rolls in a wok over a pan three-quarters full of boiling water. Steam 6 minutes.

4. To serve, add the reserved vegetable juices from step 2 to the dipping sauce. Garnish with cilantro and/or lime zest, if desired.

Makes 12 rolls

Nutrabyte

If you eat very quickly and in large bites, eat with chopsticks. Doing so will slow you down, at least until you become proficient with them.

BRUSCHETTA

Bruschetta, the hors d'oeuvre of the 1990s, replaces the taco chips and salsa of the late 1980s. While the proportions are flexible, the highest-quality ingredients are mandatory. The tomatoes must be fresh and flavorful and made into a salad no more than an hour or two before serving (about 20 minutes is ideal) or it will be too watery. Choose a European-style white bread—no squishy American-style French bread—dense but not too chewy, and preferably about 3 inches wide. Larger loaves will make the bruschetta too messy to eat. Select a high-grade vinegar, and spray your own oil using a pump sprayer (see Shopping Sources, page 306).

Yield: 10 pieces

Calories per piece: 111

Protein per piece: 3 g

Fat per piece: 1 g

Saturated fat per piece: 0.31 g

Cholesterol per piece: 0

Carbohydrates per piece: 21 g

Sodium per piece: 310 mg

Fiber per piece: 1 g

1 baguette, about 3 inches across

4 cloves roasted garlic (see page 305)

12 to 16 arugula leaves, washed and patted dry

3 medium ripe tomatoes, stemmed and chopped

2 tablespoons diced red or Spanish onion

3 tablespoons fresh minced basil

2 teaspoons balsamic vinegar

1 teaspoon sugar

$1/2$ teaspoon salt

pepper to taste

2 tablespoons pine nuts (optional)

a tomato skin rose and/or a basil leaf cluster (optional)

1. Preheat the broiler or the oven to 425 degrees. Cut the bread in half first lengthwise and then crosswise, creating 4 pieces. Hollow out the bread, leaving a thin shell (the insides could be made into croutons). Spread each bread piece with a clove of mashed roasted garlic and cover with arugula. Spray with olive oil. Set aside on a cookie sheet or broiler sheet sprayed with olive oil.

2. In a bowl combine the tomatoes, onion, basil, vinegar, sugar, salt, and pepper. Toss to combine. Taste for seasoning.

3. About 10 minutes before serving, divide the tomato mixture over the bread, and sprinkle with the pine nuts. Spray with olive oil. Broil about 4 minutes or bake about 6 to 8 minutes until the bread has crisped. Let the pieces rest about 4 minutes, then slice each piece into serving-size pieces on the diagonal. Arrange pinwheel-fashion on a plate, pointy ends toward the center and, if desired, a tomato rose and/or a basil leaf cluster in the center.

Makes 8 to 10 pieces

YOUR BASIC(ALLY) DELICIOUS MARINATED MUSHROOMS

Served as part of a salad or as a terrific cocktail snack, these are simplicity itself. They are ruled by no season and demand little besides a three-day sit in the fridge. If you have any Pesto (page 301) on hand, stir a tablespoon or so into the dressing.

Yield: 10 ounces

Calories per one ounce: 18

Protein per one ounce: 0.8 g

Fat per one ounce: 0.9 g

Saturated fat per one ounce: trace

Cholesterol per one ounce: none

Carbohydrates per one ounce: 2 g

Sodium per one ounce: 10 mg

10 ounces mushrooms, cleaned and left whole, halved, or sliced as the intended use dictates

⅔ cup canned beef consommé or double-strength beef stock

6 cloves roasted garlic (see page 305), mashed, or 1 clove raw garlic, minced

6 tablespoons best-quality balsamic vinegar

2 tablespoons walnut oil

2 tablespoons water

1 teaspoon herbs de Provence or 2 teaspoons minced fresh herb such as basil, thyme, tarragon, or parsley or a mix

2 teaspoons sugar

1 teaspoon Dijon mustard

2 bay leaves

freshly ground pepper to taste

1. Put the mushrooms in a nonmetalic bowl. Combine the remaining ingredients in a shake jar and blend. Pour over the mushrooms. Cover and refrigerate three days. The marinade may be used once more before discarding.

Makes 10 ounces

DUXELLES MELBA

A delicious way to use up aging mushrooms, these cocktail toasts may be made when the spirit strikes and then frozen. Substituting a few fresh shiitake mushrooms lends interest, as does adding a tablespoon of curry powder at Step 5.

4 slices thin-sliced white bread

6 ounces mushrooms

2 tablespoons shallots, minced

2 tablespoons chicken broth

1 ounce semisoft mild reduced-fat cheese, such as Havarti or Muenster, grated

1 tablespoon minced fresh parsley

1 tablespoon pine nuts or almonds, chopped

$1/_8$ teaspoon salt

freshly ground black pepper to taste

few gratings fresh nutmeg

Yield: 16 appetizers

Calories per appetizer: 28

Protein per appetizer: 1 g

Fat per appetizer: 0.9 g

Saturated fat per appetizer: 0.34 g

Cholesterol per appetizer: 1 mg

Carbohydrates per appetizer: 4 g

Sodium per appetizer: 65 mg

Fiber per appetizer: trace

1. Preheat the oven to 325 degrees. Spray a baking sheet with olive oil.

2. Place the bread slices in a stack and slice twice on the diagonal, making 16 triangles. Remove crusts if desired. Arrange in a single layer on the baking sheet.

3. Spray the croustades (bread triangles) with olive oil on one side. Bake 12 minutes, or until slightly crisp, in the preheated oven.

4. Wipe the mushrooms clean and mince them by hand or in a food processor. Scrape onto a kitchen towel, gather into a ball, twist the ends of the towel, and squeeze the mushrooms over the sink, extracting as much water as you can.

5. "Sauté" the shallots in the chicken broth in an 8-inch skillet. When liquid is evaporated and shallots are softened, spray the skillet with olive oil, add the mushrooms, and cook at medium-low heat, gradually increasing the heat, about 5 minutes.

6. Remove mushrooms from heat; stir in the grated cheese, parsley, and pine nuts, making duxelles. Season with salt, pepper, and nutmeg.

7. Divide duxelles over the croustades, being certain to cover the bread points or they will burn. The hors d'oeuvres may be broiled now until browned, about 2 to 3 minutes, or baked at 325 degrees until browned, about 12 minutes. You may also freeze them, uncooked, for future use.

SEVICHE

Seviche is the Latin American cousin of Japan's sashimi. Unlike sashimi, which is strictly raw, seviche is prepared by marinating the fish several hours in lemon juice. This firms the flesh, turning it opaque—in essence, cooking it. Like sashimi, the freshness of the fish is imperative. Once it's marinated, however, seviche will keep for 2 to 3 days. Seviche makes a nice lunch dish or first course as well as an appetizer. To give it a bit more body, do as a Peruvian friend of mine does: Add a boiled, cubed sweet potato.

1½ pounds scallops or delicate white-fleshed fish, such as sole, cut into bite-size pieces

1 cup plus 3 tablespoons lemon juice

1 tablespoon finely chopped Bermuda or Spanish onion

¼ green pepper, finely chopped

½ red pepper, finely chopped

½ blanched, skinned, and seeded tomato, cubed

⅓ cup lime juice (about 2 limes)

2 tablespoons orange juice, freshly squeezed preferred

freshly ground pepper to taste

Yield: 10 appetizer servings

Calories for 1 appetizer serving: 89

Protein per appetizer: 12 g

Fat per appetizer: 1 g

Saturated fat per appetizer: trace

Cholesterol per appetizer: 22 mg

Carbohydrates per appetizer: 9 g

Sodium per appetizer: 111 mg

Fiber per appetizer: trace

or

Yield: 6 first-course servings

Calories per serving: 112

Protein per serving: 19 g

Fat per serving: 1 g

Saturated fat per serving: trace

Cholesterol per serving: 36 mg

Carbohydrates per serving: 7 g

Sodium per serving: 179 mg

Fiber per serving: trace

minced fresh parsley

lettuce

1. Marinate the seafood in 1 cup lemon juice in a nonmetallic container overnight.

2. Drain seafood, discarding marinade. Rinse with water.

3. Combine the onion, green pepper, red pepper, tomato, lime, orange, and remaining lemon juices, and fish. If desired, add the remaining halves of tomato and green pepper, also chopped. Season with pepper to taste. Garnish with a bit of parsley.

4. To serve, line individual plates or a platter with lettuce and mound the mixture on top.

SOLE AND CRAB PEPPERS

These morsels may be made ahead and reheated, but for best flavor make them through Step 5, cooking just before serving. The sauce may be made ahead and reheated or omitted altogether if hoisin sauce is unavailable.

For the Peppers

4 ounces sole or other whitefish fillets

1 scallion, minced

4 water chestnuts, fresh or canned, chopped

a pinch cayenne pepper

1/2 teaspoon red wine vinegar or rice wine vinegar

1 egg white

1 teaspoon cornstarch

5 ounces crabmeat

2 medium red or green peppers

1/2 cup chicken broth

Yield: 16 appetizers with sauce

Calories per appetizer: 24

Protein per appetizer: 3 g

Fat per appetizer: trace

Saturated fat per appetizer: trace

Cholesterol per appetizer: 11 mg

Carbohydrates per appetizer: 2 g

Sodium per appetizer: 70 mg

Fiber per appetizer: trace

Note: Nutrition analysis includes sauce.

For the Sauce

1 tablespoon cornstarch
½ cup chicken broth
1 tablespoon hoisin sauce
1 teaspoon Asian sesame oil

To Prepare the Peppers

1. Put the fish in a food processor or through a meat grinder and process to a paste. Scrape into a bowl.

2. Add the scallion, water chestnuts, cayenne, vinegar, egg white, and cornstarch. Mix well.

3. Dice the crabmeat. Stir into the fish mixture.

4. Wash the peppers, cut in half, discard the seeds, and cut each half in four pieces. (Don't wash the inside of the pepper or the filling won't adhere.)

5. Pack a heaping teaspoon of filling on each pepper.

6. Spray a 12-inch nonstick skillet with olive oil. Place filled peppers in skillet, pepper-side down. Sauté at high heat until peppers are just browned, add chicken broth, cover, and steam 3 to 4 minutes. Serve hot with sauce dabbed on top or as a dip.

To Make the Sauce

1. Dissolve the cornstarch in the broth. Add hoisin sauce and sesame oil. Stir over medium heat until thickened. Sauce can be reheated.

Baked Potato Chips

A slimming alternative to potato chips is to slice a baking potato as thinly as possible (a food processor works best, of course). Pat the slices dry. Spray one or two cookie sheets with olive oil and spread out the potato slices in as close to a single layer as possible. Spray again with olive oil, and sprinkle with seasoned salt. Bake in a 350-degree oven (no need to preheat) about 10 minutes; reduce heat to 300 degrees and bake another 15 minutes or until crisp and brown.

CLAM AND HAM APPETIZERS

These clam-and-ham-stuffed shells make a delicious hot cocktail nibble. The recipe may be prepared through Step 9 early in the day, and cooked at the last minute. The appetizers reheat nicely when covered with foil. They look fabulous served on a tray covered with black, polished stones, which you can buy at some garden centers or import stores like Pier 1.

Yield: 14 appetizers

Calories in each: 20

Protein in each: 2 g

Fat in each: trace

Saturated fat in each: trace

Cholesterol in each: 6 mg

Carbohydrates in each: 1 g

Sodium in each: 78 mg

Fiber in each: trace

¹/₂ small onion, chopped

1 clove garlic, minced

¹/₂ cup chicken broth

³/₄ cup dry white wine

12 hard-shell (littleneck) clams (about 2 pounds), well scrubbed

2 teaspoons cornstarch

3 ounces lean ham, chopped

3 tablespoons dried bread crumbs

1 tablespoon minced fresh parsley

1. "Sauté" the onion and garlic in the chicken broth in a covered 2-quart saucepan until the vegetables are limp and almost transparent.

2. Add the wine (reserving 1 tablespoon for Step 3) and clams, cover pan, and steam over high heat until clams open, about 8 minutes.

3. Dissolve the cornstarch in the reserved tablespoon of wine.

4. Lift opened clams from the broth with a slotted spoon. Line a sieve, placed over a bowl, with a piece of cheesecloth, a coffee filter, or a heavy paper towel wrung out in water, and pour the broth through the sieve.

5. Pour 6 tablespoons strained broth back into the now empty saucepan. Add dissolved cornstarch and cook, whisking, over medium heat until thickened. Set aside.

6. Pull clams from their shells; discard one half of shell. Chop clams roughly.

7. Combine chopped clams, ham, and thickened broth.

8. Spoon mixture into shells. Sprinkle ½ teaspoon bread crumbs on each stuffed shell.

9. Clams may now be baked in a 425-degree oven until bubbly and browned (about 12 to 14 minutes) or held, chilled, for baking later in the day. Broil briefly if the crumbs don't brown in the oven. Garnish the stuffed, baked clams with parsley.

Nutrabyte

A teaspoon of fat equals about 4 ½ grams and has about 40 calories.

Foods to Keep on Hand

* lemon oil
* walnut or other high-quality salad oil
* roasted garlic
* fermented black beans
* Asian sesame oil and hot (spicy) oil
* mirin
* rice wine vinegar
* all manner of mustards
* all-fruit preserves or jelly
* dried cranberries
* broth concentrates in chicken, beef, mushroom, and, for fun, clam and lobster
* black or tan sesame seeds

Asian Scallop and Shrimp Flatcakes

A finger food, this is best right off the griddle but can be reheated up to a day later in a microwave oven. There's no reason to invest in premium shrimp or scallops for this, given the pungent dipping sauce.

½ pound cooked shrimp (71 to 90 count), tailed and minced

¼ pound scallops, such as previously frozen Florida bay scallops, minced

1 cup minced bell peppers, about a third each of yellow, red, and green bell peppers, seeded

4 scallions (use first 3 to 4 inches and discard remaining green), minced

½ jalapeño pepper, seeded and minced

2 tablespoons minced fresh cilantro

¾ cup each cornstarch and all-purpose flour

½ teaspoon salt

pepper to taste

1 whole egg, plus 2 egg whites

1 cup water

2 tablespoons black or tan sesame seeds, toasted (see Quick Tip, page 38; optional)

enoki mushrooms or radish or other sprouts, for garnish (optional)

¾ cup Soy-Lime Dipping Sauce (page 27)

Yield: 5 cakes

Calories per cake: 240

Protein per cake: 18 g

Fat per cake: 2 g

Saturated fat per cake: 0.50 g

Cholesterol per cake: 138 mg

Carbohydrates per cake: 36 g

Sodium per cake: 391 mg

Fiber per cake: 2 g

1. Mix together the shellfish, bell peppers, scallions, jalapeño, and cilantro in a medium-size bowl. Set aside.

2. Sift together the cornstarch, flour, salt, and pepper. Set aside.

3. Beat together until frothy the whole egg, the 2 additional egg whites, and water.

4. Whisk the egg mixture into the flour mixture. Blend in the shellfish and vegetables. Mixture may be held up to 30 minutes at room temperature or as long as 24 hours refrigerated, before cooking.

5. Spray a 10- or 12-inch nonstick skillet with olive oil and place over high heat until a few drops of water skittle when splashed in the pan. (If the water just lies there, the pan needs to be hotter; if the water immediately turns to steam, the pan is too hot.) Ladle just enough pancake mixture into the hot skillet to cover the bottom. Tip in several directions to create a uniform, thin pancake. Cook 2 to 3 minutes on each side, adjusting heat to prevent burn-ing. As soon as the pancake is flipped, sprinkle the second side with sesame seeds, if desired. Slide the finished pancake onto an ovenproof platter and keep the pancakes warm until all are cooked. Slice in wedges with a pizza cutter; serve garnished, if desired, with the enoki mushrooms or sprouts in the center; and pass the dipping sauce.

Makes 4 to 5 large cakes

QUICK TIP

To toast sesame seeds:
Place sesame seeds in a dry, 8-inch skillet over high heat. Shake the skillet fre-quently, until the seeds darken and a few begin to pop, about 1½ to 2 minutes.

CHICKEN AND PORK SKEWERS

The tasty combination of chicken and pork is for those who like it hot. If you prefer a milder flavor, reduce or omit the chili paste with garlic. Marinate the chicken and pork as much as 2 days before preparing. Soaking the wooden skewers (or use rosemary skewers) 45 minutes before grilling will keep them from scorching.

> *5 ounces boneless pork from chops or tenderloin, fat trimmed*
>
> *1 whole chicken breast, boned and skinned*
>
> *6 tablespoons reduced-sodium soy sauce*
>
> *1 tablespoon Asian sesame oil*
>
> *2 tablespoons chicken broth*
>
> *1 scallion (white part only), chopped*
>
> *a 1-inch piece of ginger root, peeled and grated*
>
> *2 teaspoons chili paste with garlic, available in the Asian section of the supermarket*

1. Put the pork in the freezer for 2 hours; place the chicken in the freezer for about 10 minutes.

2. Slice the chicken in long, thin strips, slanting the knife slightly. Cut the pork so the strips are wide as well as long by placing what was the bone end flat on the cutting surface and slicing down.

3. Place the chicken and pork in a plastic or a glass bowl with the soy sauce, sesame oil, chicken broth, scallion, and ginger root. Marinate in refrigerator 2 to 4 hours.

4. Drain poultry and meat, reserving marinade. Thread the chicken and pork alternately on skewers. You may refrigerate assembled skewers up to 12 hours before cooking.

5. Mix the marinade with the chili paste. Bring marinade to a boil for 30 seconds. Grill or broil chicken and pork skewers, brushing with chili paste marinade, 12 to 16 minutes or until done. The meat and poultry should be juicy, not overdone.

Yield: 15 skewers

Calories per skewer: 47

Protein per skewer: 6 g

Fat per skewer: 2 g

Saturated fat per skewer: 1 g

Cholesterol per skewer: 16 mg

Carbohydrates per skewer: 1 g

Sodium per skewer: 253 mg

Fiber per skewer: trace

Nutrabyte

Many recipes in this book specify Asian sesame oil to distinguish this toasted sesame oil from regular sesame oil. It is sold in smaller bottles and loses flavor if heated for a long time, so add it just before serving the dish.

CREAMY CHICKEN ENCHILADAS

These "creamy" chicken enchiladas have universal appeal. Cooked layer-cake-fashion, they are coveted family fare; assembled in tiny muffin tins, they make terrific hors d'oeuvres. Instructions for each follow. You might like to vary the chicken filling with the Black Bean and Beef Chili filling on page 243, or a minced vegetable mixture seasoned with cilantro.

Red Chili Sauce

1 small yellow onion, minced

2 cloves garlic, minced

2 tablespoons instant-blending flour

2 teaspoons chili powder

1 teaspoon unsweetened cocoa powder

1 teaspoon dried oregano

$1/2$ teaspoon cumin powder

$1/2$ teaspoon salt

1 13 $3/4$-ounce can chicken broth

"Cream" Sauce

1 cup skim milk

2 tablespoons instant-blending flour or 1 tablespoon cornstarch

2 ounces fat-free, shredded, mild cheese such as Monterey Jack or light Cheddar

Chicken Filling

3 cooked chicken breast quarters, skinned and shredded (about 4 cups)

4 ounces mushrooms, thinly sliced

3 or 4 scallions, chopped

2 teaspoons minced fresh cilantro or to taste

1 teaspoon minced canned chipotle chili peppers and about 1 teaspoon sauce or minced jalapeño to taste

Yield: 6 servings

Calories per serving: 378

Protein per serving: 40 g

Fat per serving: 9 g

Saturated fat per serving: 1 g

Cholesterol per serving: 75 mg

Carbohydrates per serving: 38 g

Sodium per serving: 891 mg

Fiber per serving: 2 g

or

Yield: 36 hors d'oeuvres

Calories each: 65

Protein each: 7 g

Fat each: 1 g

Saturated fat each: trace

Cholesterol each: 12 g

Carbohydrates each: 7 g

Sodium each: 139 mg

Fiber each: trace

1 cup canned "recipe-ready" tomatoes with a little juice

½ teaspoon salt

5 or 6 8-inch or larger whole wheat or white flour tortillas (for layer-cake
*   presentation) or 1 package 6-inch flour tortillas (for hors d'oeuvres)*

¼ cup shredded fat-free mozzarella cheese

fresh cilantro sprigs for garnish (optional)

1 minced scallion for garnish (optional)

To Prepare the Red Chili Sauce

1. Combine the onion and garlic in a 2½-quart, heavy-bottom saucepan. Spray with olive oil. Sauté over medium heat 4 minutes or until the onion is softened but not browned. Sprinkle in the flour, chili powder, cocoa, oregano, cumin, and salt. Stir over medium-high heat about 1 minute. Reduce heat to medium and whisk in the chicken broth. Continue to whisk until sauce is smooth and starting to thicken. Adjust heat so sauce just simmers. Simmer 25 to 30 minutes, until thickened.

To Prepare the Cream Sauce

1. Meanwhile combine the milk and flour in a 2-cup glass measure or other microwave-safe container. Cover with plastic wrap. Microwave on high (100 percent power) for 4 minutes or until thickened. Stir in the cheese, cover, and microwave on high (100 percent power) for an additional minute. Set aside.

To Prepare the Filling

1. If preparing the dish as an hors d'oeuvre, mince the chicken in a food processor; if preparing as an entree, leave the chicken in shreds.

2. Spray an 8-inch nonstick skillet with olive oil. Sauté the mushrooms over high heat for 5 minutes or until lightly browned. Add the mushrooms to the chicken.

3. Stir the scallions, cilantro, chili peppers with sauce, tomatoes, and salt into the chicken-mushroom mixture along with the cream sauce.

To Assemble Layer-Cake-Fashion

1. Film the bottom of a pie plate or other baking dish that has 1-inch sides with a few tablespoons of red chili sauce.

2. Dip a tortilla in the chili sauce to coat both sides. Place in the baking dish. Spread chicken-cream mixture over as if making a peanut butter sandwich. Repeat with remaining tortillas and filling, ending with a tortilla. Pour any remaining sauce on top. Sprinkle with the remaining cheese. The dish may be assembled to this point and refrigerated, up to 6 hours before baking.

3. Place in the upper third of a 350-degree oven (no need to preheat) for 25 to 30 minutes, or slightly longer if the uncooked dish has been refrigerated. Garnish and let rest 5 to 8 minutes before slicing into wedges.

To Assemble as Hors d'Oeuvres

1. Spray 3 12-cup tiny muffin tins with olive oil. Cut a package of tortillas into eighths, in wedges. Press 1 or 2 wedges into the muffin cups. Spoon in a rounded tablespoon of chicken mixture. Add a teaspoon or so of red chili sauce and top with a pinch of cheese. Press any errant tortilla tips into the filling. Bake 15 minutes in a 350-degree oven (no need to preheat) or until the cheese is lightly browned. Let the tiny tacos rest about 5 minutes before removing from the tin. If made ahead, reheat in the oven (not in the microwave—the tortillas will become too soggy).

Nutrabyte

A good way to become aware of calorie counts in foods you commonly eat is to keep a diary of everything you consume for a few days, then tally the calories and fat grams with the help of a calorie listing.

Caramelized Onion, Mushroom, and Roasted Red Pepper Tart

In this calorie-conscious tart, phyllo dough replaces the traditional crust. The flakiness is ethereal; the preparation, a snap. Prepare the onions and mushrooms up to 24 hours ahead but ready the phyllo no more than 2 to 3 hours before baking. Reduced-fat Jarlsberg is a milder substitute for goat cheese.

Yield: 8 servings

Calories per serving: 108

Protein per serving: 4 g

Fat per serving: 4 g

Saturated fat per serving: 2 g

Cholesterol per serving: 5 mg

Carbohydrates per serving: 14 g

Sodium per serving: 345 mg

Fiber per serving: 2 g

2 large white or Spanish onions, peeled, halved, and thinly sliced

2 teaspoons olive oil

4 tablespoons wine (red, white, or rosé) or vegetable broth

1 tablespoon minced fresh sage or ½ teaspoon crumbled dried sage

1 teaspoon salt

1 bay leaf

½ teaspoon dried rosemary

1 teaspoon sugar

1 clove garlic, minced, or 2 cloves roasted garlic (see page 305)

5 ounces baby portabella mushrooms or other mushrooms of your choice, sliced

1 portabella mushroom cap, sliced

2 sheets phyllo dough, thawed

3 tablespoons bread crumbs

⅓ cup roasted red pepper, from a jar and thinly sliced or 1 fresh red pepper, roasted (see Quick Tip page 44), peeled, seeded, and thinly sliced

1 tablespoon minced fresh basil

3 ounces goat cheese, crumbled, or 3 ounces reduced-fat Jarlsberg cheese, shredded

1. Spray a large skillet with olive oil. Add onions, oil, wine, sage, salt, bay leaf, and rosemary. Cover and cook over high heat, stirring occasionally, for 10 minutes. Uncover and cook over medium to medium-high heat, stirring frequently, until onions caramelize and are light brown, about 20 minutes more.

2. Sprinkle onions with the sugar; add the garlic. Cook about 3 to 5 minutes, stirring often, over medium-high heat until onions are golden brown. Scrape into a bowl and set aside.

3. Spray the same skillet, without washing it, with olive oil. Dry-sauté the mushrooms for about 4 minutes over high heat, until browned. Set aside.

4. Preheat the oven to 450 degrees. Spray a removable-bottom, 8-by-11-inch rectangular tart pan with olive oil. Lay a sheet of phyllo in the pan so there is a 1-inch overhang on one long side and about half the sheet of dough covers the pan bottom and half is draped over the other long side. Sprinkle the phyllo in the pan with 1 tablespoon of the bread crumbs and spray with olive oil. Fold the excess half-sheet of dough back into the pan, sprinkle with another tablespoon of bread crumbs, and spray again with olive oil. Lay the second sheet of phyllo so the 1-inch overhang is on the opposite long side from the first. Sprinkle with remaining bread crumbs and spray with olive oil. Lay the excess half-sheet of dough back into the pan. Tuck in the sides, and spray again.

5. Reduce heat to 375 degrees. Bake the dough 5 minutes, until golden brown. Remove from oven.

6. Spread onions evenly over phyllo. Cover evenly with the mushrooms. Divide red pepper over the mushrooms, sprinkle with basil, and dot with cheese.

7. Bake 5 to 6 minutes, until the cheese melts. Let rest 2 to 3 minutes before slicing.

   Makes 6 to 8 slices

QUICK TIP

To roast red, yellow, or orange peppers:

* halve, remove seeds, and flatten with the heel of your hand
* broil, turning the pan, until peppers are uniformly blackened
* scrape into a paper bag and roll tightly shut
* let cool; strip and discard burned skin

TOMATO AND CHÈVRE TART

Tomatoes and cheese, a standard coupling of age-proven compatibility, blend here in a tart that travels well and, like most vegetable tarts, is as tempting at room temperature as it is hot from the oven.

Yield: 6 servings
Calories per serving: 161
Protein per serving: 9 g
Fat per serving: 3 g
Saturated fat per serving: 2 g
Cholesterol per serving: 5 mg
Carbohydrates per serving: 24 g
Sodium per serving: 318 mg
Fiber per serving: 4 g

3 tablespoons chicken broth
2 medium onions, chopped (preferably mild)
1 clove garlic, minced
3 pounds tomatoes, peeled and chopped (see page 52)
8 to 10 fresh basil leaves, snipped, or 1 teaspoon dried basil
⅛ teaspoon fennel seed
1 teaspoon sugar
½ teaspoon salt
freshly ground pepper to taste
¾ cup egg substitute
½ cup yogurt cheese (page 305) or nonfat sour cream
a few gratings fresh nutmeg
2 ounces chèvre cheese, such as Montrachet or Banon (if a milder taste is
   preferred)
2 sheets phyllo dough

1. Put the broth in a 10-inch skillet over high heat. Add the onions, cover, and cook over medium-high heat until limp, about 6 to 8 minutes. Add the garlic the last few minutes of cooking.

2. Add the tomatoes, basil, fennel seed, sugar, salt, and pepper. Cook over medium-low heat, stirring occasionally, for 5 minutes. If there is more than ¼ cup liquid left, raise the heat to high to evaporate. Set the mixture aside.

3. In a bowl or a food processor, beat together the egg substitute, yogurt cheese or nonfat sour cream, and nutmeg. Set it aside.

4. Spritz a 9-inch, removable-bottom tart ring or quiche pan with olive oil. Crisscross the 2 sheets of phyllo in the pan.

5. Preheat the oven to 350 degrees. Pour the onion-tomato mixture into the pan. Add the egg mixture. Crumble the chèvre on top. Roll and crumple the pastry edges in to create a rim; don't worry if the pastry tears. Spray the pastry edge with olive oil to help it brown. Place in the bottom third of the oven and bake 45 minutes or until the center no longer wiggles when shaken. Let it rest 10 minutes before slicing.

Nutrabyte

Canola oil has an excellent fatty-acid ratio; it is the highest of all oils in healthful polyunsaturated fats and the lowest in heart-damaging saturated fat.

CHAPTER 3

THE SOUP BOWL

THE RECIPES

THE SOUP BOWL

Of soup and love, the first is best.
—SPANISH PROVERB

Many cooks today are rediscovering the natural goodness of homemade soups. Maybe it's just the down-home appeal of a good bowl of soup. Regardless, soups are a natural in *The New Gourmet Light* cooking, for a deliciously satisfying first course can be enjoyed for fewer than 100 calories, or a nutritionally balanced meal consumed for under 300 calories. Some of the soups are skinny by nature, such as Gazpacho; others have been run through the calorie reducer, such as New Wave Fish Chowder. Some are a snap to fix; others require a lengthier kitchen commitment.

CHILLED TOMATO SOUP WITH BASIL-WALNUT CREAM

This is one of my favorite summertime soups because of its delightful combination of flavors and colors. There's no need to buy perfect tomatoes for this recipe; the "seconds" or bruised tomatoes offered at many farm stands are ideal. The soup freezes well too, making it possible to enjoy the flavor of summer in the dead of February. Garnish with a dollop of Basil-Walnut Cream or Pesto.

Yield: 4 cups
Calories per cup: 106
Protein per cup: 4 g
Fat per cup: 1 g
Saturated fat per cup: trace
Cholesterol per cup: 1 mg
Carbohydrates per cup: 23 g
Sodium per cup: 430 mg
Fiber per cup: 5 g

3 pounds ripe tomatoes, cored and quartered

8 to 10 fresh basil leaves, snipped, or 1 teaspoon dried basil

2 medium onions, sliced

2 cloves garlic, minced

1 to 2 teaspoons sugar

1 tablespoon fresh tarragon, snipped, or 1 teaspoon dried tarragon

¾ teaspoon salt

freshly ground pepper to taste

½ to ¾ cup chicken broth, if needed

Basil-Walnut Cream (page 16) or Pesto (page 301) for garnish

1. Put the tomatoes in a large saucepan with the basil, onions, garlic, sugar, tarragon, salt, and pepper. Simmer on medium-high, covered, until tomatoes are completely soft and pulpy, about 20 minutes. Stir occasionally.

2. Uncover the pan, lower the heat to medium-low, and cook about 30 minutes more or until reduced by a third.

3. In batches process soup in a food processor, blender, or food mill. Strain, if desired, to remove the seeds and skins. Chill and serve the soup garnished with Basil-Walnut Cream or Pesto.

GAZPACHO

This zesty bowl of garden goodies, which is really improved the second day, is naturally low in calories. For a special treat serve with the Pesto on page 301, or garnish with minced fresh cilantro leaves.

1¾ pounds ripe tomatoes, peeled (see Quick Tip, page 52)

1 medium onion, chopped

1 cucumber, peeled, seeded, and chopped

1 green pepper, seeded and chopped

1 red pepper, seeded and chopped (optional)

1 clove garlic, minced

24 ounces tomato juice

4 tablespoons red wine vinegar

1 teaspoon salt

a few drops hot pepper sauce

2 tablespoons chopped chives (from scallion tops)

oven-dried croutons (recipe follows, optional)

cilantro leaves (optional)

Yield: 6 cups

Calories per cup: 64

Protein per cup: 2 g

Fat per cup: 1 g

Saturated fat per cup: trace

Cholesterol per cup: 0

Carbohydrates per cup: 15 g

Sodium per cup: 799 mg

Fiber per cup: 3 g

1. In a food processor or blender, combine half the tomatoes, all the juice from the same, the onion, half the cucumber, half the green pepper, half the red pepper, all the garlic, and half the tomato juice. Process until somewhat smooth.

2. Stir in the remaining tomato juice; the vinegar, salt, and pepper sauce; the remaining tomato, cucumber, and peppers; and all the chives. Chill at least 2 hours; also chill the soup bowls. Serve with oven-dried croutons and cilantro leaves, if desired.

OVEN-DRIED CROUTONS

1. Dice 4 slices of bread. Place in a single layer on a cookie sheet. Spray with olive oil. Bake in a 325-degree oven for 15 minutes; stir the cubes occasionally.

Yield: 6 cups (¼-cup serving size)

Calories per serving: 13

Protein per serving: trace

Fat per serving: trace

Saturated fat per serving: trace

Cholesterol per serving: 0

Carbohydrates per serving: 2 g

Sodium per serving: 16 mg

Fiber per serving: trace

QUICK TIP

To peel and seed tomatoes (seeding tomatoes is always optional):

* core out the stem end; cut a cross in the opposite end
* immerse in boiling water 15 to 30 seconds
* cool under running water; strip skins
* to seed, squeeze into a sieve placed over a bowl, then press the seeds in the sieve to remove juice

CAULIFLOWER "CREAM" WITH YELLOW PEPPER PUREE

Cauliflower is nothing but a cabbage with a college education.
—MARK TWAIN

In a class ahead of its cousin the cabbage or not, cauliflower is a calorie counter's dream, supplying only 28 calories a cup and a good amount of vitamin C. Here it's pureed in a soup to be served hot or cold and garnished with a swirl of Yellow Pepper Puree, an economical way to serve delicious but rather dear yellow peppers. The puree also makes a delightful dip for vegetables at cocktail time. You may substitute red peppers for the yellow. Because commercially prepared cream soups can get as much as 60 percent of their calories from fat, it makes sense to create your own using *The New Gourmet Light* way.

For the Soup

3 small leeks, white part only
3 cups chopped cauliflower (about ½ head)
1½ cups skim milk
½ cup skimmed evaporated milk
1 small potato, peeled and diced
¾ teaspoon salt
freshly ground pepper to taste
freshly grated nutmeg

For the Yellow Pepper Puree

2 yellow peppers, peeled and seeded (see Quick Tip, page 44)
1 cup loosely packed snipped fresh basil leaves or 2 tablespoons dried basil
4 tablespoons grated Parmesan-Reggiano cheese
1 tablespoon olive oil

Yield of soup: 4 cups
Calories per cup: 140
Protein per cup: 11 g
Fat per cup: 1 g
Saturated fat per cup: trace
Cholesterol per cup: 4 mg
Carbohydrates per cup: 24 g
Sodium per cup: 534 mg
Fiber per cup: 3 g

Yield of puree: 1 cup
Calories per tablespoon: 80
Protein per tablespoon: 3 g
Fat per tablespoon: 5 g
Saturated fat per tablespoon: 1 g
Cholesterol per tablespoon: 4 mg
Carbohydrates per tablespoon: 7 g
Sodium per tablespoon: 94 mg
Fiber per tablespoon: 2 g

To Prepare the Soup

1. Slice the leeks and rinse thoroughly. Place the leeks in a 1-quart saucepan with enough water to half-cover. Cover the pan; turn heat to high. When a boil is reached, reduce the heat so the liquid simmers. Uncover after 10 minutes and continue to cook until the leeks are soft, about 5 minutes more. Drain and reserve liquid.

2. Combine the cauliflower with both kinds of milk, potato, salt, pepper, and leeks in a 2-quart saucepan.

3. Cover the pan, bring mixture to a boil, and reduce heat to maintain a simmer. Simmer for 20 minutes.

4. Puree the mixture in a food processor or in batches in a blender. Thin, if desired, with the reserved liquid from Step 1, or milk. Add nutmeg and taste for seasoning adjustment. Overseason if serving the soup cold. Serve with a tablespoon of the yellow pepper puree swirled in.

To Prepare the Yellow Pepper Puree

1. Chop the peeled and seeded peppers and puree them in a food processor, blender, or food mill.

2. Add the basil, cheese, and olive oil to the peppers. The puree will be thick and chunky. It will keep up to one week chilled, or it may be frozen.

SHERRIED FIVE-MUSHROOM SOUP

Rich and robust but still light, excellent with Portabella, Eggplant, and Red Pepper Roll-Ups (page 21), Whole Wheat Vegetable Tortillas (page 23), or Bruschetta (page 29), this soup may be made up to 24 hours in advance. Buying dried mushrooms such as porcini in bulk makes "cents" (see Shopping Sources, page 306). The recipe is also successful without the whisper of Demi-Glace Gold (see Shopping Sources).

½ ounce dried porcini mushrooms

3 shallots, minced (about ½ cup minced)

3 cups rich beef broth

10 ounces button mushrooms, thinly sliced

6 ounces crimini (sometimes called brown) mushrooms, thinly sliced

2 medium portabella mushroom caps (about 5 ounces) thinly sliced, then
    sliced crosswise in thirds

3 ounces shiitake mushrooms, stemmed and thinly sliced

¼ cup dry sherry

¼ cup part-skim ricotta cheese

2 tablespoons egg substitute or 2 tablespoons of a beaten egg

1 teaspoon curry powder (optional)

1 teaspoon Demi-Glace Gold (optional)

2 bay leaves

¼ teaspoon celery seed

salt and pepper to taste

a dash cayenne

2 teaspoons minced fresh parsley, for garnish (optional)

Yield: 8 cups

Calories per cup: 56

Protein per cup: 4 g

Fat per cup: 1 g

Saturated fat per cup: 0.51 g

Cholesterol per cup: 4 mg

Carbohydrates per cup: 8 g

Sodium per cup: 26 mg

Fiber per cup: 1 g

1. Put the porcini in a glass measure with ½ cup water and microwave at high (100 percent power) for 1 minute. Set aside to soak about 10 to 15 minutes.

2. Combine the shallots and beef broth in a 2½-quart saucepan. Bring to a boil; reduce heat so liquid simmers. Cover and simmer while preparing mushrooms.

3. Spray a 12-inch nonstick skillet with olive oil. Sauté the button and crimini mushrooms, spraying as needed with olive oil, until softened (they won't brown), about 5 to 7 minutes. Scrape into a bowl.

4. Spray the same skillet again, and add the portabella caps and the shiitakes. Sauté, stirring often, for 4 to 5 minutes; add to the other mushrooms.

5. While the shiitakes cook, strain the porcini through a moistened coffee filter or piece of wet cheesecloth lining a strainer placed over the simmering broth. Mince the porcini and add to the mushroom bowl.

6. Deglaze (see Glossary) the mushroom skillet with the sherry (no heat needed), stirring to dislodge bits of mushroom on the pan's bottom. Add the reduced sherry to the broth.

7. Combine the ricotta and egg in a food processor. Blend briefly. With the machine running pour in 1 cup of broth.

8. Stir the cheese-egg mixture into the remaining broth. Maintain a bare simmer, removing the pan, if need be, from the heat for a bit. If the broth boils now, the cheese will curdle. (If this happens, process with a teaspoon of lemon juice to re-form the emulsion.) Season with the curry and demi-glace, if desired, and the bay leaves, celery seed, salt and pepper, and cayenne.

9. Simmer 10 minutes, never letting the soup boil. Garnish, if desired, with parsley.

Makes 8 cups

Nutmeg

Recipes in this book frequently specify using freshly grated nutmeg, as it is considerably more flavorful than the ground variety. Whole nutmegs—the pit of a West Indian peachlike fruit—are available at some supermarkets and specialty food shops. Mace, having a similar but stronger taste than nutmeg, is the outside sheathing that covers the nutmeg. It is sold already ground. Nutmeg grinders (similar to small pepper mills) are available, as are small, inexpensive graters that often have a hinged top to store the nutmeg.

GRILLED CORN AND TOMATO CHOWDER WITH FRESH HERB SALSA

Thick and chunky, bursting with the smoky flavor of grilled corn and tomatoes, this chowder dishes out nowhere near the 15 grams of fat found in a traditional cup. Although a recipe is given here for fresh herb salsa, the Pesto on page 301 would be equally good. Leftover herb salsa will keep in the refrigerator up to 12 days.

Yield: 6 cups chowder

Calories per cup: 111

Protein per cup: 4 g

Fat per cup: 2 g

Saturated fat per cup: trace

Cholesterol per cup: 2 mg

Carbohydrates per cup: 23 g

Sodium per cup: 199 mg

Fiber per cup: 4 g

For the Chowder

5 ears of corn, husks left on

½ head garlic

½ red onion, peeled

2 tomatoes, cored and quartered, seeds popped out with your thumb

1 teaspoon canola or olive oil

3 cups chicken broth

½ teaspoon salt

pepper to taste

For the Herb Salsa

1 bunch fresh basil, stemmed (about 1½ cups loosely packed)

½ cup tightly packed fresh parsley, stemmed

3 tablespoons chicken broth

1 tablespoon plus 1 teaspoon balsamic vinegar

4 tablespoons grated Parmesan-Reggiano cheese

1 teaspoon sugar

2 teaspoons walnut oil

½ teaspoon salt

freshly ground pepper to taste

¼ teaspoon crushed red pepper flakes

To Prepare the Chowder

1. Soak the unhusked corn in a sink full of water for 5 minutes.

2. Grill the corn with the husks on, turning to cook evenly, until the kernels are roasted, about 12 minutes. At the same time grill the garlic on a rack or on foil for about 20 minutes, or until the cloves (not the papery outer layers) are very soft and mushy. Brush the onion and tomatoes with the oil. Grill the onion until lightly blackened and softened, about 10 minutes. Grill the tomatoes until the skin is blackened and softened, about 5 minutes. Individual grill temperatures will vary and affect cooking times; err on the underdone side.

3. When the corn is cool enough to handle, husk it and cut the kernels from the cobs. Reserve about 1 cup kernels. Peel the garlic, discarding the papery outer covering.

4. In the bowl of a food processor, combine the remaining corn kernels, peeled garlic, onion, and chicken broth. Process until pureed, about 1 minute.

5. Add the tomatoes, salt, and pepper. Process just until combined. Chunks of tomato should remain. Stir in the reserved corn.

6. Place soup in a 2½-quart saucepan. Place over medium heat and simmer 10–12 minutes, stirring occasionally. Soup may be chilled and reheated or served immediately with herb salsa.

To Prepare the Herb Salsa

1. In the bowl of a food processor, combine all salsa ingredients. Process until pureed, about 1 minute.

2. To serve, place a heaping tablespoon of herb salsa on each cup of hot chowder. Let diners swirl it into the chowder themselves.

QUICK TIP

Fresh herbs are vastly superior to dried. When you can't grow your own, do buy fresh, despite the added cost.

HARVEST SOUP

A hearty soup, perfect for chilly days. Any leftovers freeze nicely.

1 1-pound package yellow or green split peas

2 carrots

1 Spanish onion

1 parsnip, peeled

3 stalks celery, stringed

½ purple-top turnip

2 cloves garlic

1 cup chopped fresh flat-leaf parsley (about ½ bunch)

1 meaty ham bone, fat removed, or 2 or 3 ham hocks

1 tablespoon minced fresh thyme or 1 teaspoon dried thyme

2 teaspoons stone-ground mustard

2 teaspoons salt or to taste

1 teaspoon ground pepper

1 teaspoon cumin

Yield: about 4 quarts

Calories per cup: 141

Protein per cup: 10 g

Fat per cup: 3 g

Saturated fat per cup: 1 g

Cholesterol per cup: 9 mg

Carbohydrates per cup: 20 g

Sodium per cup: 469 mg

Fiber per cup: 3 g

1. Place the split peas in a microwave-safe 4-quart container. Add 2 quarts water, cover, and microwave at high (100 percent power) for 30 minutes. *Alternatively, soak the peas in water to cover overnight or for 8 hours. Drain.*

2. Chop the carrots, onion, parsnip, celery, turnip, and garlic in batches in the bowl of a food processor or by hand.

3. Combine the microwaved or soaked peas, chopped vegetables, and all remaining ingredients in a microwave-safe 4-quart container. Add 10 cups water. Cover and microwave at high (100 percent power) for 1 hour and 20 minutes. *Alternatively, bring all ingredients to a simmer on the stovetop and simmer 2 hours.*

4. Remove and discard the bones. Puree the soup in batches in the food processor.

CURRIED ZUCCHINI SOUP

2 large onions, diced

1 quart plus 6 tablespoons chicken broth

1 clove garlic, minced

3 to 4 pounds zucchini, diced

1 cup cooked rice

1 tablespoon curry powder

8 to 10 fresh basil leaves, snipped, or 1 teaspoon dried basil

5 to 6 fresh sage leaves, snipped, or ½ teaspoon dried sage

1 teaspoon fresh thyme leaves or ½ teaspoon dried thyme

1 teaspoon salt (less if using canned broth)

freshly ground pepper to taste

½ cup grated low-fat Cheddar cheese

1 cup skim milk

Yield: approximately 6 cups

Calories per cup: 158

Protein per cup: 10 g

Fat per cup: 2 g

Saturated fat per cup: trace

Cholesterol per cup: 8 mg

Carbohydrates per cup: 26 g

Sodium per cup: 447 mg

Fiber per cup: 5 g

1. "Sauté" the onions in a 10-inch skillet in the 6 tablespoons of chicken broth until they're limp. Add the garlic and cook 1 minute more.

2. In a 4-quart or larger saucepan, combine the onions, garlic, zucchini, remaining broth, rice, curry powder, herbs, salt, and pepper. Cover and simmer at least 1 hour or as long as 2.

3. Puree the zucchini-onion mixture in a food processor or food mill in batches.

4. Stir in the grated cheese and milk. Heat to blend.

ROASTED THREE-ONION SOUP

Oven roasting some of the onions for this soup imparts a smoky, almost sweet flavor. The onions, shallots, and garlic may be roasted early in the day.

2 Spanish onions, halved

1 medium yellow onion, halved

2 shallots, ends discarded, halved

6 cloves garlic

2 13¾-ounce cans beef broth, plus an additional cup

¼ cup full-bodied red wine

1 teaspoon minced fresh thyme or ½ teaspoon dried thyme

1 bay leaf

1 teaspoon salt or to taste

½ teaspoon beef bouillon concentrate (see Shopping Sources, page 306)

1 teaspoon sugar

2 tablespoons instant-blending flour

1 tablespoon Cognac (optional)

freshly grated Parmesan-Reggiano cheese (optional)

Yield: about 2 quarts

Calories per cup: 55

Protein per cup: 2 g

Fat per cup: trace

Saturated fat per cup: trace

Cholesterol per cup: 0

Carbohydrates per cup: 11 g

Sodium per cup: 226 mg

Fiber per cup: 1 g

1. Spray a baking dish with olive oil spray. Roast 1 Spanish onion (reserve the other for Step 4) and the yellow onion in a foil-covered baking dish in a 350-degree oven for 30 minutes (no need to preheat). Add the shallots, and roast 30 minutes more. Add the garlic, and roast 30 minutes more. Let cool, then discard the skins.

2. Place the roasted onions, shallots, and garlic in the bowl of a food processor with 1 cup of the broth. Puree.

3. Turn the onion puree into a 2½-quart saucepan. Add all but 1 cup of the remaining broth, plus the red wine, thyme, bay leaf, salt, and bouillon concentrate. Bring to a simmer.

4. Meanwhile thinly slice the remaining onion. Spray a nonstick 10-inch skillet with olive oil. Sauté the onion over medium-high heat, stirring often,

until onion is browned and limp, about 10 minutes. Sprinkle with the sugar and flour and stir over medium-high heat, 1 minute.

5. Add the remaining broth and simmer, stirring occasionally, 4 minutes more. Add to the onion broth mixture in the saucepan. Stir in the Cognac and simmer 10 to 30 minutes. Remove the bay leaf before serving. Pass cheese at the table.

LEMON BROCCOLI SOUP

A hearty cold-weather soup that makes the most of root vegetables such as potatoes and the much-maligned turnip, this soup will keep up to 4 days.

Yield: 8 cups

Calories per cup: 74

Protein per cup: 3 g

Fat per cup: 0.4 g

Saturated fat per cup: 0.12 g

Cholesterol per cup: 2 mg

Carbohydrates per cup: 13 g

Sodium per cup: 312 mg

Fiber per cup: 3 g

2 stalks broccoli

1 small onion, peeled and chopped

1 small yellow turnip or rutabaga, peeled and diced (about 2 cups)

1 medium baking potato, peeled and diced

6 cups chicken broth

½ cup fresh minced parsley

the zest of 2 lemons (see Quick Tip, page 63), or gremolata (page 172)

6 tablespoons dry sherry

1 tablespoon fat-free sour cream

1 teaspoon sugar

1 teaspoon salt

freshly ground pepper to taste

1. Slice off and discard the bottom inch of the broccoli stalks. Peel the stalks. Chop the flowerets and stalks. You should have about 4 cups.

2. Combine the broccoli, onion, turnip, potato, chicken broth, and parsley in a 4-quart saucepan over high heat. Cover until the mixture comes to a boil, in about 6 to 8 minutes. Uncover, and adjust heat to maintain a simmer for 35 minutes.

3. Puree the mixture in a food processor. Return the soup to the saucepan and stir in the lemon zest, sherry, sour cream, sugar, salt, and pepper. Heat just to combine.

Serves 8

QUICK TIP

To zest lemons, rub the whole lemon over the finest side of a hand-held grater. Use the "nude" lemon soon; without its peel it will spoil readily.

SPIKED SQUASH SOUP WITH APPLE

Repeat "Oh, it was easy!" several times while putting together this quick soup. It's an acceptably humble response for the compliments this velvety puree will earn you.

Yield: about 2 quarts.

Calories per cup: 71

Protein per cup: 2 g

Fat per cup: trace

Saturated fat per cup: trace

Cholesterol per cup: 0

Carbohydrates per cup: 16 g

Sodium per cup: 310 mg

Fiber per cup: 2 g

1 cup cider

1 medium butternut squash, peeled, seeded, and roughly chopped

1 Granny Smith apple, peeled, cored, and roughly chopped

½ small Spanish onion, chopped (about ¾ cup)

2 14½-ounce cans chicken broth

1 teaspoon brown sugar

1 teaspoon chopped fresh thyme or ½ teaspoon dried thyme

1 teaspoon salt

freshly ground pepper to taste

a few gratings fresh nutmeg

1 tablespoon bourbon

snipped chives for garnish (optional)

8 to 10 roasted, peeled, and chopped chestnuts (optional)

1. Combine the cider, squash, apple, onion, broth, sugar, thyme, salt, pepper, and nutmeg in a 2½-quart saucepan. Cover and bring to a boil over high heat. Reduce heat to medium; simmer 35 minutes.

2. Puree the soup in batches and return to the saucepan. Stir in the bourbon. Ladle into bowls and garnish with chives and chestnuts, if desired.

PUMPKIN MAPLE SOUP

Served in small pumpkins, this soup makes a festive start to a holiday meal. Of course, it's just as good ladled into soup dishes. Fortunately, the microwave makes easy work of cooking fresh pumpkin, for it's well worth the little extra effort.

Yield: about 2 quarts
Calories per cup: 78
Protein per cup: 2 g
Fat per cup: trace
Saturated fat per cup: trace
Cholesterol per cup: 0
Carbohydrates per cup: 18 g
Sodium per cup: 293 mg
Fiber per cup: 2 g

1 pumpkin, about 3 pounds, halved and seeded, or 4 cups unsweetened
    canned pumpkin puree
½ small Spanish onion, chopped (about ¾ cup)
1 fresh jalapeño pepper, halved and seeded
1 13¾-ounce can chicken broth
⅓ cup orange juice
3 tablespoons maple syrup
1 tablespoon maple extract
1 teaspoon salt
¼ teaspoon cayenne powder, or to taste
dash ground cloves
8 small (about ½ to ¾ pound each) pumpkins with attractive stems, lids cut
    into each, stringy pulp discarded (optional)

1. Reserve the pumpkin seeds if you wish to roast them for a garnish (instructions follow). Put the pumpkin halves (from the 3-pound pumpkin) in a plastic bag with about 2 tablespoons water. Tie the bag opening and microwave at high (100 percent power) for 30 minutes or until the flesh is soft when pierced with a fork. Drain. Scrape the flesh into the bowl of a food processor. Set aside while preparing the onion.

2. To roast the seeds, rinse them thoroughly and discard the stringy orange pulp. Spray a cookie sheet with olive oil. Arrange pumpkin seeds in a single

Nutrabyte

There are times when it might be better to eat a little something fattening than a lot of something skinny.

layer and spray again with olive oil. Salt according to taste. Roast in a 350-degree oven about 30 minutes.

3. Combine the onion, jalapeño pepper, and 1 cup of the chicken broth in a microwave-safe container. Cover and microwave at high (100 percent power) for 8 minutes.

4. While the onion cooks, puree the pumpkin with the remaining chicken broth. Scrape into a 2½-quart saucepan. (If using canned pumpkin, simply scrape the puree into the saucepan. Add the remaining broth.)

5. Puree the cooked onion, jalapeño, and cooking broth in a food processor. Stir into the pumpkin puree with the remaining ingredients.

6. Simmer about 10 minutes at medium-high; do not allow to boil. Serve in soup bowls, or ladle into prepared pumpkins and heat in a microwave for 5 minutes or until soup is warmed through. Pass roasted pumpkin seeds, if desired, at the table.

NEW WAVE FISH CHOWDER

Unlike traditional chowders, this New Wave version is low in fat. As an added bonus, cleanup is a snap, thanks to microwave cooking bags. The chowder is even better the second day.

4 small potatoes, peeled and cubed

3 medium onions, thinly sliced

celery leaves from 1 bunch of celery, minced (about 1 cup)

2 pounds boneless, skinless white fish fillets, such as cod, cut into 2-inch chunks

1 8-ounce bottle clam juice

1 12-ounce can skimmed evaporated milk

2 cups skim milk

1 clove garlic, minced

2 teaspoons salt

1 bay leaf

¼ teaspoon celery seed

1 tablespoon minced fresh dill or 1 teaspoon dried dill

1 teaspoon paprika

pepper to taste

1 cup skim milk

3 tablespoons instant-blending flour

Yield: 14 cups

Calories per cup: 153

Protein per cup: 17

Fat per cup: 0.8 g

Saturated fat per cup: 0.21 g

Cholesterol per cup: 30 mg

Carbohydrates per cup: 19 g

Sodium per cup: 440 mg

Fiber per cup: 2 g

1. Line a 3-quart microwave-safe bowl with a 12-pound-size microwave cooking bag. Fold excess bag down over the bowl's rim. Place all ingredients except the last cup of milk and flour in the bag. Close bag with the tie provided or with a strip of the bag itself.

2. Microwave at medium-high (75 percent power) for 1 hour or until potatoes are tender. Lift bag and jostle ingredients 2 to 3 times during cooking.

3. Mix the remaining cup of milk and the flour. Stir into the chowder. Microwave at medium-high (75 percent power) for 15 minute more. Chowder may be served immediately or reheated.

BOUILLABAISSE OF SCALLOPS

This soup perfumes the air. Serve it with the Fire and Ice Salad (page 82) for a fine, light cold-weather meal, or serve it chilled in summer.

Yield: 8 servings

Calories per serving: 100

Protein per serving: 10 g

Fat per serving: 0.8 g

Saturated fat per serving: 0.10 g

Cholesterol per serving: 16 mg

Carbohydrates per serving: 13 g

Sodium per serving: 98 mg

Fiber per serving: 2 g

2 leeks, white part only, thinly sliced

1 medium onion, thinly sliced

4 to 5 tablespoons chicken broth or bottled clam juice

4 large tomatoes, peeled, juice reserved (see page 52), or 2 cups canned tomatoes

2 cloves garlic, minced

4 cups fish stock or 3½ 8-ounce bottles clam juice mixed with 3 ounces vermouth and 1 ounce water

2 tablespoons orange zest

2 to 3 tablespoons orange juice, freshly squeezed preferred

6 to 7 fresh basil leaves, snipped, or 1 teaspoon dried basil

a pinch of saffron

1 bay leaf

¼ teaspoon dried thyme

½ teaspoon fennel seeds

1 pound scallops or white fish fillets, cut into chunks

2 tablespoons minced fresh parsley

a bowl of freshly grated Parmesan-Reggiano

1. "Sauté" the leeks and onion in a 10-inch skillet with the broth. Cover the pan while cooking, adding more liquid if necessary. *Alternatively, combine the leeks, onion, and broth in a microwave-safe container. Cover and microwave at high (100 percent power) for 8 minutes, or until softened.*

2. When the leeks and onion are limp, add the garlic, tomatoes, reserved juice, stock, orange zest, orange juice, basil, and saffron. Tie the bay leaf, thyme, and fennel in a cheesecloth bag (a bouquet garni) and add to the skil-

let. Simmer, covered, for 30 to 40 minutes.

3. Add the scallops, raise heat to medium, and cook, covered, until scallops are opaque, about 4 to 5 minutes.

4. Remove the bouquet garni, stir in the parsley, and taste for seasoning. Ladle the finished soup into warmed bowls and pass grated Parmesan-Reggiano cheese at the table.

Nutrabyte

Things that affect how much you can eat:
* age—our BMR (the rate at which we use calories) increases up to age five, then gradually and steadily decreases, with a brief spurt in adolescence
* hormones—probably the single most important factor affecting an individual's BMR
* muscle mass—those with greater muscle mass require more calories just to hang out on the couch, because lean tissue like muscle require more calories just to exist than fatty tissue does
* illness—some illnesses increase the rate at which we metabolize food
* pregnancy—also increases calorie use rate

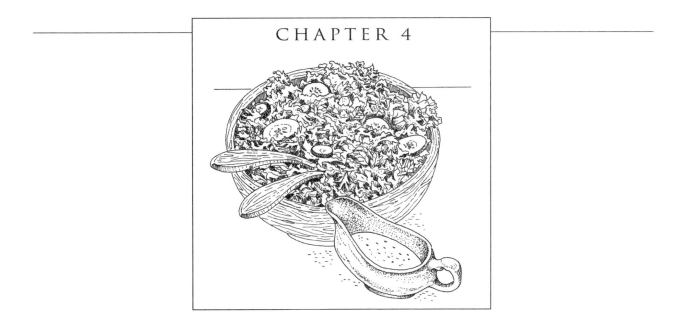

CHAPTER 4

SALADS AND THEIR DRESSINGS

THE RECIPES

Dressings

Salads

Salads and Their Dressings

Salads have risen to new heights, both in popularity and design, in recent years. Where once a few leaves of iceberg, chopped cucumber, and minced onion would suffice as a side dish, one now finds a range of rare goodies artfully presented as main-course meals. Radicchio, lamb's lettuce, and baked chèvre cheese are but a few of the salad items popular today. To support the demand, fancy green-grocers are popping up like mushrooms from coast to coast, offering an enormous selection of fresh produce from near and—thanks to modern transportation—far.

This chapter focuses on salads as a side course. The majority of the main dish salads are found in the chapter of the predominant ingredient.

The Salad Syndrome; or, the Invisible Calorie

It's become common knowledge that the culprit is the butter, not the potato, but the fats in salads remain invisible to many—that is, until they show up on the waistline. "All I ever have for lunch is a salad, and I still gain weight!" is a common lament. The demon is the salad dressing. According to the Center for Science in the Public Interest, the average adult woman gets more fat from salad dressing than from any other single food. Most dressings are very high in fat, contributing 150 to 200 calories and as much as 14 grams of fat in just 2 tablespoons to an otherwise skinny bowl of greens. *The New Gourmet Light* dressings are based mostly on stocks or consommé and contribute far fewer calories than commercial preparations. The recipes that follow are dressings for mixed green salads; beyond that are recipes for specialty salads.

VINAIGRETTES

Vinaigrette, a classic combination of oil and vinegar with or without additional seasonings, is the true French dressing. Following are several variations on the simple vinaigrette theme, all prepared in *The New Gourmet Light* way. (For more on skinny dressings, see the Primer, page 7.) First, these tips:

1. If you don't make your own naturally thick chicken or beef stock, use commercially prepared consommé or canned chicken broth. The former, because of its added gelatin, will give the best results.

2. When using homemade stock, double the amount called for in the recipe and boil it until reduced by half. This double-strength stock will give your dressings body. Don't reduce commercial broths, though, for they will be too salty.

3. If you do not use canned consommé, you will need to add salt to taste.

4. If possible, prepare the dressing at least 2 hours before serving, to let the flavors marry.

5. A dressing made with homemade stock or store-bought consommé will jell in the refrigerator. Remove it an hour before serving or heat briefly to liquefy.

HERBED FRENCH VINAIGRETTE

A true French dressing is not the mayonnaise-ketchup variety commonly called "French," but an emulsion of oil and vinegar. Here is a skinny version.

*5 tablespoons double-strength homemade beef or chicken stock or canned
    consommé*
2 tablespoons red wine vinegar
1 teaspoon sugar
½ teaspoon Dijon-style mustard
1 tablespoon extra-virgin olive oil
1 clove garlic, minced
2 teaspoons chives, minced
1 teaspoon paprika

1. Combine all the ingredients in a jar, shake well, check for seasoning, and refrigerate.

Yield: ⅔ cup
Calories per tablespoon: 13
Protein per tablespoon: trace
Fat per tablespoon: 1 g
Saturated fat per tablespoon: trace
Cholesterol per tablespoon: trace
Carbohydrates per tablespoon: 1 g
Sodium per tablespoon: 9 mg
Fiber per tablespoon: trace

APPLE-MAPLE VINAIGRETTE

Try this vinaigrette on a winter salad of tossed greens, chopped apples, a handful of raisins, and just a smattering of chopped walnuts. Maggi seasoning is a soy-based product that you'll find in the supermarket with condiments such as Worcestershire sauce (which is an acceptable substitute).

1 McIntosh apple, peeled, cored, and roughly chopped

½ cup cider

2 tablespoons white vinegar

1 tablespoon walnut oil

2 teaspoons maple syrup

1 teaspoon Maggi seasoning (optional)

½ teaspoon stone-ground mustard

½ teaspoon salt

freshly ground pepper to taste

1. Combine all ingredients in the bowl of a food processor. Turn machine to full power until apple is pureed. Store in the refrigerator up to 1 week.

Yield: 1 cup

Calories per tablespoon: 26

Protein per tablespoon: trace

Fat per tablespoon: 2 g

Saturated fat per tablespoon: trace

Cholesterol per tablespoon: 0

Carbohydrates per tablespoon: 3 g

Sodium per tablespoon: 69 mg

Fiber per tablespoon: trace

Nutrabyte

Because *The New Gourmet Light* cooking uses so little oil, buy the best. Extra-virgin olive is the first pressing of the olives and the most flavorful. Virgin quality is the next, and so on until the final pressings, which rely on hot water poured over the pits to coax the final droplets of oil. "Light" olive oil refers only to the color and flavor of the oil, not its calorie content, which remains the same as that of other olive oils, about 120 calories per tablespoon.

BALSAMIC–WALNUT OIL VINAIGRETTE

This is my "house" dressing. Buy the very best balsamic vinegar and walnut oil you can for premium flavor. Keep walnut and other oils refrigerated to prevent them from becoming rancid.

double-strength homemade beef or chicken stock or canned consommé

walnut oil (refrigerate after opening)

balsamic vinegar

1 tablespoon water

½ teaspoon prepared mustard

½ teaspoon sugar

freshly ground pepper to taste

1. In a 1-cup glass measure, pour in the consommé until the liquid reaches the ¼-cup mark. Add walnut oil until the liquid measures ⅓ cup. Add the balsamic vinegar until the liquid measures ½ cup. Add water, mustard, sugar, and pepper. Shake well, check for seasoning, and refrigerate.

Yield: ½ cup

Calories per tablespoon: 26

Protein per tablespoon: trace

Fat per tablespoon: 2 g

Saturated fat per tablespoon: trace

Cholesterol per tablespoon: trace

Carbohydrates per tablespoon: 2 g

Sodium per tablespoon: 5 mg

Fiber per tablespoon: trace

Vinegars

Once used as a medicine or as a drink when heavily diluted with water, and often used as a preservative with salt, vinegars are the darling of the gourmet food industry. Where most kitchen cabinets once stored pretty much your basic cider variety, many shelves are now crowded with enough labels and flavors to rival a modest wine cellar. Indeed, some vinegars carry a higher price tag than jug wines! Some vinegars, such as balsamic, are even aged like spirits in oak barrels. The added cost is offset by the wonderful flavor they impart.

BLACK SESAME AND MIRIN DRESSING

A sweet dressing, this is particularly tasty on a green salad of Boston or Bibb lettuce, watercress, young spinach leaves, and cilantro. A handful of canned, drained mandarin orange sections or fresh orange sections adds color and flavor too. A browse in the Asian section of the supermarket will yield the mirin, a sweet rice wine (see Glossary, page 308), the rice vinegar, and possibly the black sesame seeds; however, common tan sesame seeds are a perfectly fine substitute. This is also yummy as a basting sauce for grilled chicken breasts, with an additional tablespoon or so splashed on after cooking.

Yield: 1 cup

Calories per tablespoon: 27

Protein per tablespoon: 0.4 g

Fat per tablespoon: 0.6 g

Saturated fat per tablespoon: trace

Cholesterol per tablespoon: none

Carbohydrates per tablespoon: 5 g

Sodium per tablespoon: 90 mg

2 tablespoons black sesame seeds, toasted (see Quick Tip, page 38)

6 tablespoons orange juice concentrate, frozen or thawed

2 tablespoons grated fresh ginger root (no need to peel if the root is relatively fresh)

4 tablespoons rice vinegar

2 tablespoons mirin

2 tablespoons water or drained liquid from mandarin oranges

1. Combine all ingredients in a shake jar or food processor and blend well.
   Makes 1 cup

Nutrabyte

Looking for how many grams of fat there are in an ounce of Cheddar cheese or how many calories in fudge sauce? The bible of food values, the venerable Handbook No. 8 assembled by the USDA, is now on-line. Type in the name of food you're looking for and up comes an amazingly complete profile: http://www.nal.usda.gov/fnic/foodcomp

CAESAR SALAD DRESSING

Make this salad with romaine lettuce, freshly grated Parmesan-Reggiano or Romano cheese, and, if you like, a handful of freshly made croutons. Arrange the lettuce leaves spoke-fashion around the plate, sprinkle cheese and croutons on top, and drizzle with the following dressing. To eat, pick up the leaves in your fingers, using them as scoops to hold the croutons and cheese. Delicious! To make this into a meal, marinate ⅓ pound shrimp or ¼ pound chicken breast strips in a few tablespoons of the dressing about 20 minutes, then grill. Serve on the greens.

Yield: ¾ cup

Calories per tablespoon: 27

Protein per tablespoon: 2 g

Fat per tablespoon: 2 g

Saturated fat per tablespoon: trace

Cholesterol per tablespoon: 2 mg

Carbohydrates per tablespoon: 0.6 g

Sodium per tablespoon: 64 mg

3 eggs

5 tablespoons double-strength homemade beef or chicken stock or canned consommé or strong broth made from mushroom-base concentrate (see Shopping Sources, page 306)

juice of ½ lemon (about 2 tablespoons)

1 tablespoon extra-virgin olive oil

1 teaspoon Worcestershire sauce

1 clove garlic, minced, or 3 roasted cloves garlic (see page 305)

a few drops hot pepper sauce

freshly ground black pepper to taste

1 ounce best quality Parmesan-Reggiano cheese, grated or in long thin strips made with a potato peeler

1. To coddle the eggs, bring 2 cups water to a boil. Add the eggs, cover, and when water boils again, uncover and cook for 1½ minutes. Drain and cool under running water.

2. Separate the eggs, discarding the yolks (or add ½ yolk if you like) and slipping the whites into a food processor or the beaker of a hand-held electric blender. Add all remaining ingredients except the cheese. Blend thoroughly.

3. Drizzle over greens; top with cheese strips and croutons.
Note: For instructions on making croutons, see page 52.
    Makes 6 ounces

QUICK TIP

Lemon juice will help remove the scent of garlic from your fingers.

SESAME SEED DRESSING

This dressing and the Black Sesame and Mirin Dressing (page 76) are excellent on a concoction of baby spinach, arugula, and cilantro. That's right—treat the cilantro like a green, adding it in a ratio of about 1 part cilantro stems to 3 parts each arugula and baby spinach leaves.

2 tablespoons white or tan sesame seeds, toasted (see Quick Tip, page 38)
4 tablespoons double-strength homemade beef or chicken stock or canned consommé
2 teaspoons Asian sesame oil
2 tablespoons lemon juice
1 teaspoon sugar
freshly ground pepper to taste

1. Combine all ingredients in a jar. Shake well.

Yield: ½ cup

Calories per tablespoon: 25

Protein per tablespoon: trace

Fat per tablespoon: 2 g

Saturated fat per tablespoon: trace

Cholesterol per tablespoon: trace

Carbohydrates per tablespoon: 1 g

Sodium per tablespoon: 1 mg

Fiber per tablespoon: trace

Fresh Herb Vinaigrette

This is the dressing of choice for herb gardeners looking for ways to preserve summer's fragrant gifts, for it freezes nicely. Delicious on vine-ripened tomatoes (which have twice the vitamin C of hothouse winter tomatoes) or cold fish salads tossed with leftover corn cut from the cob.

1 cup loosely packed fresh basil leaves

½ cup loosely packed fresh tarragon leaves

2 tablespoons homemade chicken or beef stock or canned consommé

1 tablespoon raspberry or red wine vinegar

1 tablespoon olive oil

1 scant teaspoon sugar

freshly ground pepper to taste

1. Put the herbs in a bowl or measuring cup and snip repeatedly with scissors until they're reduced to about half the original volume (or process them in a food processor).

2. In a food processor or blender, combine the herbs with the remaining ingredients. Blend until herbs are mostly minced and sauce is a lovely pale green. Check for seasoning. Can be frozen.

Yield: ¾ cup

Calories per tablespoon: 13

Protein per tablespoon: trace

Fat per tablespoon: 1 g

Saturated fat per tablespoon: trace

Cholesterol per tablespoon: none

Carbohydrates per tablespoon: 0.7 g

Sodium per tablespoon: 3 mg

Fiber per tablespoon: trace

Nutrabyte

All oils contain three types of fats: polyunsaturates (good fats), considered to be beneficial fats for their ability to help rid the body of cholesterol; monosaturates, considered neutral; and saturated fats (bad fats), which are linked to elevated blood cholesterol levels.

OAK CREEK ORANGE-WALNUT DRESSING

A fresh, light, fruity dressing, particularly delicious on sharp greens like arugula and frisée—add a handful of cilantro leaves for punch. See Shopping Sources (page 306) for lemon oil or use 2 tablespoons walnut oil and 1 teaspoon lemon juice or ¼ teaspoon lemon extract.

3 tablespoons orange juice concentrate or 5 tablespoons orange juice (the concentrate will have more body)

2 tablespoons rice wine vinegar

1 tablespoon lemon oil

1 tablespoon walnut oil

2 tablespoons water

freshly ground pepper to taste

1 teaspoon lemon zest (optional)

1. Combine all ingredients in a blender or food processor and mix well.

Yield: about ½ cup

Calories per tablespoon: 40

Protein per tablespoon: 0.2 g

Fat per tablespoon: 3 g

Saturated fat per tablespoon: trace

Cholesterol per tablespoon: none

Carbohydrates per tablespoon: 3 g

Sodium per tablespoon: 77 mg

Nutrabyte

All oils are 100 percent fat and have between 100 and 120 calories a tablespoon.

JAPANESE DRESSING FOR SNOW PEAS

Yet another alternative to a mayonnaise dressing is tofu, a soybean product. The following recipe is excellent tossed with blanched snow peas or broccoli.

Yield: 1 cup

Calories per tablespoon: 20

Protein per tablespoon: 1 g

Fat per tablespoon: 2 g

Saturated fat per tablespoon: trace

Cholesterol per tablespoon: trace

Carbohydrates per tablespoon: trace

Sodium per tablespoon: 11 mg

Fiber per tablespoon: trace

4 ounces tofu

5 tablespoons double-strength homemade chicken stock or canned consommé

1 tablespoon Asian sesame oil

1 tablespoon walnut oil

2 tablespoons rice wine vinegar, available in the Asian section of your supermarket

1 teaspoon reduced-sodium soy sauce

1 quarter-size piece of fresh ginger root, peeled and grated

1. Combine all ingredients in a food processor or blender and blend. Chill.

BEYOND SIMPLE TOSSED...

No matter how innovative and imaginative your mix of greens, there are times when you yearn for something different. Perhaps a Fire and Ice Salad or the pleasant bite of Counter Slaw. These are side dishes, lunches, or light dinners; heavier offerings are found in the seafood and poultry chapters.

FIRE AND ICE SALAD

This salad gets its name from the flame of the brandy and the chill of the greens. Often when a recipe indicates flaming, it is purely for effect; here igniting the liquor renders it mellow. A wonderful salad for chilly nights.

Yield: 4 servings

Calories per serving: 119

Protein per serving: 6 g

Fat per serving: 2 g

Saturated fat per serving: trace

Cholesterol per serving: 1 mg

Carbohydrates per serving: 19 g

Sodium per serving: 321 mg

Fiber per serving: 4 g

The Salad

1 pound fresh spinach, stems and backbones removed, washed and spun
   dry (baby spinach preferred)

2 carrots, grated

½ small Bermuda onion, thinly sliced

chopped whites of 2 or 3 hard-boiled eggs

1 small portabella mushroom, stem removed and cap sliced, or 6 ounces
   regular mushrooms, cleaned and sliced

The Dressing

6 ounces canned consommé or 6 ounces double-strength homemade
   chicken or beef stock

1 tablespoon cornstarch

3 tablespoons malt or balsamic vinegar

1 tablespoon lemon juice

2 teaspoons sugar

½ to 1 teaspoon Worcestershire sauce

1 teaspoon olive oil

1 teaspoon Dijon-style mustard

½ teaspoon salt

2 tablespoons brandy or bourbon

To Prepare the Salad

1. Tear the spinach into bite-size pieces in a salad bowl. Toss with the carrots, onion, and egg whites.

2. Spray an 8-inch nonstick skillet with olive oil. Sauté the mushrooms over medium-high heat until lightly browned, about 5 minutes. Toss with the greens. Set aside while preparing the dressing.

To Prepare the Dressing

1. In a 2-cup glass measuring cup or other microwave-safe container, combine the consommé, cornstarch, vinegar, lemon juice, sugar, Worcestershire sauce, oil, mustard, and salt. Stir thoroughly to dissolve the cornstarch. Cover and microwave on high (100 percent power) for 2 minutes. *Alternatively, bring to a boil in a small saucepan for 4 minutes.*

2. Meanwhile heat the liquor over medium-high heat in a small pot with a long handle and spout. When bubbles appear at the edge of the pot, ignite the liquor. Let it burn, tipping the pot to keep the flames going, about 1 to 2 minutes. Liquor will be reduced by half before the flames die out. Combine the reduced liquor with the hot dressing.

3. Microwave the dressing at high (100 percent power) another 30 seconds, or heat over high heat another minute. Toss with the chilled greens.

BLACK BEAN AND CORN SALAD

This is an incredibly easy salad to put together, for most of the ingredients are pantry staples. It also keeps beautifully for several days, even improving in flavor as it mellows. Serve at room temperature.

Yield: 8 servings

Calories per serving: 97

Protein per serving: 4 g

Fat per serving: 2 g

Saturated fat per serving: trace

Cholesterol per serving: 0

Carbohydrates per serving: 19 g

Sodium per serving: 145 mg

Fiber per serving: 3 g

1 1-pound can black beans, drained, or 2 cups cooked black beans (see page 101)

1 17-ounce can whole kernel corn or 2 cups cooked or raw fresh corn kernels

1 large tomato, diced, or 5 tablespoons canned "recipe-ready" tomatoes

3 scallions, minced

½ jalapeño pepper, seeded and diced, or 2 tablespoons minced canned chilies

3 tablespoons minced fresh parsley

2 teaspoons olive oil

1 tablespoon minced fresh cilantro

1 tablespoon balsamic vinegar

1 tablespoon lime juice

1 clove garlic, minced

½ teaspoon salt

1. In a medium-size bowl, combine the beans, corn, tomato, scallions, jalapeño, and parsley. Set aside while preparing the dressing.

2. Combine the remaining ingredients in a screw-top jar. Shake well to combine. Toss with the bean and corn salad.

WILTED CUCUMBER SALAD

If soft-leafed lettuce dressed with vinaigrette is the national salad of France, a wilted cucumber salad is the fingerprint of Germany. Here's a reduced-calorie version that's as good the second day as the first. This salad makes a fine accompaniment to Salmon Burgers (page 204).

1 cucumber

2 teaspoons salt

2 tablespoons canned consommé

1 tablespoon red wine vinegar

1 teaspoon honey or sugar

1 teaspoon oil

freshly ground pepper to taste

Yield: 2 servings

Calories per serving: 55

Protein per serving: 1 g

Fat per serving: 2 g

Saturated fat per serving: trace

Cholesterol per serving: 0

Carbohydrates per serving: 8 g

Sodium per serving: can't be determined

Fiber per serving: 2 g

1. Peel the cucumber and seed it by slicing it in half the long way and removing the seed core with a teaspoon. Slice the cucumber very thinly by hand or in a food processor, and place in a sieve or colander. Sprinkle salt over the cucumber and let it drain 20 to 30 minutes over a bowl or in the sink; this removes excess water from the vegetable.

2. Rinse the cucumber repeatedly. Taste it to be sure the salt is removed. Press the cucumber to help remove water. Drain on an absorbent towel.

3. In a small saucepan combine the consommé, vinegar, honey, and oil. Reduce the liquid over high heat until 2 tablespoons are left. Pour it over the drained cucumber, season with pepper, and chill until serving time.

COUNTER SLAW

Cynthia Young, a fine Nantucket cook, gave me this recipe some years ago when we honeymooned at her Polpis guest house. It's quick, easy, and delicious, just the thing to take on a picnic to Great Point—or your favorite summer afternoon getaway spot. Coleslaw prepared with mayonnaise-type dressings contain as many as 225 calories and 21 grams of fat in a ¾-cup serving; this Counter Slaw lets you save room for dessert. Add grated carrots, raisins, or a bit of onion for variety.

Yield: 6 servings
Calories per serving: 76
Protein per serving: 1 g
Fat per serving: 5 g
Saturated fat per serving: trace
Cholesterol per serving: trace
Carbohydrates per serving: 9 g
Sodium per serving: 186 mg
Fiber per serving: 2 g

1 small green pepper, grated

6 cups loosely packed, shredded cabbage (about ½ small head)

⅓ cup chicken broth

2 tablespoons olive oil

2 tablespoons sugar

2 tablespoons red wine vinegar

1 teaspoon caraway seeds

½ teaspoon salt

freshly ground pepper to taste

1. In a medium-size bowl, combine the green pepper with the cabbage.

2. In a 1-quart nonaluminum saucepan, combine the broth, oil, sugar, vinegar, and caraway seeds. Bring to a boil over high heat until the sugar is dissolved, about 1 minute.

3. Toss hot dressing with the vegetables. Season to taste with salt and pepper. Cover the slaw with plastic wrap and leave it at room temperature for 4 hours. Chill until serving time.

PEAR AND HAVARTI SALAD WITH PINE NUTS

A halved pear broiled until a cloak of Havarti cheese bubbles and browns, resting on a lightly dressed bed of curly salad bowl lettuce, makes a dish of pasta tossed with Pesto (page 301) a wonderful dinner partner.

> *1 pear, any variety, slightly underripe is fine, peeled if desired*
> *2 tablespoons (1 ounce) reduced-fat Havarti cheese, grated*
> *1 tablespoon pine nuts*
> *¼ head salad bowl or other leaf lettuce*
> *4 tablespoons Herbed French Vinaigrette (page 73)*

1. Preheat the broiler. Cut the pear in half the long way, and remove its core and woody fiber leading to the stem. Sprinkle the halves with lemon juice if holding more than 20 minutes before broiling. Slice a sliver from the curved side of the pear halves so they will sit evenly. Place on a baking sheet.

2. Divide the grated cheese over the pear halves. Broil about 8 minutes, or until they are softened and cheese is bubbly and browned.

3. Meanwhile toast the pine nuts by putting them in an 8-inch skillet over high heat. Shake the pan constantly for about 1 minute, until nuts turn golden brown. Remove from skillet.

4. Wash, rinse, and dry the lettuce. Divide on two plates. Center each broiled pear half on lettuce. Drizzle 2 tablespoons dressing on each salad, and sprinkle pine nuts over.

Makes 2 servings

Yield: 2 servings

Calories per serving: 150

Protein per serving: 6 g

Fat per serving: 9 g

Saturated fat per serving: 3 g

Cholesterol per serving: 11 mg

Carbohydrates per serving: 16 g

Sodium per serving: 137 mg

Fiber per serving: 3 g

Nutrabyte

Pine nuts have about 160 calories an ounce; an ounce is 2 tablespoons. Each tablespoon contains about 50 nuts and has 40 calories. Pulse briefly in a food processor to make them go a little further. Keep refrigerated, because they get rancid quickly.

MARINATED VEGETABLE SALAD

Versatile and healthful, this salad, unlike most, is just as good the second day as the first. Although the tomatoes, cucumbers, and onions are essential, the other veggies are more a suggestion than a mandate. For example, in-season fresh raw corn kernels would make a delicious addition, as would grated carrots or jicama, anytime. Experiment too with the presentation. It's a main-dish salad when sprinkled with fat-free feta or goat cheese and served with crusty bread. Or wrap it into a roll-up. Or chop everything more finely, call it a salsa, and serve with baked tortilla chips. Whichever way you serve it, eat as much as you want. If you omit the anchovies, add a dash of salt.

Yield: 8 servings

Calories per serving: 37

Protein per serving: 1 g

Fat per serving: 0.8 g

Saturated fat per serving: trace

Cholesterol per serving: none

Carbohydrates per serving: 7 g

Sodium per serving: 6 mg

Fiber per serving: 1 g

For the Veggies

2 medium or 3 small tomatoes, stems removed

5 ounces mushrooms

1 cucumber, peeled or unpeeled

1 red bell pepper, halved and seeded

2 tomatillos (Mexican green tomatoes), papery outsides removed (optional)

¼ Spanish or Vidalia onion, peeled

For the Dressing

½ cup orange juice

4 tablespoons rice wine vinegar, either plain or flavored

3 tablespoons fresh minced basil leaves or 2 teaspoons dried basil

4 to 6 flat anchovy fillets, patted on toweling to remove oil (optional)

½ teaspoon celery seed

¼ teaspoon (or to taste) crushed red pepper

1 tablespoon sweet pepper relish (optional)

1 teaspoon olive oil

1 teaspoon lemon juice

1 teaspoon sugar (increase to 2 teaspoons if you don't use the relish)

To Prepare the Veggies

1. In a food processor fitted with a 4-millimeter slicing disk, process the tomatoes, mushrooms, cucumber, bell pepper, tomatillos, and onion. Combine in a bowl and set aside.

To Prepare the Dressing

1. Combine the orange juice, vinegar, basil, anchovies, celery seed, crushed red pepper, relish, oil, lemon juice, and sugar in a food processor or blender. Pour over the veggies and let sit at room temperature 20 minutes before serving. If refrigerated, allow to come to room temperature before serving.

   Makes about 1 quart

GRAPEFRUIT AND JICAMA SALAD

In some sections of the country, jicama may be an unfamiliar ingredient. A South American import, it is used frequently in Mexican cooking. Round, hard, and brown-skinned, it looks somewhat like a potato, has a similarly high water content, but is delightfully sweet and crunchy. Here it marries well with grapefruit to create an eminently portable salad that can withstand a few hours at room temperature. This cool, refreshing salad is also excellent with spicy, hot dishes. Serve the salad within two days as the flavors pale by the third. If the salad is served the second day, a little fresh cilantro may be in order, as this herb loses potency quickly.

Yield: 10 servings

Calories per serving: 55

Protein per serving: 0.7 g

Fat per serving: 2 g

Saturated fat per serving: trace

Cholesterol per serving: none

Carbohydrates per serving: 10 g

Sodium per serving: 153 mg

Fiber per serving: 2 g

For the Salad

½ jicama, peeled (about 2 cups loosely packed)

2 carrots

½ very small head red cabbage, tough outer leaves removed (1 cup shredded, loosely packed)

1 tablespoon minced fresh cilantro

1 small pink grapefruit

For the Dressing

3 tablespoons mirin (Japanese cooking wine; see Glossary, page 308)

1 tablespoon rice wine vinegar

2 teaspoons sugar

2 teaspoons Asian sesame oil

½ teaspoon salt

freshly ground pepper to taste

1 tablespoon black sesame seeds (see Shopping Sources, page 306; tan is an acceptable substitute), toasted

fresh whole cilantro leaves for garnish (optional)

To Prepare the Salad

1. In a food processor fitted with a julienne disk or with a hand-held grater, shred the jicama, carrots, and cabbage in thin shreds. Toss in the cilantro. Set aside in a bowl.

2. Peel the grapefruit over a 2-cup measure or other bowl to catch the juices, removing as much pith as possible with your fingers. Break the sections into bite-size pieces. Add the grapefruit to the vegetables.

To Prepare the Dressing

1. In the measure containing the grapefruit juice, mix together the mirin, vinegar, sugar, oil, salt, and pepper.

2. Toss the salad with the dressing and the sesame seeds. Garnish with cilantro leaves, if desired.

   Makes 5 cups

Pea Pod and Water Chestnut Salad with Sherry Ginger Dressing

Make the dressing, blanch the pea pods, and grate the water chestnuts early in the day, then assemble this salad at the last minute.

Yield: 4 servings
Calories per cup: 97
Protein per cup: 2 g
Fat per cup: 5 g
Saturated fat per cup: 1 g
Cholesterol per cup: trace
Carbohydrates per cup: 13 g
Sodium per cup: 157 mg
Fiber per cup: 2 g

For the Salad

½ pound pea pods, strings removed

4–6 radicchio lettuce leaves or soft-leafed lettuce such as Bibb

2 fresh mandarin oranges, peeled and sectioned, or 1 7-ounce can mandarin oranges packed in light syrup, drained

8 or 9 fresh water chestnuts, peeled and blanched, or 4 ounces canned chestnuts

broccoli or other sprouts for garnish (optional)

For the Dressing

5 tablespoons double-strength homemade beef or chicken stock or canned consommé

1 tablespoon olive oil

2 tablespoons sherry wine vinegar, available at specialty food shops

1 tablespoon reduced-sodium soy sauce

1 teaspoon Asian sesame oil

1 teaspoon peeled and grated fresh ginger root

1 scant teaspoon sugar

To Prepare the Salad

1. Bring a 2½-quart saucepan three-quarters full of water to a boil. Immerse pea pods, remove from heat, and let peas sit 4 minutes. Drain and rinse the peas under cold running water until they're no longer warm. Drain peas on absorbent towels.

To Prepare the Dressing

1. Combine the consommé, oil, vinegar, soy sauce, sesame oil, ginger root, and sugar in a jar. Shake well to combine.

2. In a small bowl combine half the dressing with the cooked pea pods. Let the mixture rest at least 15 minutes or up to several hours at room temperature or in the refrigerator.

3. Arrange the lettuce on individual plates or a serving platter. Arrange the pea pods and orange sections alternately in a circle on the lettuce.

4. Grate the water chestnuts in a Mouli grater or food processor. Arrange in the center of the pea pods and oranges. Dribble the salad with the remaining dressing. Garnish with broccoli sprouts, if desired.

GRILLED PEPPER SALAD

More than a cold side dish, this multicolored mélange of sweet bell peppers and leeks is also delicious served warmed over pasta or as an accompaniment for grilled meats, such as chicken. It's even better the second day, so you might want to double the recipe. For a variation stir in 2 tablespoons of Pesto (page 301). A tablespoon of yogurt cheese (page 305) is also a pleasing addition.

Yield: 4 servings

Calories per serving: 79

Protein per serving: 2 g

Fat per serving: 1 g

Saturated fat per serving: trace

Cholesterol per serving: 2 mg

Carbohydrates per serving: 13 g

Sodium per serving: 321 mg

Fiber per serving: 3 g

2 tablespoons minced shallots (1 large shallot)

2 cloves garlic, minced

1 cup thinly sliced leeks (2 leeks, white only)

½ cup white wine

1 tablespoon white wine vinegar

2 teaspoons dried oregano or 1 tablespoon fresh oregano

½ teaspoon salt

freshly ground pepper to taste

1 teaspoon sugar

4 sweet bell peppers, any mix of red, yellow, purple, or green (colors are only suggestions) peeled and seeded (see Quick Tip, page 44)

2 tablespoons freshly grated Parmesan-Reggiano cheese

1. Spray an 8-inch skillet with olive oil. Over medium-high heat sauté shallots and garlic, stirring often until softened. Do not allow to brown.

2. Add the leeks; continue to cook, stirring often, until softened, about 5 minutes. Add the wine, vinegar, oregano, salt, pepper, and sugar. Cook over low heat until blended and leeks are thoroughly softened, about 5–7 minutes longer.

3. Stack the peppers and slice thinly lengthwise. Add the strips to the leek mixture. Cook over low heat for 2 minutes to warm peppers. Stir in the cheese. If using Pesto and/or yogurt cheese, add now. The salad may be served at room temperature or warmed.

VEGETABLES

THE RECIPES

VEGETABLES

Vegetables in this health-aware era have come into their own. The vegetable is no longer an obligatory token item on the plate. Today we herald crisp but tender garden-fresh vegetables, not only for their flavor but for their health-enhancing qualities as well.

Predominantly carbohydrates, supplying us with fuel for energy, vegetables are the best source of antioxidants, which include beta-carotene and vitamins C and E. These nutrients, researchers believe, may help keep certain cancers, heart disease, cataracts, and rheumatoid arthritis at bay.

Antioxidants fight and may deactivate toxins, known as free radicals, released by normal cell functioning. If not kept in check, these free radicals may injure body cells and result in disease. Dark yellow and orange vegetables as well as dark leafy greens are excellent sources of beta-carotene. Broccoli is a fine source of vitamin C, and all vegetables provide vitamin E. Other vegetables supply several important minerals, such as calcium and iron, and still others are good sources of fiber. Vegetables therefore provide energy-food not only with little fat but with heaps of disease-preventive nutrition as well.

Aim for three to five servings of veggies a day—a serving is 1 cup of raw leafy greens or ½ cup of any other vegetable.

In this chapter you will find dishes suitable for both the weekday's restraint and the weekend's indulgences. As with all the recipes in this book, some can be accomplished with microwave speed, while others require more time. Some are truly sidekicks, while others demand—and receive—the spotlight. All trade on their upbringing: nothing but the freshest and the best.

ASPARAGUS

Royalty has its privileges—Louis XIV had a gardener who provided the palace kitchen with asparagus year-round. It's still a class act.

A pound of medium-size stalks holds between 16 and 20 spears, feeding 2 to 4 people, depending on the menu. Asparagus's strong suit is vitamin A as well as appreciable amounts of vitamin C, potassium, and phosphorus. To protect those nutrients, store asparagus in the refrigerator crisper in a closed plastic bag or standing in an inch or so of water.

To prepare asparagus for cooking, cut or snap the stalks where they break when bent. Peeling the stalks is a nice touch; simply lay the spear on the counter and strip with a vegetable peeler.

To boil asparagus, fill a 12-inch skillet three-quarters full of water. Add ½ teaspoon salt. Bring to a boil. Add asparagus and boil, uncovered, 4 to 8 minutes, depending on girth, until crisp-tender (bite one to check). Drain and stop the cooking with a quick splash of cold water.

To steam, tie string around spears. Place an inch of water in an asparagus steamer or a pot tall enough to hold the asparagus straight up. Steam about 6 to 8 minutes, again depending on girth. Drain as above.

To microwave, place the asparagus in a microwave-safe dish with 2 tablespoons broth or salted water. Cover and cook at high (100 percent power) 3 to 6 minutes. Test after 2 minutes; stir every minute. Let rest 2 minutes. Drain.

My favorite way to cook asparagus, however, follows . . .

HIGH-HEAT-ROASTED ASPARAGUS

Crisp-tender and delicious with Hollandaise (page 296). With timing adjustments, this cooking method works equally well with green beans too.

1 pound asparagus, ends snapped, peeled or not as you wish
juice of half a lemon, plus more juice for sprinkling
a pinch salt
ground pepper to taste

Yield: 4 servings
Calories per serving: 41
Protein per serving: 2 g
Fat per serving: 1 g
Saturated fat per serving: trace
Cholesterol per serving: 0
Carbohydrates per serving: 6 g
Sodium per serving: 130 mg
Fiber per serving: trace

Note: The analysis includes the crumb topping

1. Preheat the oven to 500 degrees. Spray a cookie sheet with olive oil. Add the asparagus; spray again with olive oil. Sprinkle with lemon juice, and season with salt and pepper. Roast in the upper third of the oven for 3 to 5 minutes or until a spear is crisp-tender when you bite into it. Season with additional lemon juice, if desired.

Note: The asparagus is also excellent roasted in a 400-degree oven. Adjust timing accordingly.

Crumb Topping
1 teaspoon olive or walnut oil
1 clove garlic, minced
2 tablespoons dried bread crumbs
1 teaspoon fresh thyme leaves
⅛ teaspoon salt
freshly ground pepper to taste
juice of half a lemon, plus additional juice for sprinkling

1. Spray an 8-inch skillet with olive oil. Add the oil and sauté the garlic over high heat about 30 seconds; don't let it brown. Add the bread crumbs, thyme, salt, and pepper, and stir-fry over medium heat until the crumbs are golden brown, about 2 minutes. Arrange crumbs over the stalks of asparagus; sprinkle with additional lemon juice.

BEANS, DRIED

Dried beans—they're inexpensive, nutritionally correct, versatile, readily available, and good. So why do you rarely cook them? Time, probably. Overnight soaking? Forget it! If you're put off from dealing with beans because of the presoaking and lengthy cooking involved, look no further than your microwave. An hour or two's stint in this kitchen timesaver is all it takes for most dried bean varieties to be ready to be turned into your favorite soup, ragout, or vegetable dish.

Just how good are beans for you? As a protein substitute, beans give you the good without the bad, the sound nutrition without the fat. Throw in a healthy dose of fiber and tip the scales with heaps of complex carbohydrates and you have a food perhaps rivaled only by that nutritional superhero broccoli. Most dried beans can be soaked and cooked by the following methods.

Microwave: Pick over 1 pound of beans, removing any stones or foreign bodies. Rinse them and place in the steamer basket of a microwave-safe 4-quart container. Cover with water to within 2 inches of the top of the container. Microwave, covered, on high (100 percent power) for 45 minutes to 1 hour. Discard water and rinse. Add fresh water as before, cover, and microwave on high (100 percent power) an additional 30 minutes to 1 hour. Test the beans from time to time; some will require less cooking time, others more. If you wish to combat the gas-producing substance in beans somewhat, discard the cooking water halfway through, adding fresh water for the remaining time. Some of the nondigestible oligosaccharides will be drained away.

Traditional Overnight Soak: Pick over 1 pound of beans, removing any foreign matter. Rinse them and cover with 2 quarts of cold water; soak overnight. Rinse beans and place in a Dutch oven or other heavy-bottomed pot. Cover with 2 quarts of water and simmer for 45 minutes to as long as 2 hours for very hard beans, such as white, black, and pinto beans.

Quick Soak: Pick over and rinse beans as above. Bring the beans to a boil and simmer for 5 minutes. Remove from heat and soak 2 hours. Rinse. Place beans in a Dutch oven or other heavy-bottomed pot. Cover with 2 quarts of cold water and simmer 45 minutes to as long as 2 hours.

Regardless of your cooking method, do not add salt to the beans until about the last 30 minutes of cooking time; salt tends to toughen them. Flavoring ingredients such as onions may be added after the initial soaking process or, if microwaving, after the first cooking cycle.

Nutrabyte

On average a woman needs about 1,800 calories a day; a man needs about 2,500. Sedentary folks will need less; athletes, more.

BLACK BEAN CAKES WITH CHILI-CORN SALSA

This small plate becomes a main dish if accompanied by a salad such as Grapefruit and Jicama Salad (page 89). Contact lens wearers might want to replace fresh jalapeño with the jarred variety; use it measure for measure and you'll avoid that eye-screaming sensation when you take out contacts after handling hot chilies. See Shopping Sources (page 306) for smoke and chili oils.

Yield: 7 cakes

Calories per cake: 158

Protein per cake: 8 g

Fat per cake: 2 g

Saturated fat per cake: trace

Cholesterol per cake: 0

Carbohydrates per cake: 30 g

Sodium per cake: 315 mg

Fiber per cake: 6 g

1 cup (½ cellophane package) raw black beans or 2 cups cooked or canned
black beans, rinsed

For the Salsa

1 cup fresh corn kernels, cut from the cob (about 2 ears)
3 small ripe tomatoes, diced
½ cup minced fresh cilantro plus a few sprigs for garnish
4 scallions, including green stalk, diced
juice of 1 lime
juice of 1 orange
1 teaspoon sugar
1 fresh jalapeño pepper, seeded and minced
1 teaspoon oil, such as smoke oil or chili oil (this will be hot), or olive oil

For the Salad

¾ cup red onion, minced
1 clove garlic, mashed
1 teaspoon cumin seed
1 teaspoon balsamic vinegar
1 teaspoon salt
1 tablespoon fat-free sour cream, for garnish (optional)
a few sprigs cilantro, for garnish (optional)

1. If using canned beans, go to Step 2. If using raw beans, rinse and cover with 4 cups water in a microwave-safe container. Cover and microwave at high (100 percent power) for 45 minutes. Discard first cooking water. Rinse, then cover with another 4 cups water. Cover and microwave again at high (100 percent power) for 20 minutes more. Test for tenderness. Discard second cooking water and rinse beans. Reserve about 1 cup beans for another purpose (such as adding to rice) and place remaining beans in a bowl.

2. Meanwhile, to prepare the salsa, place corn kernels in a glass measuring cup or other microwave-safe container, cover, and microwave at high (100 percent power) for 2 minutes. Turn corn into a medium-size bowl and add tomatoes, half the cilantro (reserve the remaining cilantro for Step 3), scallions, lime and orange juices, sugar, ½ teaspoon jalapeño (reserve the remaining jalapeño for Step 3), and oil. Stir to combine, and set aside at room temperature for no more than 4 hours.

3. Add the onion, remaining cilantro, garlic, cumin, vinegar, 4 tablespoons of the salsa juice from Step 2, salt, and the remaining jalapeño to the beans. Mash. Taste for seasoning.

4. Shape bean mixture into 6–7 patties. Spray a nonstick skillet with olive oil. Sauté cakes at medium-high heat, covered, about 5 minutes or until browned on one side. Spray again with olive oil. Cook about 4 minutes more, covered.

5. To serve, spoon a couple of tablespoons of salsa in the center of a plate. Cover with a bean cake and spoon some of the salsa and plenty of its juice on top. Top each cake with a tiny dollop of sour cream and garnish, if desired, with cilantro. Pass remaining salsa.

Makes 6 to 7 cakes

Nutrabyte

Nutrition Hotline:
Call in your nutrition questions by dialing (800) 366–1655.

BEANS, GREEN

Thanks to modern horticulture, the string in string beans has been permanently pulled. No longer do we have those pesky strings to contend with! And thanks to modern transportation methods, fresh green beans are available almost year-round (although they are often tough in the winter months). They are an excellent source of vitamin A and supply a fair amount of calcium too, for their very little 31 calories a cup.

When selecting green beans, look for those that are pliant and smooth, not coarse and tough. One pound of beans serves 4. Store the beans in the refrigerator crisper in a plastic bag; use within three days of purchase or they will be tough.

Prepare beans a large handful at a time. Align the ends and cut across. Turn beans around, realign, and cut again.

To boil a pound of beans, bring 6 cups of water to a rapid boil, with or without salt. Immerse beans and boil, uncovered, about 4 to 8 minutes, sometimes more, sometimes less. Time is a variable that is dependent on your heat source, the size and maturity of the beans, and so on. Count on inconsistency, because what works this time may not work next. During cooking remove a bean and bite into it or pierce it with a fork. It should be crunchy. If holding the beans for later use, as much as 5 hours, undercook them a bit, then cool under running water.

To steam beans, prepare as above, then place in a steamer over 2 inches of boiling water, cover, and cook until tender, anywhere from 5 to 10 minutes. Again, check during cooking for tenderness.

To microwave place the prepared beans in a microwave-safe container with ¼ cup liquid, such as broth or salted water, and cook at high (100 percent power) 8 to 12 minutes. Test for crispness after 6 minutes. Let rest 2 minutes before serving.

Either Lemon Butter Sauce (page 302) or Red Pepper Butter (page 124) is very good on beans. For a change, consider the following recipe.

Green Beans with Tomato Nuggets

1 pound cooked green beans

1 tomato, peeled, and diced (see Quick Tip, page 52)

juice of half a lemon

1 small garlic clove, minced, or 2 roasted garlic cloves (page 305)

2 teaspoons butter

⅛ teaspoon salt

freshly ground pepper to taste

Yield: 4 servings

Calories per serving: 66

Protein per serving: 3 g

Fat per serving: 3 g

Saturated fat per serving: 1 g

Cholesterol per serving: 6 mg

Carbohydrates per serving: 11 g

Sodium per serving: 94 mg

Fiber per serving: 4 g

1. Combine all ingredients in a skillet or saucepan. Heat quickly, tossing over high heat until butter is melted. Taste and correct seasoning.

Beets

While beets are generally boiled, they are delicious baked as well. Choose medium-size, smooth, firm beets for baking. Those that look shriveled or very large are apt to be too woody. The tops may be cooked like spinach and served with a few drops of fruity vinegar. Beets are a good source of potassium, calcium, phosphorus, and magnesium and contain about 35 calories per ½ cup.

To bake, prick the beats in several places with a fork. Bake in a 350-degree oven until easily pierced with a fork, about 1 hour. *Alternatively, microwave the beets at high (100 percent power) until tender. Time will vary with the number of beets cooked, about 10 minutes for 1 beet and as long as 30 minutes for 8 large beets.* Peel the beets and serve with a bit of orange juice. Garnish with grated orange zest, if desired.

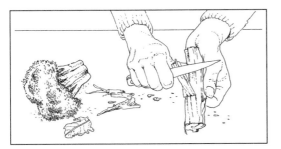

Peeling the tough outer skin from the broccoli stalk before cooking the broccoli will make the whole stalk more tetnder to eat.

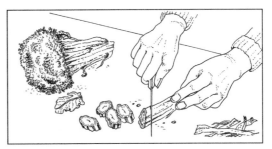

A peeled broccoli stalk is delicious to eat when it is sliced on the diagonal into thin rounds.

BROCCOLI

Another year-round vegetable, broccoli is the health addict's dream. One large cooked stalk fulfills your vitamin C requirement by half as much again, provides your need for vitamin A, and supplies goodly amounts of riboflavin, iron, calcium, potassium, and fiber.

When purchasing broccoli, look for unopened buds that are dark green, not yellow. Store broccoli in a plastic bag in the refrigerator or in the vegetable crisper for not more than four days; 1½ to 2 pounds will serve 4.

Peeling and slicing the broccoli stalks is a wonderful way to get full value from this vegetable. Cut the stalks an inch below the buds. Separate the flower stems. Remove the leaves; if they look fresh, plan to cook them, for they are rich in vitamin A. Cut the branches from the stalks, and peel the stalks, using a vegetable peeler or a small, sharp knife. Slice the stalks into rounds on the diagonal.

Boil or steam broccoli as you would green beans (see page 105); 6 to 8 minutes is about right for crisp broccoli. This vegetable also takes well to stir-frying, but watch that oil!

A peeled broccoli stalk is delicious to eat when it is sliced on the diagonal into thin rounds.

Peeling the tough outer skin from the broccoli stalk before cooking the broccoli will make the whole stalk more tender to eat.

Nutrabyte

According to a study from Johns Hopkins University, three-day old broccoli sprouts contain twenty to fifty times the amount of an anti-cancer agent as mature plants do. A mere ¼ ounce of sprouts has as much of this beneficial compound as 2 pounds of broccoli, no slouch in the nutrition department in its own right. I've not seen broccoli sprouts marketed as of this writing so have included a Shopping Source (page 307) to purchase untreated seeds (which are a must for this purpose) and a sprouter, a small plastic tray system used to grow them. It takes no time at all to set up the sprouting system, and good light isn't required. Use the sprouts in sandwiches, as a garnish, in salads, and in vegetable mixes.

Very good hot with just lemon juice, broccoli also takes well to dressing up with a cloak of Hollandaise (page 296) or Lemon Butter Sauce (page 302). And don't overlook it as a cold salad tossed with a light vinaigrette.

SESAME BROCCOLI

This recipe is a nice change from the norm. Cook the broccoli ahead, if desired, and reheat adding the sesame oil at serving time.

> *1½ pounds broccoli (1 bunch of 2 to 3 stalks)*
> *1 tablespoon Asian sesame oil*
> *1 tablespoon white or tan sesame seeds, toasted (page 38)*
> *1 tablespoon reduced-sodium soy sauce*

Yield: 4 to 6 servings
Calories per serving: 55
Protein per serving: 3 g
Fat per serving: 3 g
Saturated fat per serving: trace
Cholesterol per serving: none
Carbohydrates per serving: 5 g
Sodium per serving: 123 mg
Fiber per serving: 4 g

1. Prepare the broccoli for cooking. Boil or steam the broccoli, and drain it.

2. Toss the hot broccoli with the sesame oil, sesame seeds, and soy sauce.

CARROTS

When purchasing carrots, for the sweetest flavor buy those that have the greens attached. Although those sold in cellophane bags might have grown up in the same field, the green-topped ones will be much sweeter because they're probably fresher. Remove the greens before storing or they will sap moisture from the carrot, causing the root to shrivel. Very fresh carrots need nothing more than a good scrubbing; older ones will be more tender if peeled.

One carrot supplies you with more than the recommended daily requirement of vitamin A. Carrots are also a rich source of cancer-combative beta-carotene. Carrots are one of the few vegetables more nutritious when cooked than eaten raw; cooking breaks down the tough cell walls, making the nutrients more available.

The following recipes are uncommon ways to serve the common carrot.

Lemon-Glazed Carrots

This vegetable is easily reheated.

1 pound carrots

juice of one lemon

½ teaspoon grated ginger root

1 teaspoon honey

2 teaspoons butter

freshly grated nutmeg

⅛ teaspoon salt

freshly ground pepper to taste

1 tablespoon minced fresh parsley

Yield: 6 servings

Calories per serving: 54

Protein per serving: trace

Fat per serving: 2 g

Saturated fat per serving: 1 g

Cholesterol per serving: 4 mg

Carbohydrates per serving: 10 g

Sodium per serving: 111 mg

Fiber per serving: 1 g

1. Prepare the carrots for cooking by peeling, if desired. Bring a 2½-quart saucepan three-quarters full of water to a boil. Meanwhile slice the carrots thinly into rounds or matchsticks. Immerse the carrots and boil until tender, the time for which will depend on how they are cut. Remove one every minute after 3 minutes to test. When tender, drain.

2. In the carrot saucepan, combine the lemon juice, ginger, honey, and butter. Heat and stir until mixed. Add the carrots and cook over high heat, shaking the pan all the while, for 1 minute.

3. Turn onto a serving platter. Season with nutmeg, salt, and pepper. Garnish with the parsley.

Nutrabyte

The body converts only as much beta-carotene into vitamin A as it needs; any leftover is harmless. Excessive amounts of vitamin A, however, can cause toxic reactions.

ORANGE-CARROT PUREE

This combination of carrot and orange is excellent for do-ahead cooking because it easily reheats in a microwave.

1 pound carrots

juice of 2 oranges

grated zest of 1 orange

1 teaspoon sugar

2 teaspoons butter

½ teaspoon salt

freshly ground pepper to taste

a few gratings fresh nutmeg

1. Scrape or peel the carrots as you desire. Roughly chop them.

2. Bring a 2½-quart saucepan three-quarters full of water to a boil. Immerse the carrots, cover the pan, and boil until carrots are easily pierced with a fork, about 10 minutes.

3. Put the cooked carrots in a food processor or a food mill and puree. Add the orange juice, zest, sugar, butter, salt, pepper, and nutmeg. Mix well.

Yield: 4 servings

Calories per serving: 95

Protein per serving: 2 g

Fat per serving: 2 g

Saturated fat per serving: 1 g

Cholesterol per serving: 6 mg

Carbohydrates per serving: 18 g

Sodium per serving: 365 mg

Fiber per serving: 2 g

Nutrabyte

Ice water is far more appealing with a slice of lemon or orange.

CARROT AND SQUASH PUREE

This can also be made ahead and reheated in a microwave. It is delicious with turkey or other poultry. To vary, add a few tablespoons of nonfat sour cream with the other seasonings.

1 small butternut squash, peeled and chopped

1 pound carrots, scrubbed, peeled, and roughly chopped

2 teaspoons dark rum

a few gratings fresh nutmeg

¼ teaspoon salt

freshly ground pepper to taste

Yield: 8 servings

Calories per serving: 51

Protein per serving: 1 g

Fat per serving: trace

Saturated fat per serving: trace

Cholesterol per serving: none

Carbohydrates per serving: 12 g

Sodium per serving: 106 mg

Fiber per serving: 2 g

1. Bring a 4-quart saucepan half full of water to a boil. Add the squash, cover, and cook 8 minutes. Add the carrots, cover, and cook until both are tender, about 12 minutes more.

2. Drain and mash the vegetables either in a food mill or food processor or by hand. Add the rum and nutmeg. Season to taste with salt and pepper.

CELERY

Celery is more than mere rabbit food. Cooked, it takes on a whole new personality, but with little alteration to its naturally skinny self.

One rib of this member of the parsley family furnishes just 7 calories. It is a good source of potassium and supplies vitamins A and C as well as fiber.

Nutrabyte

A good source for printed nutrition information:

NHLBI Information Center

P.O. Box 30105

Bethesda, MD 20824–0105

NUTTED BRAISED CELERY

Try this recipe to disperse the ho-hums.

8 large ribs celery, strings pared
⅓ cup chicken broth or canned consommé
⅓ cup dry white wine
freshly ground pepper to taste
2 tablespoons finely chopped shallots
1½ tablespoons chopped walnuts or sliced water chestnuts

Yield: 8 servings
Calories per serving: 12
Protein per serving: 0.5 g
Fat per serving: 0.1 g
Saturated fat per serving: trace
Cholesterol per serving: none
Carbohydrates per serving: 2 g
Sodium per serving: 43 mg
Fiber per serving: 0.9 g

1. Slice the celery thinly on the diagonal, or julienne it. Place it in a 10-inch glass pie plate or other microwave-safe dish.

2. Pour the broth and wine over the celery. Season with the pepper. Sprinkle with the shallots. Cover with plastic wrap.

3. Microwave at high (100 percent power) for 4 minutes or until tender but crisp. Sprinkle with walnuts. Microwave, uncovered, an additional minute.

Nutrabyte

Nuts and eating light: Generally, an ounce of nuts (about 2 tablespoons, although it takes 4 tablespoons to equal 1 ounce of pine nuts) supplies about 160 calories. Some seeds, like pumpkin, have fewer calories and fat grams, but these are all calorie-dense foods with a relatively high fat content. The good news is that the fat profile of nuts and seeds is a healthy one, supplying more monounsaturated fats than saturated ones. So if you watch fat type because of heart disease and aren't particularly concerned with overall calories, nuts can be a terrific flavor booster in foods. This book uses them sparingly.

DELICIOUS "CREAMED" CORN

4 ears corn

1¼ to 1½ cups skim milk

2 tablespoons cornstarch

½ teaspoon salt

freshly ground pepper to taste

a few gratings fresh nutmeg

paprika for garnish (optional)

Yield: 4 servings

Calories per serving: 127

Protein per serving: 5 g

Fat per serving: 1 g

Saturated fat per serving: trace

Cholesterol per serving: 1 mg

Carbohydrates per serving: 27 g

Sodium per serving: 321 mg

Fiber per serving: 3 g

1. Cut the corn from the cob.

2. Spray a nonstick 10-inch skillet with olive oil. Add half the corn and sauté over medium-high heat about 3 minutes or until kernels are tender and beginning to brown lightly.

3. Meanwhile combine the remaining corn with the milk and cornstarch in the bowl of a food processor. Puree.

4. Add the pureed corn to the skillet. Stir to combine. Turn heat to low, add the seasonings, and simmer about 5 minutes. Add more milk, if necessary. Garnish with paprika, if desired, before serving.

Allowable Daily Fat Grams Based on Total Calories

Total calories:	1,200	1,500	1,800	2,000	2,500
Total fat grams:	40	50	60	65	80

FENNEL, RED PEPPER, AND TOMATO BRAISE

Cooked either in a conventional oven or in a microwave, this cool-weather veggie is particularly good with Grilled Polenta with Roasted Asparagus (page 172), as part of a vegetarian meal, or with any fish dish. The recipe here is large, serving 4 to 6 generously, depending on what else is for dinner. I always make more than we can eat at a seating because the leftovers are even better than the first go-round. Don't freeze them though. The peppers, fennel, and tomatoes all slice perfectly in a Cuisinart using the medium slicing disc.

Yield: 6 servings

Calories per serving: 50

Protein per serving: 2 g

Fat per serving: 0.5 g

Saturated fat per serving: trace

Cholesterol per serving: 0

Carbohydrates per serving: 11 g

Sodium per serving: 419 mg

Fiber per serving: 3 g

2 red peppers, seeded, thinly sliced

2 medium fennel bulbs (about 1½ to 1¾ lbs before trimming), tops trimmed, cored, halved lengthwise, and thinly sliced (reserve about 4 tablespoons, minced, feathery greens for garnish, optional)

4 ripe tomatoes (about 1 pound), thinly sliced

5 to 7 cloves roasted garlic or 2 cloves raw garlic, minced

1 teaspoon fennel seeds

1 teaspoon salt

pepper to taste

4 tablespoons chicken broth, water, or wine

4 to 6 each whole basil and parsley leaves

1. Spray an 8-inch square baking dish with olive oil. Layer in the red peppers. Spritz with olive oil spray. Layer on the fennel. Layer on the tomatoes. Divide the garlic over the mixture. Sprinkle on the fennel seeds. Season with salt and pepper. Spoon broth over. Lay on the basil and parsley. Spritz with olive oil. Cover tightly with two sheets of plastic wrap at right angles to each other if cooking in the microwave; use foil if cooking in an oven.

2. Bake in a 325-degree oven (no need to preheat) for 1 hour and 15 to 20 minutes or until the veggies are very soft. *Alternatively, cook in a microwave oven at high (100 percent power) for 10 minutes, and at 50 percent power*

for another 10 minutes. Let rest at least 5 minutes. The rest time is essential; it is part of the cooking time.

3. Stir the veggies before serving, garnished with the reserved feathery minced greens.

Serves 4 to 6

KALE, SWISS CHARD, AND SPINACH WITH DRIED CRANBERRIES

This dish is not season-bound. Buy spinach with some of the root attached—baby spinach is the most tender—rather than the stuff in cellophane bags, which is often old and has tough stems. The sautéing is a last-minute operation, although the greens can be prepared for cooking ahead of time. Quantities are more of a guideline than a mandate here.

Yield: 3 servings
Calories per serving: 103
Protein per serving: 5 g
Fat per serving: 0.9 g
Saturated fat per serving: 0.13 g
Cholesterol per serving: 1 mg
Carbohydrates per serving: 22 g
Sodium per serving: 131 mg
Fiber per serving: 4 g

1 shallot, minced (about 4 tablespoons)

5 cloves roasted garlic (see page 305), or 2 cloves raw garlic, minced

1 teaspoon brown sugar

¾ cup plus 2 tablespoons chicken broth or wine or a combination of both

5 stalks kale (about ½ bunch), the leafy green stripped from the stems and roughly chopped (about 4–5 cups loosely packed)

1 bunch Swiss chard, red or white, the leafy green stripped from the stems and roughly chopped (about 2 cups)

6 ounces spinach leaves (stems removed if tough), chopped only if large (about 2 cups loosely packed)

1 tablespoon dried cranberries or golden raisins (optional)

4 tablespoons vinegar (your choice;—balsamic will lend a rich, almost sweet flavor; champagne will be mild; raspberry or blueberry will complement the dried fruit) (see Shopping Sources, page 306)

pepper to taste

1 tablespoon toasted pine nuts (optional)

1. Combine the shallot, garlic, sugar, and 5 tablespoons of the broth (reserve remaining broth for Steps 2 and 3) in a 12-inch nonstick skillet. Cook over high heat 1 minute, reduce heat to low and cook 2 minutes more, stirring a couple of times, until the shallot is softened.

2. Add the kale and 4 more tablespoons broth; cook, stirring frequently, over high heat until the kale is reduced by half in volume, about 1–2 minutes.

3. Add the chard and 4 tablespoons reserved broth. When the chard is somewhat reduced in volume and tender (bite the kale to test), add the spinach and cranberries. Remove from heat and cover. The spinach will cook with the trapped steam.

4. When the spinach is almost done, add the vinegar and pepper. Just before serving, sprinkle with pine nuts, if desired.

Spinach

This versatile vegetable might not have made Popeye's muscles bulge, but it certainly contributed to his general well-being. A mere ½ cup of cooked spinach supplies an adult with twice the daily requirement of vitamin A, half the vitamin C, and one-fifth of the RDA of iron. Spinach is also a good source of folic acid, a B vitamin highly touted—particularly for pregnant women—by today's health reporters. All this for just 28 calories! You might also have heard that spinach is rich in calcium, but because of the presence of oxalic acid the calcium is not available to the body.

PEA AND LEEK PUREE

Leeks are very low in calories, a good source of potassium, and a fair source of vitamin C. Here they are perfectly paired with peas for a do-ahead dish.

Although *fresh* is today's culinary password, here I feel that frozen peas will pass the test. Frozen peas, however, are higher in sodium than fresh peas; the sodium content for this recipe is for fresh peas.

1 bunch leeks (about 3 stalks)
1 cup plus 2 tablespoons chicken broth
1 cup fresh or frozen peas
1 teaspoon butter
1 teaspoon freshly snipped tarragon leaves or ½ teaspoon dried tarragon
¼ teaspoon salt
lots of freshly ground black pepper to taste

1. Cut and discard the green stalks from the leeks. Slice the white of the leek in half the long way, then dice. Rinse very thoroughly in a colander.

2. Put the leeks and ¾ cup of the broth in a 1-quart saucepan. Cover and cook over high heat until tender, about 20 minutes. When the liquid is evaporated and the leeks are limp, empty into a food processor.

3. Put the peas and the remaining broth into the now empty saucepan. Cover and cook for 2 minutes at high heat (a little longer for fresh peas). Empty into the food processor, unevaporated liquid and all.

4. Add the butter, tarragon, salt, and pepper. Puree. The vegetable is ready to eat or may be reheated in the microwave before serving time.

Yield: 4 servings
Calories per serving: 68
Protein per serving: 3 g
Fat per serving: 1 g
Saturated fat per serving: trace
Cholesterol per serving: 4 mg
Carbohydrates per serving: 11 g
Sodium per serving: 160 mg
Fiber per serving: 3 g

LEEK AND THREE-CHEESE PIE

Serve this pie with a salad and creamy risotto flecked with zucchini or asparagus for a vegetarian meal that will please even the staunchest meat and potato lovers. Leftovers heat very nicely in the microwave.

Yield: 4 to 6 servings

Calories per serving: 119

Protein per serving: 12 g

Fat per serving: 3 g

Saturated fat per serving: 2 g

Cholesterol per serving: 10 mg

Carbohydrates per serving: 11 g

Sodium per serving: 624 mg

Fiber per serving: trace

1 bunch leeks (about 4), whites only, chopped and well rinsed

1 cup chicken broth

½ cup egg substitute

¾ cup skimmed evaporated milk

¾ cup skim milk

1 teaspoon salt or seasoned salt

freshly ground pepper to taste

½ teaspoon Dijon-style or stone-ground mustard

several gratings fresh nutmeg or a few shakes of ground nutmeg

2 ounces fat-free Swiss cheese, diced

2 ounces goat cheese, crumbled

3 tablespoons grated Parmesan-Reggiano cheese

1. Combine the leeks and broth in a 4-cup glass measure or other microwave-safe container. Cover with plastic wrap. Microwave on high (100 percent power) for 8 minutes. Stir. Cover again and microwave an additional 2 minutes on high. Drain while mixing egg substitute and milk.

2. Preheat oven to 325 degrees. Combine the egg substitute, both milks, salt, pepper, mustard, and nutmeg in a food processor. Process about 30 seconds.

3. Layer the leeks in a 10-inch glass pie pan or other oven-safe dish. Cover with egg-milk mixture. Dot with cheeses and sprinkle with Parmesan-Reggiano.

4. Bake in the upper third of the oven for 45 minutes. Let rest 5 to 10 minutes before slicing into wedges.

Mushrooms

A whole new world of exotic mushrooms has come to market, with flavors that whisper of earth and woods. Some are dried and imported, such as cèpes (rhymes with *step*), chanterelles, and morels; others are being cultivated and marketed fresh, such as shiitake and enoki. All are expensive but deliver a wealth of flavor for a token calorie tax.

While nutritionally weak, mushrooms contain a mere 20 calories a cup.

FETTUCCINE WITH CÈPES

This wonderful pasta dish makes a great first course for a dinner party or a delicious main dish for a casual supper. The sauce may be easily made ahead and reheated just before tossing with freshly cooked fettuccine.

1 ounce dried cèpes, also called porcini, or other dried mushrooms

boiling water

2 tablespoons minced shallots

1 clove garlic, minced

1½ cups beef stock or canned beef broth

1 cup tomato sauce (see page 303) or canned sauce

lots of freshly ground pepper to taste

8 ounces fresh fettuccine noodles

2 teaspoons olive oil

1 tablespoon minced fresh parsley

freshly grated Parmesan-Reggiano cheese

Yield: 4 servings

Calories per serving: 233

Protein per serving: 9 g

Fat per serving: 4 g

Saturated fat per serving: .60 g

Cholesterol per serving: 43 mg

Carbohydrates per serving: 42 g

Sodium per serving: 393 mg

Fiber per serving: 3 g

1. Cover the dried mushrooms with boiling water and soak for 20 minutes.

2. Spray a 10- or 12-inch nonstick skillet with olive oil and sauté the shallots over medium-low heat until limp. Add the garlic and cook 30 seconds more.

3. Add the beef stock and boil over high heat until reduced to 1 cup. Add the tomato sauce and boil until reduced to 1½ cups.

4. Drain the mushrooms and chop them. The juice may be used only if strained twice through a coffee filter. Add mushrooms to sauce base. Stir to combine. Season with freshly ground pepper.

5. Cook the fettuccine noodles according to package instructions. Drain the noodles and toss with the olive oil. Toss the fettuccine with cèpe sauce. Sprinkle minced parsley on top. Pass cheese at the table.

SHERRIED MUSHROOMS

For a treat add ½ to 1 ounce of dried mushrooms such as cèpes. Soak the dried mushrooms for 20 minutes, drain, and rinse, adding them at the end of Step 2.

12 ounces mushrooms, cleaned

2 tablespoons sherry or Madeira

3 tablespoons nonfat yogurt or yogurt cheese (page 305)

a few fresh gratings nutmeg

⅛ teaspoon salt

freshly ground pepper to taste

1 tablespoon minced fresh parsley

Yield: 4 servings

Calories per serving: 37

Protein per serving: 2 g

Fat per serving: trace

Saturated fat per serving: trace

Cholesterol per serving: 0

Carbohydrates per serving: 5 g

Sodium per serving: 81 mg

Fiber per serving: 1 g

1. Spray a 10- or 12-inch nonstick skillet with olive oil. Add the mushrooms and cook over medium-high heat, shaking the pan often, until the mushrooms are lightly browned and all their moisture has evaporated.

2. Add the sherry and shake the pan while the wine evaporates.

3. Stir in the yogurt, and season with nutmeg, salt, and pepper. To serve, garnish with the parsley.

Onions

While not exactly nutritional powerhouses, onions do contribute lots of flavor for a minimal calorie cost.

Never store onions near potatoes, because they will sprout quickly due to the moisture the potato gives off.

SCOTCH ONIONS

This deliciously simple vegetable goes very well with roasted poultry. It may be made as much as a day ahead and gently reheated.

1 pound pearl or small white boiling onions

1 cup chicken broth

½ cup water

½ teaspoon salt

freshly ground pepper to taste

1 teaspoon olive oil

2 tablespoons Scotch

1 tablespoon minced fresh parsley (optional)

Yield: 4 servings

Calories per serving: 73

Protein per serving: 2 g

Fat per serving: 1 g

Saturated fat per serving: trace

Cholesterol per serving: 1 mg

Carbohydrates per serving: 10 g

Sodium per serving: 280 mg

Fiber per serving: 2 g

1. Slice the ends from the onions and put a cross in the root end to prevent them from exploding.

2. Cover the onions with water in a 2½-quart heavy-bottom saucepan and bring to a boil. Boil onions for 2 minutes, drain, and cool under running water. Slip and discard skins from the onions.

3. Return onions to the saucepan with the broth, water, salt, pepper, and oil. Cover and boil gently until the liquid is almost absorbed and the onions are tender. Onions that are 1½ inches in diameter will be done in about 12 minutes. If the onions are easily pierced with a fork before the liquid is absorbed, lift them from the pot with a slotted spoon and boil liquid at high heat, uncovered, until only 2 to 3 tablespoons remain. Or add more broth or water and extend cooking time if needed.

4. Remove the cover from the pan. Add Scotch with heat turned high. Boil, uncovered, until a semisyrupy liquid remains. To serve, dribble a spoonful of sauce over onions. Sprinkle with the parsley, if desired.

PEPPERS

Roasting a pepper, red or green, is actually to broil it, then allow it to cool in a tightly closed bag. The steam loosens the charred skin, which then pulls off as easily as old paint—if you've broiled it sufficiently but not overdone it. The broiling process cooks the flesh, turning it yet a deeper scarlet. It has a mild, sweet taste quite unsurpassed by other vegetables. It may then be marinated and served at room temperature as a salad; sautéed with any combination of vegetables; or pureed with herbs and a touch of vinegar. As a puree it is delicious over other vegetables such as green beans, broccoli, and the like, or over fish or even poultry. It is wonderful on spinach fettuccine as a fine first course or as a casual dinner.

A red pepper is nothing more than a green pepper allowed to mature and ripen on the vine. Yet because most peppers are harvested when green, red peppers are somewhat scarce and often expensive. Although you can sometimes ripen a green pepper that has begun to blush by putting it with a cut apple in a paper bag for a day or two, it is likely to decay before becoming scarlet. When they are available, take advantage of their high vitamins A and C content by making up the following puree and freezing it.

To Roast Peppers

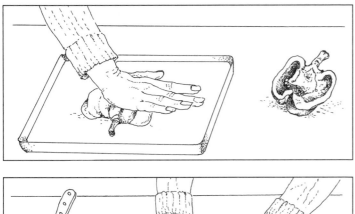

1. Place a seeded, halved pepper, skin side up, on a flat surface. Flatten pepper with the heel of your hand.

2. Broil pepper until it is completely blackened, cool in a tightly closed bag, then peel away and discard the charred skin.

To Julienne Peppers

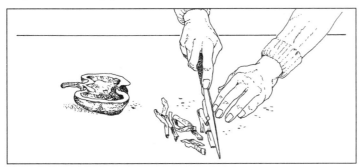

A roasted or raw pepper is often sliced into julienned strips for use in cooking.

RED PEPPER BUTTER

This delicious sauce can be made ahead and reheated at serving time.

4 large red bell peppers (about 4 pounds)
2 tablespoons minced fresh parsley
8 to 10 fresh basil leaves, snipped, or 1 teaspoon dried basil
1 clove garlic, minced
1 teaspoon sugar
½ teaspoon balsamic vinegar or lemon juice
½ teaspoon salt
freshly ground pepper to taste

Yield: 9 servings
Calories per serving: 14
Protein per serving: 0.4 g
Fat per serving: 0.1 g
Saturated fat per serving: trace
Cholesterol per serving: none
Carbohydrates per serving: 3 g
Sodium per serving: 125 mg
Fiber per serving: 0.8 g

1. Cut the peppers in half. Remove and discard the seeds and inner membranes. Flatten peppers with the heel of your hand and place skin side up on a baking sheet lined with foil. Broil the peppers until they're completely blackened and charred. The skin will not peel off easily unless it's burned, so don't be shy about doing so. Don't let the peppers dry out, however. Roll the peppers up in the foil then wrap the lot in a kitchen towel. Let cool.

2. With your fingers peel and discard the loosened skin from the peppers.

3. Combine the peppers with the parsley, basil, garlic, sugar, vinegar, salt, and pepper in a food processor. Puree. If using a food mill or blender, puree the peppers first, then combine them with the other ingredients.
   Yield 2⅓ cups

Pasta with Red Pepper Butter

Use the above recipe to coat 12 ounces fresh linguine. Cook and drain the noodles according to package directions. Toss with the "butter." Remember to heat the plates when serving pasta. Pass grated cheese at the table, if desired. Serves 4 to 6.

MARINATED ROASTED PEPPERS

Roasted red peppers are delicious when marinated in oil (tiny amounts, of course!), vinegar, and herbs and served at room temperature as a vegetable side dish. This recipe is best made a day ahead.

1 tablespoon oil (walnut oil recommended)

1 tablespoon balsamic or malt vinegar

2 tablespoons beef stock or canned consommé

1 clove garlic, minced

8 fresh basil leaves, snipped, or 1 teaspoon dried basil

2 red bell peppers roasted, peeled, and sliced

2 green bell peppers roasted, peeled, and sliced

⅛ teaspoon salt

freshly ground pepper to taste

1 tablespoon minced fresh parsley

Yield: 4 servings

Calories per serving: 56

Protein per serving: 1 g

Fat per serving: 4 g

Saturated fat per serving: trace

Cholesterol per serving: trace

Carbohydrates per serving: 6 g

Sodium per serving: 69 mg

Fiber per serving: 1 g

1. Combine the oil, vinegar, stock, garlic, and basil. Pour the mixture over peppers. Sprinkle the peppers with salt, pepper, and parsley just before serving.

WOK SAUTÉ OF PEPPERS AND BROCCOLI

This is a basic method for sautéing any combination of vegetables with roasted red peppers. Likely combinations are sliced napa, pea pods, zucchini, and so forth. The use of a wok cuts down on the amount of fat needed and also allows you to push the quicker-cooking vegetables up on the rim out of heat's way. If you're using a traditional flat skillet, just add the slowest-cooking vegetable first. These vegetables may be readied for cooking ahead of time, but stir-fry them at the last moment. Their freshness will be compromised if reheated.

4 tablespoons chicken broth or canned consommé

1 small clove garlic, minced

1 cup broccoli flowerets, sliced, and stems, peeled and julienned

1 teaspoon olive oil

1 cup mushrooms, sliced

3 red bell peppers, roasted, peeled (see page 44), and julienned

¼ teaspoon salt

freshly ground pepper to taste

1 tablespoon minced fresh parsley

1. Heat the wok over high heat. Add the broth and garlic and cook, stirring constantly, for 30 seconds.

2. Add the broccoli and cook over high heat, stirring until crisp-tender, about 1 minute. Push the broccoli up onto the sides of wok (or remove from the wok and keep warm).

3. Add the oil and mushrooms. Cook, stirring, over high heat, about 1 minute. Push the mushrooms up onto the sides of wok.

Yield: 4 servings

Calories per serving: 44

Protein per serving: 2 g

Fat per serving: 1 g

Saturated fat per serving: trace

Cholesterol per serving: trace

Carbohydrates per serving: 7 g

Sodium per serving: 149 mg

Fiber per serving: 2 g

Nutrabyte

Focus on food, never eat mindlessly. Eat well, savor it, enjoy it. When time, not food, is the priority, don't waste calories on potato chips or candy bars just to fill up. Munch apples, eat an orange, grab an "engineered" product like Slim-Fast or Met-Rx, or a power bar. Don't waste calories on nutritionally empty yet calorie-charged snacks.

4. Add the red peppers. Cook over high heat, stirring constantly, until heated through, about 30 seconds longer.

5. Push all the vegetables down to the bottom of wok to heat through. Season with salt and pepper. Sprinkle with parsley and serve.

POTATOES

Shopping for a plain old potato poses a surprisingly large number of choices. There are many varieties, from round white to long russet, from new potatoes to mature. There are waxy spuds and mealy ones, some sold loose and others in bags. What's a body to do? Short of memorizing every variety and its particular use, let this be a simple guide. Purchase new potatoes, those that look like they're suffering from bad sunburn with chafed and peeling skin, for salads, boiling, and steaming. New potatoes are less likely to break in tossing because their high-moisture/low-starch ratio means they absorb less of the cooking liquid. Happily, new potatoes will absorb less of the dressing too. Choose the mature potatoes for mashing and baking. Their low-moisture content makes for fluffier mashed and baked potatoes.

Purchase only as many potatoes as you can use within 2 weeks, and, if possible, don't store them in the refrigerator. Excessive cold converts the potato's starch to sugar, affecting the flavor. Store potatoes in a cool, dark spot. At room temperature they should keep 2 to 3 weeks. If kept in the light, green spots develop that give the tuber a bitter taste.

Ounce for ounce, a plain baked potato has about the same number of calories as a banana. Nutritionally and economically the humble potato is an excellent buy. It's high in energy-sustaining carbohydrates, yet low in fat. Given their good amount of iron and potassium, some calcium, phosphorous, vitamins B1 and C, and niacin, it seems sensible to enjoy potatoes. The trick is to enhance the flavor without inflating the calorie count. The following recipes are such an attempt.

Nutrabyte

Just 10 potato chips will bulk you up with 114 calories and 8 grams of fat.

POTATO AND ARTICHOKE GRATIN

A "flash-y" dish, quick to do but a step above the ordinary.

3 potatoes, scrubbed, thinly sliced in a food processor

1 9-ounce package frozen artichoke hearts, thawed, or 5 fresh artichoke hearts, thinly sliced

1½ cups skim milk

¾ cup skimmed evaporated milk

2 ounces goat cheese

1 teaspoon minced fresh tarragon

1 teaspoon salt

freshly ground pepper to taste

a few gratings nutmeg

2 tablespoons bread crumbs

1 tablespoon grated Parmesan-Reggiano cheese

Yield: 4 servings

Calories per serving: 216

Protein per serving: 14 g

Fat per serving: 4 g

Saturated fat per serving: 3 g

Cholesterol per serving: 11 mg

Carbohydrates per serving: 33 g

Sodium per serving: 790 mg

Fiber per serving: 4 g

1. Spray an 8-by-10-inch baking dish with olive oil.

2. Bring the potatoes and water to cover to a boil on the stovetop and simmer until crisp-tender, about 15–20 minutes. Drain. Spread the potatoes and artichokes in the baking dish. *Alternatively, combine the potatoes with 1 cup water in a microwave-safe container and microwave at high (100 percent power) for 8 minutes.*

3. Add skim milk and skimmed evaporated milk to the potatoes. Crumble the goat cheese on top.

4. Add tarragon, salt, pepper, and nutmeg. Sprinkle with bread crumbs and Parmesan-Reggiano cheese.

5. Place in the upper third of the oven. Turn heat to 425 degrees (no need to preheat) and bake 30 minutes or until top is browned and milk is bubbly.

MASHED POTATOES AND LEEKS WITH SHIITAKES

All right, it isn't exactly purely whipped potatoes with a stick of butter and cream, but it is perfectly delicious and will be welcomed by mashed potato lovers who'd rather cut back on the calories. If you keep roasted garlic on hand, try squeezing 2 or 3 cloves into the milk mixture for a true taste treat. This dish reheats in an oven or microwave beautifully. To use the leftover buttermilk, see page 164.

Yield: 4, ½-cup servings
Calories per serving: 193
Protein per serving: 6 g
Fat per serving: 1 g
Saturated fat per serving: trace
Cholesterol per serving: 3 mg
Carbohydrates per serving: 39 g
Sodium per serving: 376 mg
Fiber per serving: 5 g

4 cups loosely packed, chopped white of leek (from about 3 large leeks),
 rinsed well

1 cup chicken broth

½ ounce dried porcini or other wild mushrooms, soaked 5 minutes in ½ cup
 hot water (optional)

5 shiitake mushrooms, stems removed, sliced

2 tablespoons sherry

3 tablespoons nonfat sour cream

¼ cup buttermilk or skim milk

1 teaspoon butter (optional)

1 teaspoon fresh minced dill or ½ teaspoon dried dill weed

½ teaspoon salt

pepper to taste

a few gratings fresh nutmeg or ¼ teaspoon ground nutmeg

2 large Prince Edward Island or other large boiling potatoes, peeled, quar-
 tered, and boiled until tender

2 tablespoons grated Parmesan-Reggiano cheese

1 tablespoon freshly minced parsley

1. Preheat the oven to 300 degrees. Combine the leeks and ¾ cup chicken broth (reserve the remaining ¼ cup for Step 4) in a 1-quart microwave-safe container. Cover with plastic wrap and microwave on high (100 percent power) for 10 minutes or until the leeks are tender. Put leeks into a food processor and set aside.

2. Meanwhile line a sieve with a moistened paper coffee filter placed over a bowl. Strain the porcini, reserve the liquid, and rinse well.

3. Spray a nonstick 8-inch skillet with olive oil and "sauté" the drained porcini and shiitake mushrooms over high heat, stirring frequently, about 5 minutes or until softened and lightly browned. Add the strained porcini liquid and the sherry and stir over high heat until the pan is nearly dry, about 1 to 2 minutes more. Set aside.

4. Meanwhile heat the remaining chicken broth and the sour cream, buttermilk, butter, dill, salt, pepper, and nutmeg in a small heavy saucepan over medium-high heat until the mixture just comes to a boil.

5. Add this hot liquid to the leeks along with the potatoes. (*Alternatively, puree the leek in a food processor and force the potatoes through a ricer. Stir in the liquid. Combine the leeks with the potatoes.*) Scrape the leek-potato mixture into an ovenproof 1½- or 2-quart baking dish, preferably deeper than it is wide.

6. Cover the potatoes with the mushrooms, cheese, and parsley. The dish may be held, refrigerated, up to 24 hours or baked now until set, about 10 to 15 minutes if all the ingredients are still warm from the preparation; bake longer if they are chilled or at room temperature.

Serves 4 generously

Summer Squash

Summer squash is a good supplier of vitamins A and C, with a virtually free calorie count—about 15 calories in ½ cup. And—joy of joys!—it tastes good too.

DILLED SUMMER SQUASH

Good stuff, even without a dollop of butter.

3 small summer squashes, chopped

2 tablespoons minced fresh dill

salt and pepper to taste

1. Place the squash in a small saucepan with about ⅓ cup of water. Cover and bring to a boil. Gently boil about 4 to 5 minutes, stirring a couple of times. Remove cover if water hasn't evaporated.

2. Mash the cooked squash with the dill, salt, and pepper.
   Serves 4

Yield: 4 servings

Calories per serving: 27

Protein per serving: 1 g

Fat per serving: trace

Saturated fat per serving: trace

Cholesterol per serving: none

Carbohydrates per serving: 6 g

Sodium per serving: 2 mg

Fiber per serving: 2 g

ZUCCHINI SAUTÉ

This recipe works well with any of the summer squashes. While it may be readied for cooking in advance, sauté it just before serving. Don't be put off by the amount of salt (it's washed out).

3 small zucchini

2 teaspoons salt

1 whole clove garlic, minced or 2 cloves roasted garlic (page 305)

a few gratings fresh nutmeg

lots of freshly ground pepper to taste

1. Cut the ends from the zucchini and grate either by hand or in a food processor. Place the squash in a sieve and toss with the salt. Let the veg-

Yield: 4 servings

Calories per serving: 23

Protein per serving: 2 g

Fat per serving: 0.2 g

Saturated fat per serving: trace

Cholesterol per serving: none

Carbohydrates per serving: 5 g

Sodium per serving: 271 mg

Fiber per serving: 2 g

etable rest at least 20 minutes. The salt draws excess moisture from the vegetable.

2. Rinse the salted zucchini very thoroughly under running water, tossing and squeezing the vegetables in your fingers to rinse out the salt. Squeeze the zucchini against the sieve to remove the water. Taste to be sure the salt is removed.

3. Spray a 10-inch nonstick skillet with olive oil, and place over medium-high heat. Add the squeezed zucchini and garlic and sauté, stirring constantly, until just heated through, about 2 minutes. Season with nutmeg and pepper.

Zucchini Boats with Eggplant Caviar

Make the eggplant caviar for this dish a day or two before serving, and prepare and assemble the boats early in the day. Bake or reheat at dinnertime. Or pile the eggplant caviar into hollowed, salted, and drained tomatoes for cool dining on sun-sweltering days. Leftover eggplant caviar can have another life as an hors d'oeuvre mounded on cucumber slices, stuffed in blanched mushroom caps for broiling, or spread on croustades and sprinkled with Parmesan-Reggiano cheese.

Yield: 6 servings
Calories per serving: 55
Protein per serving: 2 g
Fat per serving: 4 g
Saturated fat per serving: 1 g
Cholesterol per serving: 1 mg
Carbohydrates per serving: 5 g
Sodium per serving: 380 mg
Fiber per serving: 1 g

For the Eggplant Caviar

1 medium eggplant, a little over a pound

1 tomato, blanched, peeled, seeded, and chopped (see page 52)

1 clove garlic, minced

1 tablespoon red wine or raspberry vinegar

1 tablespoon extra-virgin olive oil

1 tablespoon minced fresh parsley

1 tablespoon pine nuts

a few drops hot pepper sauce

½ teaspoon salt

freshly ground pepper to taste

For the Zucchini Boats

3 small zucchini

½ teaspoon salt

2 tablespoons grated Parmesan-Reggiano cheese

To Prepare the Eggplant Caviar

1. Preheat oven to 400 degrees. Cut off the ends of the eggplant and pierce it in several places with a fork. Bake eggplant until soft, about 30 minutes. Cool slightly. *Alternatively, microwave at high (100 percent power) for 12 minutes or until soft.*

2. Skin the eggplant, cut it into quarters, and scoop out and discard the seeds. Put the pulp in a food processor.

3. Add the tomato, garlic, vinegar, oil, parsley, pine nuts, pepper sauce, salt, and pepper. Blend but leave the mixture chunky. Taste for seasoning.

4. Refrigerate the eggplant caviar at least 2 hours to marry flavors. May be frozen without flavor loss up to 2 months.

To Prepare the Zucchini Boats

1. Cut the zucchini in half lengthwise. Scoop out troughs with a teaspoon. Cut a thin slice off of the bottom so that the zucchini will sit flat.

2. Bring a 2½-quart saucepan half full of water to a boil. Add the zucchini and blanch 3 minutes. Drain. *Alternatively, wrap zucchini in plastic wrap. Microwave at high (100 percent power) for 2 minutes.*

3. Preheat oven to 350 degrees. Place the zucchini boats in an oven-safe serving dish that has been sprayed with olive oil and is just large enough to hold them. Season with salt. Mound eggplant caviar into each. Sprinkle with cheese. Bake 30 minutes or until bubbly and cheese is browned.

Note: Boats may be held for several hours, even a day, before cooking.

RATATOUILLE

Ratatouille is a medley of eggplant, zucchini, onions, peppers, and tomatoes, heady with the perfume of sweet basil. It takes a bit of time to prepare but is best made a day ahead. It also freezes well. Make it when summer's produce is at its peak, and serve it beside a cold poached salmon or a simple roasted chicken. All by itself it makes for a most satisfying lunch. For an all-vegetable meal, serve with rice.

1 small eggplant, about ½ pound

3 teaspoons extra-virgin olive oil

1 medium zucchini

4 tablespoons chicken broth or canned consommé

2 green peppers, diced

2 medium onions, diced, about 1¾ cups

1 clove garlic, minced

1 pound tomatoes, blanched and peeled (page 52), juices reserved

10 fresh basil leaves, snipped, or 1 teaspoon dried basil

1 teaspoon salt

freshly ground pepper to taste

1 tablespoon minced fresh parsley

1. Cut the ends from the eggplant and slice it into rounds ½-inch thick. Stack the slices and cut the rounds into 6 or 8 wedges.

2. Spritz with olive oil a nonstick skillet large enough to hold the eggplant in one layer. Add 2 teaspoons of the extra-virgin olive oil and turn the heat to high. When hot, add the eggplant and cook over high heat until tender and lightly browned, about 8 minutes. Lower heat if eggplant starts to burn. Spritz with olive oil again if needed. Shake pan vigorously by the handle during cooking to keep the eggplant from sticking, and to turn it. Transfer to a casserole.

3. While the eggplant cooks, cut the ends from the zucchini, slice it into rounds, stack the slices, and cut them into wedges.

Yield: 6 servings

Calories per serving: 74

Protein per serving: 2 g

Fat per serving: 3 g

Saturated fat per serving: trace

Cholesterol per serving: trace

Carbohydrates per serving: 12 g

Sodium per serving: 355 mg

Fiber per serving: 3 g

Nutrabyte

Web site with nutrition information: www.amhrt.org
This site of the American Heart Association is chock-full of nutrition, fitness, and health information.

4. Spray the skillet again; add the rest of the oil, along with the zucchini; and cook over high heat until lightly browned. Shake the pan often during cooking. Spritz with olive oil again if needed. Transfer zucchini to the casserole with the eggplant.

5. Add the broth to the now empty skillet; add the peppers, onions, and garlic; cover the skillet; and cook over medium-low heat until the vegetables are limp. If there is visible liquid after cooking, raise the heat to high to evaporate. Add these ingredients to the eggplant mixture.

6. Add the tomato pulp and juices to the casserole.

7. Add the basil to the eggplant-tomato mixture. Season with salt and lots of freshly ground pepper. Toss to mix well. Sprinkle parsley on top.

8. Casserole may be baked, covered, at 350 degrees (no need to preheat) for about 35 minutes or until heated through, or cooked over low heat, covered, on top of the stove. Be careful the vegetables don't burn on the bottom. *Alternatively, it may be microwaved at high (100 percent power) for 15 minutes, covered with plastic wrap.* Serve warm, at room temperature, or cold.

WINTER SQUASH

Hard-shelled squash, commonly called winter squash, is available much of the year. Some varieties, such as acorn and buttercup, are marketed throughout the year.

Squash is indigenous to the New World and was unknown in Europe until explorers returned home with the new vegetable. When North American Indians introduced the English settlers to *askootasquash,* meaning "eaten raw," the Europeans shortened the name to *squash* and proceeded to cook it. Cooking is still the norm.

The common varieties include:

Acorn: ribbed dark green skin.

Butternut: dark green with stripes of gray; blossom end is turban-shaped.

Nutrabyte

Most varieties of winter squash provide a tasty source of beta-carotene, along with significant amounts of riboflavin and iron. They supply approximately 35 to 70 calories per ½ cup.

Hubbard: smooth, buff-colored skin, with a bulbous end.

Turban: two-toned, with the top knot blue-gray and the remainder an orange with stripes.

Spaghetti squash: a yellow gourd of Asian origin. When cooked, its bland but pleasantly crunchy strands resemble thin spaghetti.

Winter squashes are long-keeping vegetables. They do best in a cool, dry, well-ventilated spot, where they will keep 1 to 4 weeks.

Winter squashes can be roasted whole, avoiding peeling and cutting, which can be difficult, or boiled or microwaved. *To roast whole,* wash thoroughly and prick in several places with a fork. Roast 45 to 90 minutes in a 375-degree oven or until a skewer or thin knife pierces the skin easily. Cut open; discard seeds and skin. Mash, and season.

To microwave, halve the squash; discard the seeds now or after cooking, as you wish. Place in a microwave-safe casserole dish with ½ inch of water. Cover with plastic wrap or a lid for the dish. Microwaving times are difficult to predict because they will vary enormously with the size and amount of vegetable.

To boil, peel and cube the flesh, discarding seeds. Cover with water by 2 inches and boil until the flesh is soft when pierced with a fork. Drain, mash, and season. (I find boiling the least preferable, because the vegetable becomes somewhat waterlogged.)

BRAISED BUTTERCUP SQUASH WITH CURRIED FRUITS

Hearty and rich, even without added fats, this is a fine winter veggie. Leftovers reheat beautifully in the microwave. Buttercup squash is round and dark green.

4 to 5 ounces mixed dried fruits or dried apricots, diced

1 yellow onion, peeled and diced

1 teaspoon mushroom or chicken base concentrate (see Shopping Sources, page 306), blended in 2 cups water, or 2 cups chicken broth

1 small buttercup squash, peeled, seeded, and diced into uniform, ½-inch

Yield: 4 servings

Calories per serving: 188

Protein per serving: 4 g

Fat per serving: 0.8 g

Saturated fat per serving: trace

Cholesterol per serving: 0

Carbohydrates per serving: 46 g

Sodium per serving: 492 mg

Fiber per serving: 6 g

pieces (about 3 cups)
¾ to 1 cup orange juice
1 tablespoon curry powder or to taste (this will be spicy)
1 1-inch piece ginger root, unpeeled and grated
½ teaspoon salt
1 tablespoon minced fresh parsley for garnish (optional)

1. Combine the dried fruits with ½ cup hot water in a microwave-safe container. Microwave at high (100 percent power) for 2 minutes. Set aside.

2. In a 10-inch skillet, combine the onion and broth. Bring to a boil and simmer 5 minutes, until onion is translucent. Add squash and cook, covered, over medium-low heat for 10 minutes, or until squash is tender when pierced with a fork.

3. Mix together the orange juice, curry powder, ginger root, and salt. Add to the squash, along with the softened fruits and their juice, and simmer until blended, about 2 minutes. Serve garnished with parsley, if desired.

Makes 4 generous servings

BOURBON SQUASH SOUFFLÉ

A puffy presentation of pureed butternut squash combined with bourbon and a hint of maple syrup, this soufflé is just the thing when you want a vegetable dish of distinction. Everything except beating the egg whites can be readied far in advance of the actual cooking, making it an easy-to-prepare party dish. If you prefer, you can make the soufflé in its entirety and freeze it, uncooked. Turn the freezer to its coldest setting. Cover the soufflé with aluminum foil or plastic wrap and freeze solidly. If the soufflé was frozen in a freezer-to-oven dish, bake it frozen and double the cooking time. In a more fragile dish, thaw for 30 minutes, then bake, again doubling the cooking time. Some of the dramatic puff is sacrificed in this method, but it is convenient.

The recipe prepared through Step 2 is an excellent everyday way to serve the vegetable.

Yield: 6 servings

Calories per serving: 115

Protein per serving: 6 g

Fat per serving: 1 g

Saturated fat per serving: trace

Cholesterol per serving: 2 mg

Carbohydrates per serving: 20 g

Sodium per serving: 272 mg

Fiber per serving: 2 g

1 medium butternut squash, about 1¼ pounds

2 tablespoons bourbon

3 tablespoons maple syrup

½ teaspoon salt

freshly ground pepper to taste

a few gratings nutmeg

3 tablespoons cornstarch

1½ cups skim milk

¼ cup egg substitute

1 tablespoon grated Parmesan-Reggiano cheese or dried bread crumbs

4 egg whites

a pinch cream of tartar

1. Preheat the oven to 400 degrees. Peel the squash, chop into eighths, and discard the seeds. Bring a 2½-quart saucepan two-thirds full of water to a boil, immerse the squash, and cook it until tender, about 20 minutes. Drain.

2. Mash the squash with the bourbon, maple syrup, salt, pepper, and nutmeg. Set the mixture aside.

3. Dissolve the cornstarch in the milk. Set over medium-high heat and whisk until thickened, about 3 minutes. Set aside.

4. In a food processor or a bowl with a hand-held mixer, beat the egg substitute into the squash puree. Beat in the thickened milk. Set aside or refrigerate.

5. Spray a 1-quart soufflé dish or other straight-sided baking dish (preferably with a 6-inch diameter) with olive oil. Sprinkle in cheese or bread crumbs. Shake the dish to evenly distribute. Make a collar for the dish by folding a length of aluminum foil, long enough to encircle the dish with a 2-inch overlap, into thirds. Spray the nonseamed side of the foil with olive oil, or butter it heavily. Wrap this collar, seam side out, tightly around the dish; secure it with a straight pin or paper clip.

6. When you're ready to complete this soufflé, beat the egg whites until foamy. Add the cream of tartar. Beat until soft peaks form. Scoop the egg whites on top of the squash mixture. Fold them in gently. Ladle (pouring can deflate the whites) the soufflé mixture into the soufflé dish.

7. Put 1 inch water in an 8-inch square baking dish. Put the soufflé dish in the baking dish on top of the stove. Turn heat to high; simmer for 5 minutes. Baking pan and all, slide soufflé into the bottom third of a preheated oven. Check the soufflé after 35 minutes. If the top is browning too fast, cover loosely with foil. Cook 15 to 25 minutes more. Soufflé is done when a skewer inserted slightly off center comes out dry. Remove collar and serve immediately.

SPAGHETTI SQUASH PRIMAVERA

Spaghetti squash may be tossed with just a hint of butter and seasoned with salt and pepper, or you can gussy it up, as it is here. It is delicious with either Pesto (page 301) or Red Pepper Butter (page 124).

    This casserole will satisfy some appetites as a complete meal, though meat eaters may want to add a few ounces of lean Canadian bacon or ham.

1 2-pound spaghetti squash

2 teaspoons butter

2 ounces grated Parmesan-Reggiano cheese

½ bunch broccoli flowerets, sliced

1 cup shelled fresh peas (about 1 pound in the pod)

1 small zucchini, julienned

¾ cup sliced mushrooms

1 teaspoon salt

freshly ground pepper to taste

Yield: 4 servings

Calories per serving: 208

Protein per serving: 13 g

Fat per serving: 7 g

Saturated fat per serving: 4 g

Cholesterol per serving: 17 mg

Carbohydrates per serving: 26 g

Sodium per serving: 874 mg

Fiber per serving: 8 g

1. Cut the squash in half the short way. Place it, cut side down, with 1 inch of water in a baking dish just large enough to hold it.

2. Bake at 350 degrees until the shell is easily pierced with a fork and the flesh shreds when pulled with a fork, about 45 minutes. *Alternatively, wrap the halves in plastic wrap and microwave at high (100 percent power) for 10 minutes or until tender.* Cool, scoop out, and discard the seeds. Pull the strands from the squash into a bowl. Discard the tough skin. Toss the squash strands with the butter and the cheese.

3. While the squash is baking, prepare the vegetables. Bring a 2½-quart saucepan three-quarters full of water to a boil. Add the broccoli and boil 1 minute; add the peas and cook 1 minute more; add the zucchini and cook 30 seconds more. Drain and cool all the vegetables under running water. Set vegetables aside.

4. Spritz a nonstick 8-inch skillet with olive oil. Sauté the mushrooms in the skillet until lightly browned.

5. In a large bowl combine the cooked spaghetti squash, drained vegetables, and mushrooms. Season with salt and pepper and toss well to combine. Spoon into a casserole. Recipe is ready to eat, or set the dish aside, then reheat, covered, in a 350-degree oven for 30 to 35 minutes and uncover the last 10 minutes of cooking. *Alternatively, heat in the microwave at high (100 percent power) 5 to 8 minutes or until warmed through.*

TOMATOES

While genetic engineering promises vine-ripened tomatoes at your supermarket every day, right now the only really good tomato is still a local tomato. It doesn't matter where "local" is—though New Jerseyites will disagree—it only matters that the tomato is allowed to ripen on the vine to develop peak flavor. To preserve that flavor, never refrigerate tomatoes or ripen them on a sunny windowsill; room temperature and regular light are the ideal conditions to ripen and store tomatoes.

Although tomatoes, or a not-so-reasonable facsimile, can be purchased all year long, the season for most local tomatoes is midsummer to September, depending on your location. "Seconds," bruised or misshapen tomatoes, are perfect for many uses at about half the price of the perfect specimens.

An uncooked tomato supplies a little over half an adult's daily need for vitamin C, for a meager 35 calories.

The recipes that follow are for those sun-dappled months when local tomatoes abound.

CHEESE-FROSTED TOMATOES

Select small- to medium-size local tomatoes for this quick vegetable dish. While farm-stand tomatoes need only a spritz of your own olive oil, supermarket tomatoes will benefit from a drizzle of extra-virgin olive oil. To cook on a covered grill, place them on a sheet of aluminum foil on an upper rung. Tomatoes may be prepared for cooking hours before baking.

Yield: 6 servings
Calories per serving: 49
Protein per serving: 3 g
Fat per serving: 2 g
Saturated fat per serving: 1 g
Cholesterol per serving: 4 mg
Carbohydrates per serving: 6 g
Sodium per serving: 197 mg
Fiber per serving: 1 g

6 ripe tomatoes, peeled and cored (see Quick Tip, page 52)

¼ teaspoon salt

freshly ground pepper to taste

6 teaspoons Pesto (page 301), or 15 leaves fresh basil, snipped, or 3 teaspoons dried basil

6 tablespoons grated Parmesan-Reggiano cheese

1. Slice a thin round off the base of each tomato so it will stand upright. With a melon baller, make a deep well where the tomatoes' cores were. Place the tomatoes in a baking dish.

2. Preheat oven to 325 degrees. Season tomatoes with salt and pepper. Spritz with olive oil. Place a teaspoon of Pesto or the basil in each tomato well. Divide the cheese over the top and bake for 20 minutes. If desired, broil until the cheese is lightly browned.

TOMATOES STUFFED WITH FRESH MOZZARELLA, OLIVES, AND CROUTONS

As good as fresh sliced tomatoes are, a quick turn in the oven makes them even better. After you've been cooking *The New Gourmet Light* way for a while, the teaspoon of oil looks like so much! A recipe aside: Don't buy ricotta for this recipe, but if you have some on hand, it's a nice addition.

Yield: 6 servings
Calories per serving: 72
Protein per serving: 4 g
Fat per serving: 3 g
Saturated fat per serving: 1 g
Cholesterol per serving: 7 mg
Carbohydrates per serving: 8 g
Sodium per serving: 301 mg
Fiber per serving: 2 g

6 small tomatoes, one thin end sliced off, insides scooped out, with a
   ¼-inch shell left
½ teaspoon salt
2 slices best-quality white, chewy, European-style bread, such as a peasant
   bread or baguette, with crust, cubed (about 1 ounce or 1 cup loosely
   packed)
1 ball fresh mozzarella (about 2½ ounces), preferably skim or part-skim,
   cubed
2 tablespoons part-skim ricotta (optional)
¼ cup minced fresh basil or other fresh herb, such as oregano or thyme, or a
   combination
2 tablespoons diced, pitted green or black olives, or a combination (about 5
   to 6 medium olives)
2 whole scallions, minced
½ teaspoon sugar
2 teaspoons toasted pine nuts (optional) (see page 87)
1 teaspoon walnut or olive oil (optional)

1. Sprinkle the cored tomatoes with salt, and invert them to drain, about 10 to 20 minutes.

2. Spray an 8-inch skillet with olive oil and place over high heat. When the pan is hot, add the bread, spray again, and reduce heat as needed, stirring often, until the bread is browned, about 8 to 10 minutes. (Croutons can be prepared as much as 8 hours ahead.)

3. Preheat oven to 400 degrees. Combine the cheeses, basil, olives, and scallions in a bowl; stir to combine. Stir in the croutons just when ready to bake.

4. Rinse the tomatoes, shake them to dispel water, and sprinkle the insides with sugar. Divide the cheese mixture among the tomatoes. Bake for 15 to 18 minutes, or until lightly browned on top.

Serves 4 to 6 depending on the menu

VEGGIE MADNESS

Why not? After all, there's "Chocolate Madness" on every dessert cart. So, vegetables aren't quite as addicting as chocolate—few people actually crave a good, juicy carrot—but this is still a pretty good recipe for those vegetable addicts among us. Go ahead, go mad. Your hips will never regret it.

Watch the veggies closely during microwave cooking. Many factors affect timing.

Yield: 6 servings

Calories per serving: 50

Protein per serving: 3 g

Fat per serving: 2 g

Saturated fat per serving: trace

Cholesterol per serving: 4 mg

Carbohydrates per serving: 8 g

Sodium per serving: 34 mg

Fiber per serving: 3 g

1 stalk broccoli, stems peeled and thinly sliced, flowerets chopped

½ cup chopped cauliflower

1½ carrots, cut in thin sticks

7 tablespoons chicken broth

½ zucchini, sliced in thin sticks

½ red bell pepper, sliced in thin strips

½ summer squash, sliced in thin sticks

4 ounces mushrooms, sliced

¼ cup Spanish onion, chopped

⅓ cup minced fresh parsley

1 teaspoon salt

freshly ground pepper to taste

1 tablespoon fresh minced tarragon or 1 teaspoon dried tarragon

1 clove garlic, minced

1 shallot, minced

1 tablespoon lemon juice

2 teaspoons butter

1. In a microwave-safe bowl, combine the broccoli, cauliflower, carrots, and 4 tablespoons chicken broth. Cover with plastic wrap and microwave at high (100 percent power) for 4 minutes.

2. Uncover and remove from microwave; add the zucchini, red pepper, summer squash, mushrooms, and onion. Stir to combine. Sprinkle with parsley. Season with salt and pepper.

3. Combine the tarragon, garlic, shallot, lemon juice, butter, and 3 tablespoons broth in a 1-cup glass measure or other microwave-safe container. Heat at high (100 percent power) for 1 minute or until butter is melted. Pour mixture over the veggies.

4. Cover veggies again with plastic wrap and cook at high (100 percent power) for 4 minutes more or just until crisp-tender.

STIR-FRIED ASIAN VEGGIES

Light and clean tasting. If you don't have a julienne disk for your food processor, use the large side of a hand-held grater and grate rather than julienning by hand.

1 small jicama, peeled and julienned (about 2 cups loosely packed)

3 ounces (about 1 cup) loosely packed daikon, peeled and julienned

3 ounces (about 2) baby bok choy, thinly sliced, or 1 cup loosely packed napa cabbage

1 carrot, julienned

1 clove garlic, minced

2 scallions, including most of the green, minced

2 teaspoons grated, unpeeled ginger root

1 tablespoon oil, such as peanut, olive, or canola

1 cup bean sprouts

2 tablespoons mirin (Japanese cooking wine)

1 tablespoon rice wine vinegar

Yield: 4 servings

Calories per serving: 104

Protein per serving: 2 g

Fat per serving: 4 g

Saturated fat per serving: 0.5 g

Cholesterol per serving: none

Carbohydrates per serving: 17 g

Sodium per serving: 125 mg

Fiber per serving: 5 g

1. In a bowl toss together the jicama, daikon, bok choy, and carrot.

2. Spray a wok with olive oil. Stir-fry the garlic, scallions, and ginger root about 1 minute, until fragrant.

3. Add the oil and the tossed-together veggies. Stir-fry until crisp-tender, about 4 to 5 minutes. Add the bean sprouts, mirin, and vinegar. Toss over high heat just to warm through, and serve.

    Serves 4

Nutrabyte

Olive and canola oils are considered healthy oils because their ratio of polyunsaturated and monounsaturated fats to saturated fat is better than that of other oils, such as coconut oil, which has a higher ratio of saturated to polyunsaturated or monounsaturated fat.

GRILLED VEGGIES

An idea more than a recipe, these are terrific with Grilled Brined Chicken Breasts (page 178) or Salmon Burgers (page 208). If you have rosemary skewers on hand, it's fun (but not necessary) to use them as a rack for the veggies.

Yield: 4 servings
Calories per serving: 140
Protein per serving: 5 g
Fat per serving: 1 g
Saturated fat per serving: trace
Cholesterol per serving: none
Carbohydrates per serving: 31 g
Sodium per serving: 253 mg
Fiber per serving: 6 g

1 bulb fennel, stalks removed, cored and quartered

1 red pepper, seeded and halved

2 medium portabella mushroom caps

1 Vidalia or Spanish onion, peeled and sliced in ¼-inch slices

1 medium eggplant, sliced on the diagonal in ½-inch-thick slices

¾ cup fat-free bottled dressing of choice, such as Lemon and Garlic or
*   Balsamic and Olive Oil*

2 tablespoons hoisin sauce, available in the Asian section of the
*   supermarket*

2 tablespoons chicken broth or wine or orange juice

1 tablespoon minced fresh dill or 1 teaspoon dried dill

2 teaspoons lemon juice

1 teaspoon sugar

½ teaspoon minced garlic from a jar or 1 clove garlic, minced

1. Put the fennel, red pepper, mushroom caps, onion, and eggplant in a bowl.

2. Mix together in a jar the bottled dressing, hoisin, broth, dill, lemon juice, sugar, and garlic. Shake well and pour all but ½ cup over the veggies. Let sit at least 5 minutes and as long as overnight.

3. Grill, basting with the remaining ½ cup marinade. Slice the red pepper and mushroom caps before serving.

    Serves 2 to 4 depending on menu and appetite

FOUR-VEGETABLE PIE WITH FRESH MOZZARELLA CHEESE

Whether served as an elegant side dish or as the star of an all-vegetable meal, this dish will garner much-deserved raves. It can be prepared through Step 5 early in the day. Adjust microwave timing for your own oven.

Yield: 4 to 6 servings
Calories per serving: 130
Protein per serving: 7 g
Fat per serving: 6 g
Saturated fat per serving: 3 g
Cholesterol per serving: 12 mg
Carbohydrates per serving: 13 g
Sodium per serving: 451 mg
Fiber per serving: 3 g

1 medium eggplant, cut in half lengthwise, then thinly sliced crosswise

8 plum tomatoes, thinly sliced lengthwise

½ bulb fennel, diced

½ cup diced Spanish onion

3 tablespoons chopped fresh basil

½ teaspoon seasoned or regular salt

freshly ground pepper to taste

1 tablespoon lemon juice

2 tablespoons bread crumbs

2 tablespoons grated Parmesan-Reggiano cheese

1 teaspoon dried oregano

½ teaspoon salt

freshly ground pepper to taste

4 ounces fresh part-skim mozzarella cheese, thinly sliced

1 tablespoon excellent-quality oil, such as olive or walnut

1. Place the eggplant in a single layer on cotton or paper towels. Sprinkle with salt and let rest 10 to 15 minutes.

2. Turn eggplant over, salt the other side, and let rest another 5 to 10 minutes. Rinse and pat dry.

3. Spritz a 10-inch glass pie plate or other microwave-safe dish with olive oil. Form a ring of eggplant slices up along the sloped edge. Leave the center of the dish empty. Intersperse the tomato slices between the eggplant slices. Spritz with olive oil again.

4. Combine the fennel and onion. Fill the center with this mixture; some will spill onto the eggplant as well.

5. Sprinkle basil on top. Season with salt and pepper and sprinkle with lemon juice. Spritz again with olive oil.

6. Cover with plastic wrap. Microwave at high (100 percent power) for 12 minutes.

7. While the vegetable pie cooks, combine the bread crumbs, Parmesan-Reggiano, oregano, salt, and pepper in an 8-inch nonstick skillet. Spray with olive oil. Stir to brown lightly over medium-low heat, for about 1 minute.

8. Remove plastic wrap from pie. Make a ring with the cheese slices, leaving a small circle empty in the middle of the pie. Divide the bread crumbs between this center and the outside perimeter of the pie. Drizzle oil over all.

9. Place pie in the upper third of the oven, turn heat to 425 degrees, and bake until lightly browned, about 5 to 8 minutes, or broil until crumbs are browned. Let rest 5 to 10 minutes before slicing in wedges.

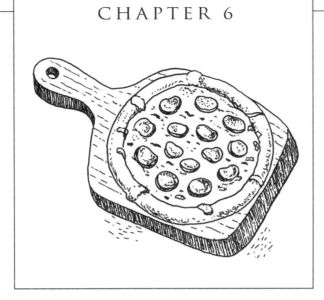

PIZZA, PASTA, AND GRAINS

THE RECIPES

Pizza

Pasta

Grains

PIZZA, PASTA, AND GRAINS

Pizza, pastas, and grains—these yummy, stick-to-the-ribs foods fit right into *The New Gourmet Light* cooking style, given attention to a few details like excess oils and heavy cheeses. Some of the recipes call for rather expensive ingredients, such as cèpes, or seasonally available produce, such as Sweet 100s, a particularly sweet cherry tomato, but their extra flavor allows scrimping on fats.

FRESH MOZZARELLA AND TOMATO PIZZETTA

Assemble this pizzetta no more than an hour before serving or the tortilla will get soggy. Fresh mozzarella, the kind sold in brine and available at some specialty food stores, makes a delicious change from the supermarket variety, which is usually wrapped in plastic.

1 large, burrito-style flour tortilla (sold refrigerated in the supermarket dairy section)

1 large, fully ripe tomato, thinly sliced, slices cut in half

2 ounces fresh mozzarella cheese, cut into strips

4 or 5 fresh basil leaves, snipped, or ½ teaspoon dried basil

⅛ teaspoon salt

freshly ground pepper to taste

1. Preheat oven to 475 degrees. Place the tortilla on a baking sheet; spray with olive oil. Arrange the tomato slices, overlapping them spoke-fashion, on the tortilla.

2. Cover the tomato with the cheese strips.

3. Sprinkle basil over cheese, spray with olive oil, then season with salt and pepper.

4. Bake about 6 minutes, until cheese is melted. Then broil until lightly browned, about 3 minutes more. Cool slightly before cutting into quarters with a pizza cutter.

Yield: 4 servings

Calories per serving: 97

Protein per serving: 5 g

Fat per serving: 4 g

Saturated fat per serving: 2 g

Cholesterol per serving: 11 mg

Carbohydrates per serving: 10 g

Sodium per serving: 138 mg

Fiber per serving: 1 g

PIZZA DOUGH

Many markets sell uncooked pizza dough—or, time allowing, you can make your own. I've had poor luck freezing commercial dough, as it seems to be much harder to roll out once frozen, so if you use only a half-package you might want to roll out the dough and, if you've got room, freeze it, uncooked, for a ready-made pizza base another night. For best results use a perforated-bottom pizza pan, which will keep this very thin crust crispy. To accommodate different tastes, do "halvsies" (suggestions follow). *Note:* All the ingredients except those for the Clam and Canadian Bacon Pizza are for half of a 16-inch pie.

Yield: 16 slices
Calories per slice: 109
Protein per slice: 3 g
Fat per slice: 1 g
Saturated fat per slice: trace
Cholesterol per slice: none
Carbohydrates per slice: 21 g
Sodium per slice: 68 mg
Fiber per slice: trace

1 package (¼ ounce) dry yeast
1 teaspoon sugar
3½ cups all-purpose flour, sifted into a large bowl
½ teaspoon salt
1 tablespoon olive oil
1 cup warm water
cornmeal for rolling

1. Proof the yeast according to package instructions in ¼ cup warm water (105 to 115 degrees) with 1 teaspoon sugar. Place in a warm spot. Yeast will foam and bubble in about 5 to 8 minutes.

2. Make a well in the center of the flour in a bowl. Add the salt, olive oil, warm water, and yeast mixture. Stir to combine, then turn out onto a floured surface and knead 5 to 10 minutes or until smooth and elastic and no longer sticky. Return to bowl; place in a warm, draft-free spot; cover loosely with a towel; and let rise until doubled, about 1¾ to 2 hours.

3. Punch down. Divide in half. Roll each half out onto a floured surface with a sprinkle of cornmeal into a circle about 18 inches wide. Sprinkle pizza pan with cornmeal and lay dough on it, folding in edges.
   This recipe makes 2 16-inch pizzas crusts.

CLAM AND CANADIAN BACON PIZZA

Clams and Canadian bacon combine to make a delicious, albeit unusual, pizza.

cornmeal for rolling

½ pound commercial pizza dough, or ½ Pizza Dough recipe (page 153)

½ bulb roasted garlic (see page 305)

3 ounces diced Canadian bacon (about ⅔ cup) or lean ham

1 10-ounce can whole baby clams, drained

2 ounces (about 8) stemmed fresh shiitake mushrooms, thinly sliced

1 ounce Parmesan-Reggiano cheese, grated (about ⅓ cup)

*2 tablespoons each minced fresh basil and oregano or 1 tablespoon each
    dried basil and oregano*

salt and freshly ground pepper to taste

Yield: 8 slices
Calories per slice: 204
Protein per slice: 16 g
Fat per slice: 4 g
Saturated fat per slice: 1 g
Cholesterol per slice: 33 mg
Carbohydrates per slice: 25 g
Sodium per slice: 341 mg
Fiber per slice: 1 g

1. Preheat oven to 500 degrees. Spray a 16-inch perforated-bottom pizza pan with olive oil. Sprinkle with cornmeal. Roll out the dough into a circle about 18 inches in diameter. To facilitate the rolling, use a little cornmeal on the floured rolling surface, lift the dough onto your fists, and twirl and stretch it into a circle as well as rolling it. The circle doesn't have to be perfect; you can stretch and coax it to fit the pan. Lay the dough onto the pan. Form a crust by rolling up the edges.

2. With a flexible rubber spatula, mash the garlic evenly over the dough. Cover with the bacon, clams, mushrooms, cheese, herbs, and salt and pepper. Spray with olive oil.

3. Bake in the upper third of the oven 10 to 12 minutes, reducing the heat to 425 degrees if the edges begin to burn. Let rest 5 minutes before slicing with a pizza cutter.

    Makes 8 slices

Red Pepper Butter with Corn Pizza

Note: To accommodate different tastes, you can do "halvsies" and top a single crust with 2 different toppings. This recipe as well as the ones on pages 156 and 157 can be mixed and matched. The ingredients here will top half of a 16-inch pie. Double them to top a whole pizza.

½ pound commercial pizza dough, ½ recipe Pizza Dough (page 153),

> *or 1 16-inch unbaked pizza crust*

1 ear of corn, unshucked

½ cup Red Pepper Butter (page 124)

1 tablespoon fresh minced basil

2 teaspoons fresh minced oregano or 1 teaspoon dried oregano

2 tablespoons grated Parmesan-Reggiano cheese

salt and pepper to taste

Yield: 4 slices

Calories per slice: 149

Protein per slice: 5 g

Fat per slice: 2 g

Saturated fat per slice: 0.67 g

Cholesterol per slice: 2 mg

Carbohydrates per slice: 28 g

Sodium per slice: 181 mg

Fiber per slice: 2 g

1. Preheat oven to 500 degrees. Wet the unshucked ear of corn. Microwave at high (100 percent power) for 3 minutes. Cool slightly, husk, and cut the kernels from the cob.

2. Spread the Red Pepper Butter thinly over half of the uncooked pizza crust. Sprinkle first with corn and then with herbs and cheese. Salt (if desired, but the cheese is salty), and season with pepper. Top the other half as desired with the Classic or BBQ Chicken topping.

3. Bake 12 to 18 minutes, until browned and bubbly.

> Covers ½ of a 16-inch pizza

BBQ Chicken Pizza

The ingredients here are for a half of a 16-inch pie. See note on page 155.

For BBQ Sauce

¾ cup minced onion

2 tablespoons bourbon

2 tablespoons hoisin sauce (available in the Asian section of the supermarket)

2 tablespoons reduced-sodium soy sauce

2 tablespoons orange or pineapple juice

2 cloves garlic, minced

1 teaspoon paprika

1. Combine all ingredients in a small saucepan and bring to a boil. Cover and cook at medium heat for 20 minutes. Uncover and boil about 2 minutes more, until sauce is reduced to about ½ cup. Sauce can be made several days in advance.

For Pizza

½ pound commercial pizza dough, or ½ recipe Pizza Dough (page 153, or 1 16-inch unbaked pizza crust)

1 recipe BBQ sauce (about ½ cup)

1 tablespoon minced fresh basil

½ chicken breast, grilled just 3 minutes per side (it will be underdone), shredded, juices reserved

salt and pepper to taste

1. Preheat oven to 500 degrees. Spread ½ cup BBQ sauce over half of a 16-inch unbaked pizza crust. Top with basil and chicken. Season with salt and pepper. Top the other half as desired with Classic or Red Pepper Butter and Corn topping

2. Bake pizza 12 to 18 minutes, until browned and bubbly.
      Covers ½ of a 16-inch pizza

Yield: 4 slices

Calories per slice: 200

Protein per slice: 11 g

Fat per slice: 3 g

Saturated fat per slice: 0.45 g

Cholesterol per slice: 17 mg

Carbohydrates per slice: 31 g

Sodium per slice: 463 mg

Fiber per slice: 2 g

CLASSIC PIZZA

The ingredients here are for a half of a 16-inch pie. See note on page 155.

½ pound commercial pizza dough, or ½ recipe Pizza Dough (page 153),
*   or 1 16-inch unbaked pizza crust*
½ cup homemade tomato or pizza sauce from a jar
1 tablespoon minced fresh basil
2 teaspoons minced fresh oregano or 1 teaspoon dried oregano
1 ball (about 2 ounces) fresh water-packed mozzarella, preferably part-skim,
*   thinly sliced*
1 ounce grated Parmesan-Reggiano cheese
salt and pepper to taste

Yield: 4 slices
Calories per slice: 197
Protein per slice: 10 g
Fat per slice: 6 g
Saturated fat per slice: 3 g
Cholesterol per slice: 14 mg
Carbohydrates per slice: 25 g
Sodium per slice: 361 mg
Fiber per slice: 1 g

1. Preheat oven to 500 degrees. Spread half of a 16-inch unbaked pizza crust thinly with pizza sauce (a thick base will make the crust soggy). Sprinkle with basil and oregano, top with cheeses, and season with salt and pepper. Top the other half as desired with Red Pepper Butter and Corn or BBQ Chicken toppings.

2. Bake 12 to 18 minutes, until browned and bubbly.
   Covers ½ of a 16-inch pizza

Nutrabyte

For hearty cheese flavor without hefty calories and fat values, choose Parmesan. The more expensive, such as a Parmesan-Reggiano, the better, guaranteeing superior flavor for the smallest caloric tag. A tablespoon of shredded Parmesan-Reggiano has 20 calories and 1 gram of fat. A tablespoon of Cheddar, by contrast, has 57 calories and 4½ grams of fat.

SHRIMP, ASPARAGUS, AND LEMON PEPPER PASTA

Let this recipe be guided by seasonal availability. Use asparagus, for example, only when it's fresh and priced reasonably. Otherwise, choose broccoli flowerets, green beans, sugar snap peas, or pea pods. The veggies and sauce can be prepared several hours in advance and held, refrigerated, until serving time. Undercook the veggies initially so as not to turn them to mush when reheating.

Yield: 4 servings

Calories per serving: 448

Protein per serving: 34 g

Fat per serving: 10 g

Saturated fat per serving: 4 g

Cholesterol per serving: 234 mg

Carbohydrates per serving: 55 g

Sodium per serving: 590 mg

Fiber per serving: 4 g

For the Shrimp, Marinade, and Vegetables

1 pound frozen shrimp (31 to 40 count), thawed

juice of 2 lemons (about 8 tablespoons)

1 teaspoon olive oil

1 clove garlic, minced

freshly ground pepper to taste

1 bunch (1 pound) asparagus, tough stalks snapped off, remaining stalks snapped in thirds

8 to 10 shiitake mushrooms (about 3 ounces), stems discarded, caps sliced

1 7-ounce jar red pepper halves (not packed in brine), drained and thinly sliced, or 2 red peppers, peeled and seeded (see page 44)

4 tablespoons wine (red or white)

For the Sauce

1¼ cups rich chicken broth

1 tablespoon butter

⅓ cup egg substitute, shaken vigorously

dash each salt and pepper

For the Pasta

*8 ounces cooked lemon pepper penne cooked or plain penne cooked tossed
with the zest of 2 lemons and fresh pepper to taste, drained (reserve
about ½ cup pasta cooking water)*

4 tablespoons finely grated Parmesan-Reggiano cheese

*3 tablespoons minced fresh basil leaves and a few whole basil leaves for
garnish (optional)*

To Prepare the Shrimp and Vegetables

1. Marinate the shrimp for about 20 minutes (or as long as 24 hours) in half the lemon juice (reserve the remaining 4 tablespoons for Step 1 of the sauce preparation), the oil, the garlic, and the pepper.

2. Preheat a grill. Spray a 10- or 12-inch skillet with olive oil spray. Over the high heat stir-fry the asparagus and mushrooms, adjusting heat to prevent burning, until tender, about 5 minutes. Shake the pan several times to rotate the veggies. The last minute of cooking, add the red pepper. Then add the wine and set mixture aside on the stovetop.

3. Grill the shrimp, basting with the marinade, about 4 minutes on each side. Combine the shrimp with the veggies and set aside.

To Prepare the Sauce

1. While the shrimp cook, begin the sauce. In a small saucepan combine the remaining 4 tablespoons lemon juice, the chicken broth, and the butter. Boil rapidly 8 minutes or until reduced to about ¾ cup.

2. Meanwhile beat the egg substitute with an immersion blender or by hand in a small, heavy-bottomed saucepan. Dribble in the hot broth mixture (from Step 4) while whisking. Cook over gentle heat, whisking with the immersion blender about 3 to 4 minutes (longer by hand), until the sauce is thickened to the consistency of melted ice cream. Remove from heat.

To Finish the Dish

1. Briefly reheat the veggies and shrimp, if need be. Toss the veggies, sauce, 5 or more tablespoons reserved pasta water, cheese, and 2 tablespoons of the minced basil with the pasta. Add more reserved pasta water (or wine) if the dish looks too dry. Serve in shallow soup bowls garnished with remaining basil and, if desired, whole basil leaves.

Serves 4

LINGUINE WITH FRESH TOMATO SAUCE

While I wouldn't attempt this with anything less than garden-ripened tomatoes, several of the other ingredients are easily varied. Use, for example, other combinations of herbs, such as parsley, tarragon, mint, or thyme. The important thing is to have about ⅓ cup fresh, minced, tightly packed herbs, with basil in the starring role. A fruity vinegar such as raspberry instead of the Champagne vinegar is nice. Or try 1 or 2 cloves of raw garlic instead of roasted ones. Substitute anything hot, such as ¼ teaspoon jalapeño or a couple of dried hot small chilies (remove them before serving), for the hot pepper flakes. Use all goat cheese or all Parmesan-Reggiano—you get the idea. I love this on a flavored pasta such as lemon pepper (see Shopping Sources, page 306).

Yield: 3 servings

Calories per serving: 269

Protein per serving: 13 g

Fat per serving: 9 g

Saturated fat per serving: 3 g

Cholesterol per serving: 12 mg

Carbohydrates per serving: 37 g

Sodium per serving: 327 mg

Fiber per serving: 3 g

3 medium tomatoes, chopped (about 12 to 13 ounces, or 1¾ cup)

1 ounce Parmesan-Reggiano cheese, grated

1 ounce goat cheese, flavored with herbs or plain, as you wish

¼ cup tightly packed, minced fresh basil

1 teaspoon minced fresh oregano or ¾ teaspoon dried oregano

2 tablespoons minced fresh cilantro or 1 tablespoon dried cilantro

5 black kalamata olives, pitted and chopped (about ¾ ounce)

4 cloves roasted garlic (see page 305) or 2 small or 1 large clove raw garlic, minced

1 tablespoon Champagne vinegar

½ teaspoon sugar

tiny pinch hot pepper flakes or 2 dried small chilies, removed just before
*   serving*

salt and pepper to taste

10 leaves arugula, rinsed and stems removed (optional)

4 ounces (dry, ¼ package) hot cooked pasta such as penne or linguine,
*   drained and spritzed with olive oil*

1 tablespoon pine nuts, toasted

1. Combine the tomatoes, cheeses, basil, oregano, cilantro, olives, garlic, vinegar, sugar, hot pepper flakes, and salt and pepper. Stir to combine, cover with plastic wrap, and leave at room temperature up to 3 hours. (Don't prepare farther in advance or it will be too watery.)

2. Line shallow bowls with the arugula leaves, if desired. Toss hot pasta with the tomato mixture. Divide between the bowls. Sprinkle with pine nuts.

    Serves 2

Chèvre

Goat cheeses, collectively known as chèvres, have long been popular in Europe. In America they have become the darling of foodies and the star in many a recipe. Chèvres can be creatively turned out in various guises from stuffing for pasta to soufflés. Consequently, the import and local manufacture of these distinctive handmade cheeses have grown greatly.

The flavor of chèvre is best described as clear, tangy, and fresh. Banon (wrapped in chestnut or grape leaves) is the mildest; Cortin de Chazignol is the sharpest; and Bucheron and Montrachet are perhaps the best known.

LINGUINE WITH PESTO

A plain name for a deliciously easy dish. Serve it at room temperature with a salad and garden-ripe tomatoes or Sweet 100s (tiny, sweet cherry tomatoes) tossed in for a meatless meal. Or toss in a few shrimp that have been grilled on rosemary skewers, or a few strips of grilled chicken breast.

Yield: 4 servings

Calories per serving: 244

Protein per serving: 9 g

Fat per serving: 3 g

Saturated fat per serving: 0.58 g

Cholesterol per serving: 2 mg

Carbohydrates per serving: 45 g

Sodium per serving: 188 mg

Fiber per serving: 2 g

8 ounces linguine, fresh if possible, cooked and drained
¾ cup Pesto (page 301)
¼ teaspoon salt
freshly ground pepper to taste
freshly grated Parmesan-Reggiano cheese

1. Toss the linguine with the Pesto, salt, pepper, and cheese. Serve at room temperature. *Note:* If the dish is chilled, add a few tablespoons chicken broth or white wine and warm briefly in a microwave (50 percent power) just to room temperature.

Serves 4

Nutrabyte

Diets, it seems, come and go like fashion trends. High-protein diets have sometimes been the rage. Their slant is that protein requires a lot of energy to digest, so some of its calories are cannibalized, so to speak, in that process. But when protein is mixed with either fat or carbohydrates—even in minimal amounts, as it is in most everything we eat—that effect is greatly reduced.

PENNE WITH SWEET 100S

Here's a quick pasta dish that complements a light fish or chicken dish or stands proudly on its own. A couple of ingredient notes: Roasted garlic light cream cheese is recommended (and marketed by Kraft), but you can substitute any light cream cheese or cheese spread, such as those marketed by Alouette. The idea is to use a flavored, reduced-fat, and reduced-calorie soft cheese such as a cream cheese.

The sweetness of the cherry tomatoes is integral to the success of this dish. Californians can buy "Sweet 100s," tiny, oh-so-sweet cherry tomatoes in season during spring. Living on the East Coast, I don't have access to these, but I can get a wonderful cherry tomato from Mexico. The bottom line is to use only homegrown or premium tomatoes that are sweet and ripe. Of course, any type of flavorful tomato will be fine.

Yield: 2 servings

Calories per serving: 318

Protein per serving: 13 g

Fat per serving: 5 g

Saturated fat per serving: 2 g

Cholesterol per serving: 10 mg

Carbohydrates per serving: 57 g

Sodium per serving: 694 mg

Fiber per serving: 5 g

For the Dressing

½ cup buttermilk, shaken well

2 tablespoons light cream cheese, roasted garlic recommended

2 tablespoons chicken broth

3 tablespoons minced fresh basil

2 tablespoons minced fresh mint

1 tablespoon minced fresh cilantro

2 cloves roasted garlic (see page 305)

½ teaspoon salt

fresh ground pepper to taste

For the Pasta

3 to 4 ounces pea pods, blanched and drained

8 ounces Sweet 100s or other sweet cherry tomatoes, halved

½ teaspoon sugar

4 ounces penne, cooked according to package instructions

a few whole basil leaves (optional)

grated Parmesan-Reggiano (optional)

1. In a glass measure combine the buttermilk, cream cheese, chicken broth, basil, mint, cilantro, garlic, salt, and pepper. Set aside.

2. In a medium bowl combine the pea pods and tomatoes; season with sugar, and stir to combine.

3. When ready to serve, heat both the dressing and the veggies, separately, in the microwave (70 percent power) for 1 minute each. Toss with the hot pasta. Garnish with the basil and pass the cheese, if desired.

Serves 2

PENNE WITH BROCCOLI RABE, WHITE BEANS, AND HAM

A quick pasta dish that lends itself to many variations, this is particularly good with lemon pepper pasta (see Shopping Sources, page 306). Adding a teaspoon of lemon oil (see Quick Tip, page 242) or lemon zest to plain pasta would to some extent equate the same flavor. Broccoli rabe is a somewhat new-to-market green that looks like overgrown broccoli leaves with tiny undeveloped broccoli heads as flowers. It has a pungent, pleasantly bitter taste. If you have any beans left over from the London Broil on Arugula and White Bean Salad (page 238), this is the perfect place to use them, or see that recipe or Chapter 5, Vegetables, for instructions on cooking white beans from scratch; they freeze beautifully for up to 6 months.

Yield: 2 servings
Calories per serving: 362
Protein per serving: 18 g
Fat per serving: 2 g
Saturated fat per serving: trace
Cholesterol per serving: 7 mg
Carbohydrates per serving: 64 g
Sodium per serving: 607 mg
Fiber per serving: 8 g

½ bunch broccoli rabe, stems discarded

1 clove garlic, minced

1 shallot, minced

1¼ cups rich chicken broth (best made from chicken base concentrate; see Shopping Sources, page 306) or canned broth enriched with 1/2 cube bouillon

¼ cup wine, red, rosé, or white (or broth)

½ cup plus 2 tablespoons cooked or canned (drained and rinsed) white beans (see page 101 for cooking instructions)

½ teaspoon dried rosemary

freshly ground pepper to taste

2 to 3 ounces low-sodium cooked ham steak, chopped

4 ounces hot cooked penne or other pasta

grated Parmesan-Reggiano cheese (optional)

1. Preheat the oven to 350 degrees. Spread the broccoli rabe over a cookie sheet that's been sprayed with olive oil. Roast in the upper third of the oven for 6 minutes. Stir and flip over, spray with olive oil, and roast an additional 2 minutes. Remove from oven, chop roughly, and set aside.

2. Spray a 12-inch nonstick skillet with olive oil. Sauté the garlic and shallot over high heat 1 minute, reducing heat if they start to brown.

3. Add the chicken broth, wine, ½ cup of the beans, rosemary, and pepper. Bring to a boil over high heat while partially mashing the beans with a potato masher. Add the remaining 2 tablespoons beans. When the sauce boils, reduce heat to low and simmer 5 minutes. Taste to correct seasoning. (Sauce can be made up to 1 hour in advance to this point, but you'll need more liquid, such as wine, broth, or pasta cooking water, to keep it juicy.)

4. Just before serving (add a spoonful of pasta cooking water or wine if mixture seems dry), stir in the ham and broccoli rabe. Heat just to warm, and toss with hot pasta. Pass grated cheese, if desired.

Serves 2 very generously

CHICKEN AND PASTA SALAD WITH GOLDEN RAISINS AND CAPERS

Here is a delicious pasta salad with absolutely no added fat, thanks to a dressing based on egg whites instead of the more traditional yolk and/or oil dressing. Use a food processor to make quick work of julienning the vegetables. To roast peppers, refer to the illustrated directions on page 44, or purchase a jar of roasted peppers (don't buy those packed in brine) from the Italian section of your market. Serve the salad at room temperature.

Yield: 4 servings

Calories per serving: 477

Protein per serving: 39 g

Fat per serving: 5 g

Saturated fat per serving: 1 g

Cholesterol per serving: 73 mg

Carbohydrates per serving: 70 g

Sodium per serving: 1133 mg

Fiber per serving: 7 g

For the Salad

1½ cups water

1 teaspoon chicken base concentrate (see Shopping Sources, page 306)
    or 1 cube chicken bouillon

4 split chicken breasts, with bones, skinned

1 leek, white only, julienned

1 summer squash, julienned

1 zucchini, julienned

1 carrot, julienned

8 ounces penne or bowtie pasta, cooked according to package instructions

½ cup roasted red peppers, thinly sliced

¼ cup golden raisins

2 tablespoons capers, or to taste

For the Dressing

2 egg whites

1 tablespoon lemon juice

2 tablespoons fat-free mayonnaise

1 tablespoon honey

2 teaspoons curry powder

½ teaspoon cumin powder

1 teaspoon Dijon-style mustard

1 teaspoon prepared horseradish

1 teaspoon salt

freshly ground pepper to taste

1 tablespoon minced fresh parsley (optional)

To Prepare the Salad

1. In a skillet just large enough to hold the chicken, bring the water and chicken base concentrate to a boil. Add the chicken, cover, and bring back to a boil; then reduce heat to a simmer. Cook 15 minutes or until chicken flesh feels firm.

2. Remove chicken with a slotted spoon, and set it aside to cool. Reserve the broth.

3. While the chicken is cooking, combine leek, summer squash, zucchini, and carrot in a 4-cup glass measuring cup or other microwave-safe container. Add 3 tablespoons water, cover with plastic wrap, and microwave on high (100 percent power) for 4 minutes. *Alternatively, steam the vegetables until crisp-tender.*

4. Drain vegetables and combine them in a bowl with the pasta, red pepper, raisins, and capers. Set aside.

To Prepare the Dressing

1. To make the dressing, beat the egg whites and lemon juice in the bowl of a food processor or with an immersion blender for 30 seconds or until frothy. Bring the chicken cooking broth to a boil. Dribble 4 tablespoons of the hot broth into the whites with the processor or immersion blender on full power. Add remaining ingredients except parsley. Taste to correct seasoning.

To Assemble

1. Discard the bones from the chicken. Shred the meat into the pasta-vegetable mixture. Toss with the dressing. Garnish with parsley, if desired.

Risotto

A creamy risotto is a wonderful side dish. When embellished with summer squash, zucchini, diced tomato, and a bit of Parmesan-Reggiano cheese, it's a deliciously satisfying main dish as well. For proper results check the Italian section of your market for arborio, a short-grain rice.

1 small onion, minced

1 cup arborio rice

1 13¾-ounce can chicken broth

1 cup water

1 teaspoon chicken base concentrate (see Shopping Sources, page 306)
or 1 chicken bouillon cube

1 small summer squash, diced (optional)

3 tablespoons grated Parmesan-Reggiano cheese (optional)

Yield: 4 servings

Calories per serving: 207

Protein per serving: 5 g

Fat per serving: 1 g

Saturated fat per serving: trace

Cholesterol per serving: none

Carbohydrates per serving: 43 g

Sodium per serving: 697 mg

Fiber per serving: 1 g

1. Combine the onion and rice in a 2-quart heavy-bottom saucepan. Spritz with olive oil. Lightly toast the rice mixture over medium-low heat about 3 minutes, stirring often.

2. While the rice toasts bring the chicken broth, water, and chicken base concentrate or bouillon cube to a boil in a 1-quart saucepan. *To microwave, combine toasted rice and all remaining ingredients except squash and Parmesan-Reggiano in a microwave-safe 2½-quart dish. Stir, cover, and microwave on high (100 percent power) for 8 minutes. Add squash, stir, cover, and microwave on high for an additional 5 to 6 minutes. Stir in Parmesan-Reggiano, if desired; let stand 5 minutes before serving.*

3. Add about ½ cup of broth to the rice. Stir, cover, and adjust heat so rice just simmers in the hot broth.

4. Continue to add the broth, gradually, stirring after each addition. The rice should absorb the liquid before more is added. When about three-fourths of the liquid has been added, stir in the summer squash, if desired. When all the liquid is absorbed, stir in the Parmesan-Reggiano, if desired. Let the risotto sit about 2 minutes before serving.

CONFETTI RICE SALAD

Carbohydrates, the bugaboo of the diet world for years, is no longer a dirty word. The diet conscious, particularly those who exercise regularly, need complex carbohydrates for energy; otherwise, the body will break down proteins for fuel, proteins better used to build and maintain tissues. Sadly, most carbohydrates taste better when lathered with fats: the butter on the bread, the sour cream on the potato, the dressing on the salad. Here's a cool salad—great for picnicking because it's ultimately portable—that makes the most of the carbohydrates and the least of the fat. A few smoked shrimp would make a wonderful addition.

Yield: 6 servings

Calories per serving: 190

Protein per serving: 3 g

Fat per serving: 5 g

Saturated fat per serving: 1 g

Cholesterol per serving: none

Carbohydrates per serving: 33 g

Sodium per serving: 180 mg

Fiber per serving: 2 g

2 medium tomatoes

2 medium green peppers

1 medium red pepper

3 cups cooked rice

2 tablespoons minced fresh parsley

10 fresh basil leaves, snipped, or 1 teaspoon dried basil

½ teaspoon salt

freshly ground pepper to taste

2 tablespoons olive oil

1 tablespoon plus 2 teaspoons rice wine vinegar, available at specialty foods stores or Asian markets

1. Dice the tomatoes. Seed and dice the peppers.

2. Place the vegetables in a bowl with the rice, parsley, basil, salt, and pepper. Sprinkle all with oil and vinegar.

3. Spray a 1-quart mold or 6 1-cup ramekins with olive oil. Fill each ramekin three-quarters full with rice mixture, and press salad down with a glass or any utensil slightly smaller than the diameter of the ramekin. Cover with plastic wrap and chill at least 3 hours. (*Note:* For a decorative design, on the bottom of each ramekin fashion a "flower" from a thin carrot slice and a "stem" from a parsley stem.)

4. To unmold, run a flexible-bladed metal spatula between the salad and the mold. Invert a plate on mold, flip over, and lift mold off.

RICE STICK NOODLE SALAD WITH SESAME SHRIMP

An East-meets-West recipe, this ties signature Asian flavors—ginger, scallion, miso, and Thai fish sauce—with California notions like carrot juice and plenty of veggies. You may need to give the 800 number in Shopping Sources a call to get ingredients your market doesn't have, although those on both coasts are likely to carry the necessaries. The rice stick noodles are truly optional to the success of the recipe. Serve this salad with anything that will be enhanced by these Asian flavors, such as the Tuna Spring Rolls (page 26), or use this as a filling for rice paper wrappers (see the spring roll recipe for instructions). Consult the Index for recipes to use the odd perishables, such as carrot juice, if you don't drink it!

The dressing here is equally terrific on a mix of cilantro (used as a salad green), grated cabbage and carrot, papaya, and shredded romaine.

Yield: 8 servings

Calories per serving: 123

Protein per serving: 7 g

Fat per serving: 2 g

Saturated fat per serving: trace

Cholesterol per serving: 42 mg

Carbohydrates per serving: 19 g

Sodium per serving: 430 mg

Fiber per serving: 1 g

For the Dressing

4 tablespoons chicken broth, preferably made from chicken base concentrate (see Shopping sources, page 306)

2½ teaspoons cornstarch

2 teaspoons miso (yellow recommended)

2 scallions, white and green parts, minced

5 tablespoons carrot juice (or apple juice, if carrot is unavailable)

3 tablespoons lemon juice (juice of ½ lemon)

1 tablespoon Thai fish sauce or soy sauce

1 tablespoon unpeeled, grated ginger root

1 tablespoon dry sherry

1 clove garlic, minced, or 2 to 3 cloves roasted garlic (see page 305)

1 teaspoon hoisin sauce

2 teaspoons Asian sesame oil

a few drops Asian hot oil

For the Salad

3 to 4 ounces shiitake mushrooms, stemmed and thinly sliced

6 ounces medium shrimp, thawed if frozen

juice of ¼ lemon

2 teaspoons tan or black sesame seeds

2 medium to large carrots, shredded with a medium Cuisinart disk or by
hand (about 2 cups)

⅛ small red cabbage, shredded with a medium Cuisinart disk or by hand
(about ¾ cup)

4 ounces rice stick noodles, cooked according to package instructions and
cut with scissors

1 tablespoon each minced cilantro and basil, for garnish, or a few whole
basil leaves (optional)

To Make the Dressing

1. Combine the 4 tablespoons chicken broth and the cornstarch in a small bowl. Stir and microwave at high (100 percent power) for 30 seconds. Stir.

2. Add the miso, scallions, carrot and lemon juices, fish sauce, ginger root, sherry, garlic, hoisin, and sesame and hot oils. Set aside.

To Make the Salad

1. Spritz an 8-inch skillet with olive oil. Add the mushrooms, spritz again, and sauté until softened, about 3 minutes. Scrape into a medium bowl.

2. Spritz the same skillet again. Add the shrimp. Sauté, tossing frequently, until heated through, about 2 to 3 minutes. Season with lemon juice while cooking. Add sesame seeds the last minute to brown. Add shrimp mixture to the mushrooms; stir in the carrots and cabbage.

3. Heat the dressing 1 minute in the microwave at high (100 percent power). Toss with the veggies and the cooked noodles. Garnish, if desired, with minced herbs or basil leaves.

Makes about 2 quarts

Nutrabyte

Redefine what constitutes dinner. Instead of potato, meat, a veggie, and bread, think:

* a meat (or better yet, chicken or fish), 2 veggies, and a salad

* a meat, a veggie, a salad, and bread

* a potato, served with assorted toppings like minced scallion, fresh herbs, shredded low-fat cheese, yogurt, or poppy seeds and served with another veggie and a salad

* 3 veggies with a bread

* a pasta and a veggie or salad

* a grain or rice dish like risotto, loaded with veggies and served with a salad

* 2 or 3 small plates

The point is to serve not less food but less fat-dense and calorie-dense foods.

GRILLED POLENTA WITH ROASTED ASPARAGUS

This is terrific as part of a vegetarian meal or with just a small piece of fish, chicken, or beef. It needs very little to complement it. My favorite counterpart is the Fennel, Red Pepper, and Tomato Braise (page 114). Make this when you have leftover chilled polenta (chill in a round cake pan), or buy premixed polenta, ready to grill.

Yield: 1 serving

Calories per serving: 129

Protein per serving: 8 g

Fat per serving: 4 g

Saturated fat per serving: 2 g

Cholesterol per serving: 7 mg

Carbohydrates per serving: 16 g

Sodium per serving: 449 mg

Fiber per serving: 2 g

For Each Diner

1 2- to 3-inch wedge of polenta

1 teaspoon poppy seeds or sesame seeds

arugula leaves (optional)

5 to 6 spears High-Heat-Roasted Asparagus (page 100)

⅓ ounce coarsely grated (use the wide side of hand-held grater),
*   best-quality Parmesan-Reggiano cheese*

pepper to taste

a pinch gremolata (directions follow)

For the Gremolata

grated zest of 2 to 3 lemons, equaling 2 tablespoons zest

2 tablespoons finely minced parsley (or experiment with other herbs,
*   such as arugula or basil)*

2 cloves garlic, minced

To Prepare the Gremolata

1. To zest the lemon, grate the yellow peel only, not the white part, on the finest side of a hand-held grater. (The nude lemon is vulnerable without its skin and will rot quickly. Use it within 1 or 2 days.) Combine all ingredients and mix well. Leftovers keep up to 4 days.

To Prepare the Polenta-Asparagus Wedge

1. Spray one side of the polenta wedge with olive oil. Press poppy or sesame seeds into it. Place seed side down on a wire mesh rack on the grill. *Alternatively, spray a nonstick skillet with olive oil and place the polenta wedge, seed side down, over high heat.* Grill or sauté, adjusting heat to prevent burning, until lightly browned. Spray top side, press seeds into it, and flip. Brown.

2. Place on a plate garnished with arugula if you like. Crisscross asparagus over the wedge, and top with cheese, pepper, and gremolata.

Yields 3 to 4 tablespoons

Unopened Flower Buds

Two spices in your kitchen are actually unopened flower buds: cloves, from a kind of evergreen tree, and capers, from a Mediterranean shrub. Capers are priced by their size, the smaller the more costly. They are most frequently preserved in vinegar, occasionally in salt. Used in salads, sauces, and as a garnish for egg dishes, they lend a distinction totally their own. They will keep in the refrigerator for up to one year. Cloves are dried flower buds; they come powdered or whole. Add a few to a bouquet garni destined for a tomato dish for a pleasant, peppery sweet taste.

POULTRY

THE RECIPES

POULTRY

Just 4 ounces of chicken, a typical half-breast serving without skin, supplies about half an adult woman's protein needs for less than 150 calories. But ½ cup of skinned, boned chicken is hardly something to feast on, and certainly no culinary inspiration. This chapter offers more tempting treatments.

Chicken, like red meat, must be inspected for wholesomeness, but there's no law stating it must be graded—a letter classification (A or B) based on the bird's physical appearance. Chickens wearing a Grade A shield do so because the processor has paid USDA inspectors to grade the product, a cost that the producer, and ultimately the consumer, must pay for. And it's not likely you'll spot a Grade B shield boldly displayed on a chicken breast—who wants the world to know your product is second best? This is not to say that nongraded birds are necessarily of poor quality, only that they've not been graded. You can be assured they'll be less expensive, and in some cases, just as good.

GRILLED BRINED CHICKEN BREASTS WITH GINGERED ORANGE SAUCE

Since discovering this age-old preservation method, I hate to cook a chicken breast without having brined it first. With brining, a chicken breast or lean meat can be grilled with no added fat and *still* be moist and flavorful. The process—heating, followed by cooling, a brine in which food is then marinated—isn't cumbersome but does require planning. To prevent partial cooking the brine should be completely cooled before the food is added. I like to throw it together after dinner (it's about a 5-minute job) and refrigerate the brine overnight. The chicken breasts then bathe in the brine 90 minutes before grilling. As a general rule of thumb, the larger the piece of meat, such as a whole chicken (brine a 4-pounder about 8 to 12 hours) or a pork tenderloin, the longer it should be brined. Too long a bath, however, results in mushy meat. Shrimp need a paltry 30 minutes.

While the brined, grilled breast, sans sauce, is excellent, many embellishments and crusts, to use the current culinary lingo, are delicious. The Pesto sauce (page 301), the Red Pepper Butter (page 124), the Blackened Tomato Salsa (page 304), the Hollandaise (page 296)—all are complementary to chicken. A recipe follows here for Gingered Orange Sauce. If I have more than one sauce on hand, I like to do a smorgasbord kind of thing, with a different sauce on each breast.

Brine can be flavored in infinite ways; here is a basic recipe for 4 cups brine, enough for 4 to 6 chicken breasts (double the recipe if you need more) with variations. Kosher salt has no additives, but regular table salt is fine. Use a brine only once. The brine will cool—refrigerated—in about an hour but can be refrigerated indefinitely.

Yield: 4 servings

Calories per serving: 161

Protein per serving: 27 g

Fat per serving: 3 g

Saturated fat per serving: 1 g

Cholesterol per serving: 73 mg

Carbohydrates per serving: 4 g

Sodium per serving: 771 mg

Note: The gingered orange sauce is included in the nutritional analysis.

For the Basic Brined Breasts

3½ cups water

¼ cup salt, kosher recommended

2 to 3 garlic cloves (no need to peel), flattened with the side of a wide knife

1 teaspoon dried herb of choice, such as herbs de Provence, oregano, or thyme, or 8 to 10 sprigs fresh thyme or other fresh herb

several whole peppercorns
½ cup orange juice
4 boneless, skinless chicken breasts

To Make the Brine

1. Bring the water, salt, garlic, herbs, and peppercorns just to a boil to dissolve the salt; a 30-second boil should do it. Remove from heat, stir in orange juice, and refrigerate until at least room temperature or colder.

2. Submerge the chicken breasts in brine, weighting them down, if necessary, for 1½ to no more than 2 hours.

Cooking the Chicken

1. Discard the brine; there's no need to rinse the chicken. Heat a grill and add some soaked wood chips to partially smoke the meat.

2. As the breasts grill, smear them on both sides with sauce, or a crust of choice. Pass extra sauce at the table.

Brine Variations

Experiment with whole cloves and cinnamon, all manner of herbs, juniper berries, cumin, coriander seeds—you get the idea.

Nice with poultry:

4 cups water
¼ cup brown sugar, honey, or maple syrup
6 to 8 fresh sage leaves or 1 teaspoon dried sage
¼ cup salt
1 small onion, chopped
3 whole cloves

Nutrabyte

On average each adult American eats 138 pounds of fat a year. That's about 6 ounces or ¾ cup of fat a day.

Nice with shrimp:

> *4 cups water*
>
> *2 teaspoons sugar*
>
> *2 scallions, chopped*
>
> *¼ cup salt*
>
> *1 dried chili pepper*
>
> *2 bay leaves*

Gingered Orange Sauce

This sauce is also delicious on swordfish with a teaspoon of minced fresh dill added. Consider embellishing with curry powder and/or basil if that suits the food and the mood.

> *1⅓ cups orange juice*
>
> *4 teaspoons grated, unpeeled fresh ginger root*
>
> *2 teaspoons honey*
>
> *2 teaspoons Dijon mustard*

1. Combine the ingredients in a small saucepan. Bring to a boil, reduce heat to medium-high, and boil until reduced to ½ to ¾ cup, about 4 to 5 minutes. Use sauce to baste the chicken on both sides while the chicken cooks; serve any remaining sauce at the table.

   Yields 1½ cups

BEER AND MUSTARD CHICKEN

Here's a chicken dish to savor with rice and a steamed veggie such as cock-tail carrots and broccoli flowerets. You can do the dish up to 1 hour before serving, holding it in a warm (200-degree) oven. Or you can do the dish through Step 4 early in the day, refrigerate the parts, and finish just before serving, adjusting cooking times to accommodate the chilled ingredients.

1 teaspoon olive oil

1 clove garlic, minced

4 boneless, skinless chicken breasts, dusted with 1 tablespoon instant-
blending flour mixed with salt and pepper to taste

12 ounces mushrooms, sliced

2 leeks, white and very little green only, chopped (about 3 cups)

1 12-ounce beer, preferably lager

½ cup fat-free sour cream

2 tablespoons sweet or sweet and hot mustard

2 tablespoons chutney

1 teaspoon balsamic vinegar

1 tablespoon fresh minced tarragon or 1 teaspoon dried tarragon

1 tablespoon minced fresh parsley (optional)

1. Spray a nonstick skillet with olive oil. Add 1 teaspoon olive oil, and cook the garlic 30 seconds at high heat. Add chicken breasts. Sauté over medium-high heat about 3 to 4 minutes. Turn breasts, cover, and cook an additional 3 to 4 minutes or until chicken breasts are slightly pink in the center. Remove chicken to a platter.

2. Spray the pan again, if necessary; add the mushrooms and sauté until browned, about 5 minutes. Add to the chicken.

3. Add leeks and beer to the skillet. Boil, covered, or medium-high heat until leeks are softened, about 5 to 7 minutes.

Yield: 4 servings

Calories per serving: 306

Protein per serving: 33 g

Fat per serving: 4 g

Saturated fat per serving: trace

Cholesterol per serving: 68 mg

Carbohydrates per serving: 31 g

Sodium per serving: 204 mg

Fiber per serving: 3 g

4. Over medium heat stir into the leeks the sour cream, mustard, chutney, vinegar, and tarragon. Cook, stirring, about 1 minute.

5. Return chicken and mushrooms to skillet. Stir. Simmer over medium-low heat, covered, to complete cooking the chicken, about 4 minutes. Taste for salt and pepper. Sprinkle with parsley, if desired, and serve immediately.

Serves 4

Nutrabyte

Portion control is vital to weight control. Invest in a small food scale and use it until you can pretty well judge what a 3- or 4-ounce portion looks like.

CURRIED CHICKEN BREASTS WITH SHIITAKES AND ASPARAGUS

This is a calorie-controlled but flavor-bold meal that you can put together in half an hour; serve it with jasmine rice. The rather mild curry can be adjusted up or down to suit your tastes. Keep orange juice concentrate in the freezer, measuring out what's needed without thawing, or just keep the concentrate in the fridge for up to two weeks. The coconut milk is widely available in the Asian section of the market, or see Shopping Sources (page 306).

Yield: 4 servings

Calories per serving: 385

Protein per serving: 34 g

Fat per serving: 7 g

Saturated fat per serving: 4 g

Cholesterol per serving: 68 mg

Carbohydrates per serving: 44 g

Sodium per serving: 435 mg

Fiber per serving: 3 g

5 to 6 ounces (about 14–15 medium) fresh shiitake mushroom caps,
    thinly sliced

4 boneless, skinless chicken breasts

5 tablespoons orange juice concentrate

6 tablespoons white wine or chicken broth

½ teaspoon salt

freshly ground pepper to taste

1 pound asparagus, tough ends of stalk snapped off and discarded

juice of ½ lemon (about 2 tablespoons)

⅛ teaspoon salt, kosher recommended

1 cup unsweetened, reduced-fat coconut milk, shaken vigorously

4 tablespoons minced fresh basil

1 tablespoon golden raisins (optional)

1 teaspoon curry powder

½ teaspoon ground cumin

2 cups hot cooked rice, such as Jasmine

fresh basil or cilantro leaves for garnish (optional)

Nutrabyte

Chill canned broth before opening. The fat will coagulate for easy removal.

1. Preheat the oven to 400 degrees. Spray with olive oil an ovenproof baking dish just large enough to hold the chicken. Spread the mushrooms in the bottom. Cover with the chicken. Pour the orange juice concentrate and wine over the chicken; season with salt and pepper. Cover with foil. Place in the bottom third of the oven and set the timer for 17 minutes.

2. Meanwhile spray a cookie sheet with olive oil. Arrange the asparagus in a single layer. Season with lemon juice and salt.

3. Prepare the sauce by combining the coconut milk, basil, raisins, curry powder, and cumin in a small, heavy-bottomed saucepan. Bring to a boil and simmer, stirring frequently, for 6 to 8 minutes or until reduced to ⅔ to ¾ cup.

4. When the timer goes off, put the asparagus in the upper third of the oven. Set the timer for 5 minutes.

5. When the timer goes off again, remove the chicken and test an asparagus spear by biting it—it should be crisp-tender. Thin spears will be done, but thicker ones will need another 3 minutes. Rotate if needed.

6. Drain the chicken cooking juices into the reduced coconut milk. Leave the chicken covered loosely with the foil while boiling the sauce, stirring occasionally, until the sauce is reduced to about 1¼ cups, about 4 to 5 minutes more.

7. To serve, place a scoop of rice in the center of a plate or shallow wide soup bowl. Place a chicken breast (the mushrooms will stick to the bottom) on half the rice mound. Scatter the asparagus in a haphazard fashion over the chicken and rice. Ladle about ⅓ cup of sauce. Garnish, if desired, with basil or cilantro leaves.

Serves 4

Nutrabyte

While it is true that egg yolks are high in cholesterol, containing about 213 milligrams each, the American Heart Association does not suggest that they must be eliminated from the diet altogether. The current advice is to eat no more than 3 whole eggs per week.

CHICKEN SAUTÉ WITH CÈPES

Gone are the days when I made my own reduction sauces (demi-glace). These days I dial 1–800 and little flavor bombs of rich stock reductions arrive in the mail. I add these, bit by precious bit, to simmering skillets, here a sauté of chicken and wild mushrooms. In years past I would have then swirled in tablespoon(s) of butter too. Older and wiser, I now forgo that step, and still we lick our plates *and* the serving platter.

Look to Shopping Sources (page 306) for the company that furnishes this reduction base, or make your own by reducing homemade chicken stock until thick and gelatinous. But don't let want of the product keep you from enjoying this fine dish. Instead of adding the Poulet de Glace Gold, reduce the broth at Step 6 a little more than called for and swirl in a tablespoon of nonfat sour cream. This will thicken the sauce in much the same fashion as the reduction base and be delicious.

Since discovering brining (page 178), I'm loath to cook chicken breasts any other way, but decidedly it is not necessary to the success of this recipe. The sauté goes very nicely with couscous, kasha, barley, polenta—almost any starch except potatoes.

Yield: 4 servings

Calories per serving: 174

Protein per serving: 30 g

Fat per serving: 2 g

Saturated fat per serving: trace

Cholesterol per serving: 68 mg

Carbohydrates per serving: 8 g

Sodium per serving: 350 mg

Fiber per serving: 1 g

½ *ounce dried cèpes (also called porcini), available in specialty food stores and major supermarkets*

1 tablespoon minced shallot

2 large or 3 medium cloves roasted garlic (see page 305) or 1 clove minced garlic

10 ounces regular mushrooms, washed and sliced

1 tablespoon wine (red or white), chicken broth, or water

4 boneless, skinless chicken breasts, brined or not as you wish

½ *teaspoon salt*

½ *cup chicken broth or 1 teaspoon chicken base concentrate (see Shopping Sources, page 306)*

3 tablespoons red wine or fruity vinegar such as raspberry

1 teaspoon Poulet de Glace Gold or 1 teaspoon homemade chicken stock
   reduction or 1 tablespoon nonfat sour cream
1 tablespoon dry sherry
1 tablespoon minced fresh parsley
freshly ground pepper to taste

1. Put the cèpes in a glass measure. Add water to the 1-cup mark. Cover and microwave at high (100 percent power) 2 minutes. *Alternatively, combine cèpes in a small saucepan with ¾ cup water and bring to a boil for 2 minutes. Set cèpes aside to soak for at least 15 minutes.*

2. Line a sieve with a moistened paper coffee filter or cheesecloth or thick paper towel, and place over a bowl. Pour the cèpes and their soaking liquid through; allow to drain thoroughly. Dice the cèpes if larger than bite-size. Scrape into another bowl. Let the soaking juices settle so grit sinks to the bottom. Reserve the juices.

3. Preheat the oven to 150 degrees. Place a 10-inch skillet over high heat and spritz with olive oil. Add the shallot, garlic, mushrooms, and wine. Cook, stirring often, 3 to 4 minutes or until the mushrooms are softened and limp. Add to the cèpes.

4. Add the chicken to the skillet, spritz with olive oil, cover, and sauté over high heat 3 minutes. Turn (season with ½ teaspoon salt if chicken is *not* brined), spritz again with olive oil, cover, and sauté another 3 minutes. Remove to an ovenproof platter and place in the warmed oven.

5. While the chicken cooks, pour the mushroom soaking juices (taking care not to disturb the settled grit) into a glass measure with the chicken broth or chicken base concentrate. If using concentrate, add water so liquid measures 1 cup in all. Set aside.

6. After removing the chicken, deglaze the skillet with vinegar, stirring with a wooden spoon to dislodge the goodies on the bottom. Boil until liquid is reduced to about 1 tablespoon. Add the mushroom soaking liquid, Poulet de Glace Gold (if using sour cream, add at end), and sherry. Stir and boil about 2 to 3 minutes to reduce somewhat (longer if not using Poulet de Glace). Add the mushrooms and cèpes. Stir; boil about 1 minute.

7. Add the chicken, spoon sauce over, reduce heat to very low, cover, and simmer about 5 minutes. If the dish needs to be held, remove from heat and then reheat rather than simmering, or chicken will be tough. Just before serving, season with parsley and pepper.

Serves 4

Nutrabyte

To avoid saturated fat:

* limit meats and animal foods
* skin poultry
* avoid whole milk and cheese
* avoid tropical oils in packaged foods

PARCHMENT CHICKEN WITH TOMATO VINAIGRETTE

This Tomato Vinaigrette is one with panache. The feather in its cap is a dash of vinegar—just the right touch for a moist and juicy chicken breast. Because the sauce is actually better the second day, make some ahead; it will keep under refrigeration for about a week. The Hollandaise, the Bearnaise, or the Pesto, all in Chapter 11, would also be appropriate.

Yield of Chicken: 1 serving

Calories per serving: 164

Protein per serving: 28 g

Fat per serving: 3 g

Saturated fat per serving: 1 g

Cholesterol per serving: 73 mg

Carbohydrates per serving: 5 g

Sodium per serving: 420 mg

Fiber per serving: 1 g

For the Chicken

1 boneless, skinless chicken breast

⅛ teaspoon salt

freshly ground pepper to taste

2 tablespoons Tomato Vinaigrette (recipe follows)

2 or 3 mushrooms, sliced

parchment paper, available in specialty food shops

To Prepare the Chicken

1. Preheat oven to 425 degrees. Place chicken breast on a square of parchment paper (see page 222 for instructions on wrapping food in parchment paper hearts, if preferred). Sprinkle the chicken with salt and pepper, spoon on the Tomato Vinaigrette, and place mushrooms on top. Fold the paper around the chicken as you would for a sandwich. Place on a baking sheet and cook for 12 to 15 minutes.

2. To serve, open and discard the paper and spoon juices over chicken.

For the Tomato Vinaigrette

1½ pounds tomatoes (2 to 3 large), quartered
1 tomato, peeled and chopped
1 tablespoon raspberry or red wine vinegar
4 to 6 fresh basil leaves or 1 teaspoon dried basil
1 tablespoon minced fresh parsley
1 teaspoon sugar
½ teaspoon salt
3 to 4 drops hot pepper sauce

To Prepare the Vinaigrette

1. Place the 2 to 3 large tomatoes in a heavy-bottomed saucepan, cover, and bring to a boil over medium heat. Simmer, uncovered, 45 to 50 minutes or until somewhat reduced.

2. Puree the tomatoes in a food processor, blender, or food mill. Strain the tomatoes into a bowl to remove the seeds and skin.

3. Add the remaining tomato to the bowl along with the vinegar, basil, parsley, sugar, salt, and pepper sauce. Stir to combine.

Note: A wonderfully versatile sauce, Tomato Vinaigrette may be a thick but thinning hot or cold soup, tossed with marinated chilled zucchini as a salad, or used as a braising sauce for grilled chicken.

Yield of Vinaigrette: 1¾ cups
   (serving size 2 tablespoons)
Calories per serving: 14
Protein per serving: trace
Fat per serving: trace
Saturated fat per serving: trace
Cholesterol per serving: 0
Carbohydrates per serving: 3 g
Sodium per serving: 82 mg
Fiber per serving: trace

Nutrabyte

A gram of carbohydrate and a gram of protein each supply 4 calories; a gram of fat supplies 9 calories.

POACHED CHICKEN BREASTS WITH MUSTARD HOLLANDAISE

Reheating a traditional Hollandaise is a bit like spacewalking: There's little room for error. You won't find yourself in orbit, though, with *The New Gourmet Light* version; it may be made early in the day and reheated over low heat. Or you may choose to keep it warm in a bowl set atop an electric warming tray. Serve this dish with Pea and Leek Puree (page 117) and some broccoli or a rice pilaf.

Yield: 4 servings

Calories per serving: 192

Protein per serving: 27 g

Fat per serving: 7 g

Saturated fat per serving: 2 g

Cholesterol per serving: 66 mg

Carbohydrates per serving: 3 g

Sodium per serving: 253 mg

Fiber per serving: trace

1 scallion or ½ small onion, minced

1 sprig fresh tarragon or ½ teaspoon dried tarragon

1 cup water

4 chicken breasts, with bones, skinned

juice of ½ lemon

1 recipe Hollandaise (page 296)

1 tablespoon stone-ground mustard, or to taste

minced fresh parsley or watercress (optional)

1. In a food processor or blender, combine the scallion, tarragon, and water. Blend.

2. Pour into a skillet just large enough to hold the chicken. Add chicken, with the meatier side down. Add lemon juice; add water to cover. Bring to a boil, then immediately reduce to a simmer. Cover and cook 15 to 20 minutes or until the chicken flesh feels firm when poked with a finger.

3. Remove the chicken with a slotted spoon (cooking liquid may be reserved for making stock).

4. Meanwhile make *The New Gourmet Light* Hollandaise (see page 296). Stir in the mustard and set aside.

5. Lift the chicken from bones in one piece and place on warmed plates. Spoon Hollandaise over and garnish with parsley or watercress, if desired.

POACHED CHICKEN BREASTS WITH HONEY-MUSTARD SAUCE

Quick, delicious, and very low in fat. The Honey-Mustard Sauce holds for a few days, so prepare it at your leisure. It's also terrific without the dill as a dip for pretzels (add a little more mustard). If you are on a very cholesterol-restrictive diet, use ¼ cup egg substitute to equal 2 eggs.

Yield: 10 servings

Calories per serving: 27

Protein per serving: 2 g

Fat per serving: 0.7 g

Saturated fat per serving: 0.17 g

Cholesterol per serving: 22 mg

Carbohydrates per serving: 4 g

Sodium per serving: 46 mg

For the Honey-Mustard Sauce

4 boneless, skinless chicken breasts

1 egg plus 2 additional egg whites

1 tablespoon honey

1 tablespoon sweet-hot mustard or mustard of choice

2 teaspoons stone-ground or other grainy mustard such as Pommery

1 teaspoon cornstarch

½ cup skim milk

3 tablespoons white vinegar (Note: not wine vinegar)

1 tablespoon minced fresh dill (optional)

To Cook the Chicken

1. To poach the chicken, fill a skillet just large enough to hold it three-quarters full of water. Bring to a boil. Add chicken, cover, reduce heat, and poach 15 to 20 minutes in barely simmering water. A boil, no matter how brief, will toughen the meat. Drain. *Alternatively, to microwave the chicken, place it in a microwave-safe dish, cover with plastic wrap, and cook at high (100 percent power) 6 to 8 minutes, or until chicken is done. Let rest 5 minutes.*

To serve, nap the chicken with Honey Mustard Sauce.

To Prepare the Sauce

1. In the bowl of an immersion blender or in a food processor, beat together the eggs, honey, and mustards. Stir the cornstarch into the milk to dissolve it and add this to the egg mixture. Process.

2. Pour the mixture into a small, heavy-bottomed saucepan and place over medium heat, whisking with an immersion blender for about 3 to 4 minutes, or until the sauce thickens. Gradually reduce heat as needed to prevent curdling. Occasionally scrape down sauce from the sides of the pan with a flexible-bladed spatula. Sauce will thicken when removed from heat. Off heat, whisk about 1 minute. Add vinegar and return to low heat, whisking, 1 minute more. Remove from heat. Stir in the dill, if desired.

Makes ¾ cup sauce

Stir-Fried Chicken and Vegetables

The signature of the world's oldest cuisine, the stir-fry, may be tailored to fit the modern principles of good nutrition perfectly. This recipe is rich in carbohydrates, while frugal with both proteins and fats. Just 10–12 ounces of poultry or meat with the bountiful use of vegetables and rice easily feeds 4. Stir-fries are also quick to cook once the chopping and slicing are accomplished, a task that can often be done as much as 5 hours in advance. This stir-fry is made spicy with hot red pepper and chili paste—both may be omitted if a milder dish is preferred. All this dish needs is a side of rice or Chinese noodles to complete the meal. The Asian ingredients are available at most major markets.

Yield: 4 servings

Calories per serving: 225

Protein per serving: 25 g

Fat per serving: 7 g

Saturated fat per serving: 2 g

Cholesterol per serving: 59 mg

Carbohydrates per serving: 14 g

Sodium per serving: 380 mg

Fiber per serving: 2 g

2 tablespoons reduced-sodium soy sauce

1 tablespoon rice wine or semisweet sherry

1 tablespoon rice wine vinegar (white wine vinegar may be substituted)

1 teaspoon Asian sesame oil

2 tablespoons plus ⅓ cup chicken broth

2 teaspoons sugar

1 clove garlic, minced

1 stalk green onion, minced

a 1-inch piece ginger root, peeled and grated

¾ pound skinless, boneless breast of chicken

1 tablespoon olive or peanut oil

½ red bell pepper, sliced

½ green bell pepper, sliced

8 ounces fresh mushrooms, sliced

1 cup Chinese cabbage, sliced

1 carrot, julienned

4 ounces snow peas, strings removed

½ to 1 teaspoon minced hot chili pepper (optional)

½ to 1 teaspoon chili paste with garlic (optional)

2 teaspoons cornstarch

1. Combine the soy sauce, wine, vinegar, sesame oil, 2 tablespoons of the broth, sugar, garlic, onion, and ginger root in a measuring cup. Mix well. Pour it into a plastic bag.

2. Cut the chicken into thin strips and marinate in the above soy mixture for 2 hours in the refrigerator or 20 minutes at room temperature.

3. Heat the oil in a wok or heavy 10-inch skillet until very hot. Lift the chicken from the soy marinade a few pieces at a time (reserving the marinade for Step 7). Stir-fry in hot oil until flesh firms and becomes opaque, about 4 minutes.

4. Remove the chicken with a slotted spoon or chopsticks and drain on paper towels. Continue stir-frying until all the chicken is cooked.

5. Add the peppers and mushrooms to the wok. Add a bit of chicken broth or spritz with olive oil, if necessary. Stir-fry for 1 minute. Add the Chinese cabbage and stir-fry another minute. Add the carrots and snow peas, and stir-fry about 1 minute more or until pea pods are done.

6. Stir in the chili pepper and paste, if desired.

7. Moisten the cornstarch in the remaining ⅓ cup chicken broth; combine it with the reserved marinade from Step 3. Add to the vegetables in the wok along with the cooked chicken. Stir over high heat until thickened. Serve with boiled rice or noodles.

OLD-FASHIONED CHICKEN POT PIE

Phyllo pastry, available in the frozen food section of the market, makes pastry dishes possible in this waist-not-want-not style of cooking. Plan accordingly, though, as the pastry leaves require about 4 hours at room temperature to thaw. For a pretty and easy-to-serve presentation, use main-portion-size ramekins or other individual ovenproof dishes. Microwaving a fryer chicken (about 3 to 4 pounds) in a covered dish for about 20 minutes will yield 4 cups cooked, chopped chicken. Turn the chicken once during cooking.

Yield: 4 servings

Calories per serving: 366

Protein per serving: 46 g

Fat per serving: 6 g

Saturated fat per serving: 1 g

Cholesterol per serving: 110 mg

Carbohydrates per serving: 27 g

Sodium per serving: 497 mg

Fiber per serving: 5 g

½ large (about 1 cup) Spanish onion, chopped

2¼ cups chicken broth

2 carrots, julienned (about 1 cup loosely packed)

4 stalks celery, julienned (about 1 cup loosely packed)

1 cup frozen peas

4 cups cooked chicken, chopped, skin removed, juices reserved
   (about ½ cup), and defatted (see Quick Tip, page 291)

3 tablespoons instant-blending flour

¾ cup white wine

2 cloves roasted garlic (see page 305) (optional)

2 tablespoons fresh minced parsley

1 tablespoon fresh minced tarragon

½ teaspoon salt

freshly ground pepper to taste

3 leaves phyllo pastry, thawed

2 teaspoons bread crumbs

1. Preheat the oven to 400 degrees. In a 10-inch skillet over high heat, cook the onion in ½ cup of the chicken broth until softened, about 5 minutes, reducing heat if necessary.

2. Off heat, stir in carrots, celery, peas, and chicken. Set aside.

3. Whisk the flour into the wine. Whisk the mixture with the remaining

chicken broth, the reserved chicken juices, and the garlic over medium-high heat, until thickened, about 3 minutes.

4. Stir in the parsley, tarragon, salt, and pepper. Stir the mixture into the chicken and veggies.

5. Spray the ramekins or a 9-by-12-by-2-inch baking dish with olive oil. Spoon in the chicken-veggie mixture. Loosely layer a sheet of phyllo over. Spray with olive oil. Sprinkle with 1 teaspoon bread crumbs. Cover loosely with another sheet of pastry, spray, sprinkle with remaining 1 teaspoon crumbs, loosely cover with last pastry sheet, and spray again. (If using ramekins, cut the phyllo leaves into sixths first.) Bake in the upper third of the oven until bubbly, about 30 minutes for the single baking dish and less for ramekins. Serve immediately.

Serves 4 generously

CHICKEN BOUILLABAISSE

Bouillabaisse—a mélange of tomatoes and leeks flavored with saffron—is a natural in low-fat cookery. Use this recipe as a starting point and let your imagination run. Without the chicken this could be a sauce for white fish and/or shellfish, or you could simmer vegetables such as zucchini, summer squash, and fresh corn kernels in the bouillabaisse until cooked, then spoon it over slabs of grilled bread and pass freshly grated Parmesan-Reggiano cheese at the table. Low-fat, low-calorie, fabulously flavorful and satisfying. Serve this bouillabaisse with Risotto (page 168) or with plain rice. This is excellent the second day.

Yield: 6 servings

Calories per serving: 155

Protein per serving: 16 g

Fat per serving: 3 g

Saturated fat per serving: .62 g

Cholesterol per serving: 46 mg

Carbohydrates per serving: 17 g

Sodium per serving: 430 mg

Fiber per serving: 3 g

3 leeks, white part only, chopped

2 cloves garlic, minced

1 shallot, minced

¾ cup chicken broth or white or rose wine

5 to 6 tomatoes (about 1½ to 1¾ pounds), peeled and chopped, juice reserved

¼ cup orange juice or the juice of 1 orange

zest of 1 orange (optional)
1 bay leaf
1 teaspoon dried thyme
1 teaspoon sugar
1 teaspoon salt
freshly ground pepper to taste
½ teaspoon fennel seed
¼ teaspoon ground saffron or a pinch of saffron threads
1 cut-up broiler chicken, skinned (about 2 pounds), wings discarded

To Microwave

1. Combine the leeks, garlic, shallot, and chicken broth in a 4-cup glass measuring cup or other microwave-safe dish. Cover and microwave at high (100 percent) power for 6 minutes.

2. Add all the remaining ingredients except the chicken. Stir, cover, and cook at high (100 percent power) for 6 minutes.

3. Place the chicken in a single layer in a 1-gallon microwave-safe container. Add leek and tomato mixture. Cover. Microwave at high (100 percent power) for 15 minutes; stir and microwave at medium (50 percent power) for 30 minutes more. Let rest 5 minutes before serving.

To Cook in a Crock-Pot or Other Slow Cooker

1. Combine the leeks, garlic, shallot, and chicken broth in an 8-inch skillet and sauté over medium-high heat, stirring often, until the leeks are softened, about 10 minutes. Scrape into a Crock-Pot or other slow cooker.

2. Add all remaining ingredients. Cover and cook at high heat 1 hour, then reduce heat to low and simmer 4 to 5 hours longer. Stir occasionally. Remove cover the last hour of cooking.

CHICKEN BAKED IN A SALT CRUST

Meats and poultry roasted in a crust of salt are amazingly succulent, flavorful, and juicy. The moistened salt forms a shell, locking in moisture that would otherwise evaporate. Happily, the salt doesn't penetrate the food either. For this family meal a broiler is stuffed with rice seasoned with a garlic puree (made mild by a long simmer), trussed to keep the legs from breaking through the salt crust, then roasted. Carve the bird and serve on a platter with the natural juices retrieved from the carving board. The rice stuffing may be prepared a day ahead or early in the day, the chicken stuffed and packed in salt just before roasting. Although the bird does take 2 hours to cook, it is not lengthy to prepare for roasting, and all you need to complete the meal is a green vegetable or salad.

Yield: 4 servings

Calories per serving: 424

Protein per serving: 41 g

Fat per serving: 10 g

Saturated fat per serving: 3 g

Cholesterol per serving: 112 mg

Carbohydrates per serving: 40 g

Sodium per serving: 384 mg

Fiber per serving: 1 g

1 2- or 3-pound broiler chicken

1 whole head garlic, cloves separated

2½ cups cooked rice

1 small tomato, diced

4 to 5 fresh basil leaves or 1 teaspoon dried basil

½ teaspoon salt

freshly ground pepper to taste

10 cups kosher salt

1¾ cups water

1. Prepare the bird for roasting by cutting off the excess fat at the cavity opening. Cut off the wing tips at the joint, add them to your bone collection for making stock, or discard. Set aside the bird while preparing the stuffing.

2. Separate but don't peel the garlic cloves. Bring a 1-quart saucepan three-quarters full of water to a boil. Boil the garlic cloves 1 minute, lift with a slotted spoon to a sieve, and cool under running water. Slip skins off. Return peeled cloves to boiling water and simmer 30 minutes. Drain, reserving 2 to 3 tablespoons cooking water. Puree the garlic in a food processor, adding reserved cooking water as needed, or force through a fine mesh sieve with a wooden spoon.

3. Combine the cooked rice, garlic puree, tomato, basil, salt, and pepper. Adjust seasoning, if necessary.

4. Stuff the cavity of the chicken with the rice mixture, but don't pack too tightly; any remaining rice may be heated in a small casserole the last 20 minutes of roasting. To truss the bird—a process that will keep the legs from breaking through the salt crust during baking—follow the illustrations on the following two pages or use another trussing technique. Pack any stuffing that might have come loose back into the cavity.

5. Preheat oven to 475 degrees.

6. Line a roasting pan large enough for the chicken with a sheet of aluminum foil that extends 10 inches over the short sides.

7. Moisten the kosher salt with some of the water, but don't use all the water at once. The paste should be just wet enough to hold together when packed with your hands. Place about a third of the paste on the foil-lined roasting pan. Place the chicken on top. Pack the remaining salt all around the bird, covering any exposed spots. Pull the foil up snug to the bird; use it to help pack down the salt. Roast in the lower third of the preheated oven for 2 hours.

8. To serve, peel back the foil. Break and discard the top salt crust. Lift the chicken from the roasting pan by the trussing string to a cutting board or plate, one that will trap the juices. Snip and discard string. Brush away any clinging salt. Pull and discard skin from bird. To carve, cut off legs first, then cut them in half at the joint. Cut off breast meat. Flip bird, remove skin, and cut back in half. Scoop stuffing onto serving platter. Dribble juices from cutting board onto chicken.

How to Truss a Chicken

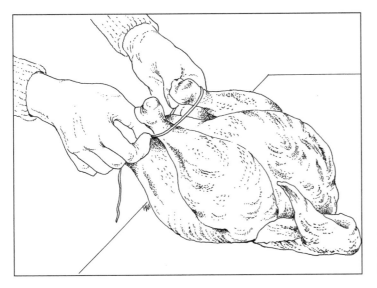

1. Fold a 3- or 4-foot length of butcher's twine in half, then lay the midsection over the knee joints of the whole chicken.

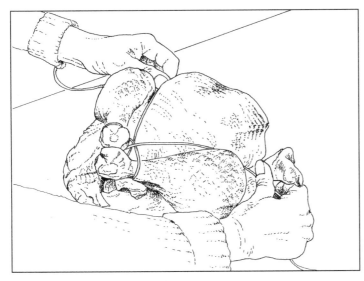

2. "Lasso" the leg ends by pulling the twine up, then lay the twine in the hollow between the leg and the breast.

(continued on next page)

How to Truss a Chicken

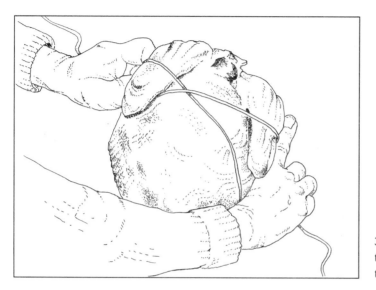

3. Flip the chicken over and cross the twine. Pull the wings snug to the body by laying the twine over them.

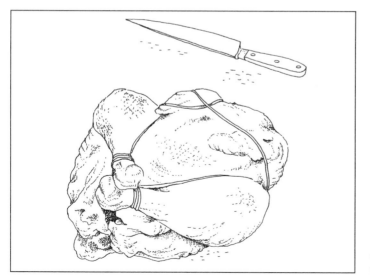

4. Flip the chicken back over so the breast side is up. Knot the twine and cut off the excess.

TURKEY CUTLETS IN CRANBERRY-CURAÇAO SAUCE

This recipe was inspired by the ubiquitous Thanksgiving staple of home-ec classes everywhere—cranberry-orange relish. I always loved it. Thankfully, it fits right in with calorie-conscious eating, given a few adjustments. The recipe makes about twice the relish you'll need. Pass the remainder at the table or enjoy it as a snack mixed with vanilla or plain low-fat yogurt. Serve the cutlets with Bourbon Squash Soufflé (page 137) and rice.

Yield: 4 servings

Calories per serving: 235

Protein per serving: 28 g

Fat per serving: 4 g

Saturated fat per serving: 0.77 g

Cholesterol per serving: 69 mg

Carbohydrates per serving: 15 g

Sodium per serving: 730 mg

Fiber per serving: 1 g

1 navel orange, unpeeled and cut into chunks

½ cup whole, fresh, or frozen cranberries (see Quick Tip, page 202)

½ cup orange juice

1 1-inch piece of ginger root, peeled and grated

2 tablespoons fruit-only marmalade

2 tablespoons walnuts

1 tablespoon low-fat mayonnaise mixed with 2 tablespoons Dijon or Dijon-
  naise mustard

1 pound turkey cutlets

salt and pepper to taste

4 tablespoons curaçao or other orange-flavored liqueur

2 teaspoons chicken base concentrate (see Shopping Sources, page 306)
  dissolved in ¾ cup hot water

1 teaspoon arrowroot or 2 teaspoons cornstarch

1 teaspoon ground dried sage or 1 tablespoon minced fresh sage

fresh sage leaves for garnish (optional)

1. Combine the orange, cranberries, ¼ cup of the orange juice (reserve the other ¼ cup for Step 7), ginger root and 1 tablespoon of the marmalade in a food processor. Pulse to chop coarsely.

2. Add the walnuts. Pulse just until combined; do not grind. Set this cranberry-orange relish aside.

3. Brush the mayonnaise-mustard mixture over the turkey cutlets. Season with salt and pepper.

4. Spray with olive oil a skillet just large enough to hold the turkey. Brown the turkey over high heat, 2 minutes on each side.

5. Remove the cutlets to a platter. Deglaze the skillet with curaçao, scraping up the turkey bits with a wooden spoon.

6. Add the chicken base concentrate, dissolved in the water, to the skillet. Boil, stirring, for about 30 seconds.

7. Dissolve the arrowroot in remaining orange juice; add to the skillet. Stir over medium-high heat until thickened, about 2 minutes. Add the remaining tablespoon of marmalade and the sage. Stir in ½ cup of the reserved cranberry-orange relish.

8. Return turkey to the skillet. Spoon sauce over. Cover and simmer 3 to 4 minutes, until turkey is just cooked through. Remove to a platter, spoon sauce over, and garnish, if desired, with fresh sage leaves.

Serves 4

QUICK TIP

When fresh cranberries are in season, throw a cellophane bag or two into the freezer. The berries will keep until next year's harvest and can be used without thawing, just as you would fresh ones.

CHINESE TEA–SMOKED TURKEY

Tea smoking is a lovely way to impart smoked flavor to fish or poultry without a major investment of time or expensive equipment. You need a wok or any pan with a tight cover, such as an electric skillet, and Chinese black tea. While the instructions are written for a boned turkey, you may use a turkey breast or even a chicken. Start the recipe a day before serving, and if using a frozen turkey or breast, 2 days before. The smoked turkey may be served sliced warm or at room temperature or used in other recipes, such as a turkey salad. It is wonderful sliced for the buffet table, accompanied with small pumpkin biscuits and pots of herbed jellies.

Yield: 12 servings

Calories per serving: 153

Protein per serving: 29 g

Fat per serving: 3 g

Saturated fat per serving: 1 g

Cholesterol per serving: 68 mg

Carbohydrates per serving: none

Sodium per serving: 328 mg

Fiber per serving: none

1 4-pound boned turkey or turkey breast

1 tablespoon whole black peppercorns

3 tablespoons kosher salt

2 tablespoons Chinese black tea or contents of 4 Chinese tea bags (available
*   at specialty food shops)*

2 tablespoons uncooked regular rice

2 tablespoons brown sugar

1. Thaw the turkey if it is frozen, and wipe it dry.

2. Combine the peppercorns and salt in a small skillet and sauté over medium-high heat until the mixture is fragrant, about 2–3 minutes. Let the mixture cool, and rub it into the turkey breast. Wrap the turkey in aluminum foil and refrigerate overnight.

3. Rinse the turkey breast free of the peppercorn-salt mixture. Steam the breast in a steamer over 3 inches of water for 40–50 minutes. Remove the breast from the steamer and let it stand at room temperature (or refrigerate overnight) until cool (about 2 to 3 hours); pat thoroughly dry. *Note:* This step is important, for if the meat is not cool and continues to "sweat," the moisture will prevent it from browning in the smoking step.

4. Line a wok or other deep pot that has a tight-fitting lid with a double

thickness of aluminum foil. Combine the tea, rice, and sugar. Spread over the foil. Set a rack in the pot. Place the breast on rack, skin side up. Cover and place over medium heat until the tea leaves crackle or wisps of smoke escape. Smoke the turkey for 10 minutes. Remove the lid. If the meat is not browned, cover and smoke 5 minutes longer. Discard skin before serving. Turkey is ready to serve or use in any turkey recipe.

Smoked Foods

Smoking foods, used as a preservation technique in a time before refrigeration, has enjoyed a revival. Many restaurants feature smoked foods or garnish dishes with smoked tidbits. Smoked turkey breasts, hams, fishes, and shellfish are available by mail from many a modern smokehouse. Those on sodium-restricted diets should know that most smoked foods are treated heavily with salt. Some companies will supply salt-free smoked foods.

FISH AND SHELLFISH

THE RECIPES

FISH AND SHELLFISH

Few foods are as calorie economic or as nutritionally rich as fish. Yet fish varies in calorie count from variety to variety. So-called fat fish (tuna, salmon, trout, and pompano), with a higher percentage of natural oils, are higher in calories than lean fish (cod, flounder, and red snapper). But a fat fish may need less oils added to it during cooking to avoid drying out.

All fish is high in protein and relative low in fat. A 3½-ounce serving of flounder supplies 30 grams of protein (three-quarters of the daily requirement for a 120-pound woman) and 8 grams of fat for a very reasonable 202 calories. A similar-size serving of beef rump supplies somewhat less protein (24 grams) and three times the amount of fat (27 grams) for 347 calories. All other things being equal, substituting fish for beef two nights a week for twelve weeks would save 3,500 calories—which, if not converted into energy, transforms into a pound of fat.

Care must be taken in the purchase and storage of fish, perhaps more so than with any other food, or the delicate flavor suffers. A reputable store is one supplied daily, not twice a week—don't hesitate to ask when the product came in. Keep fish in a bowl of ice (protected in a plastic bag) in the refrigerator if held more than 1 day. Remember to replenish the ice and pour off the water.

SALMON BURGERS

Start a new tradition on the Fourth of July with these culinarily correct burgers. The patties can be made early in the day and grilled at your convenience. Grill them slowly—I'm not going to try to suggest times, because there are too many variables: temperature of fish at cooking, thickness of burgers, grill heat, and so on. I love these with grilled veggies (page 146).

1 to 1¼ pounds salmon steaks or fillets, skinned

½ medium shallot

2 tablespoons fresh dill or 1 teaspoon dried dill weed

1 teaspoon brown sugar

1 to 2 teaspoons lemon juice

1 teaspoon capers, drained

½ teaspoon minced jalapeño pepper from a jar or to taste

½ teaspoon salt

2 tablespoons bread crumbs

sweet-hot mustard or other favorite mustard

3 deli-style buns

lettuce leaves (optional)

1 recipe Hollandaise (page 296) or Wasabi Cream (page 228) (optional)

Yield: 3 servings

Calories per serving: 395

Protein per serving: 31 g

Fat per serving: 17 g

Saturated fat per serving: 4 g

Cholesterol per serving: 76 mg

Carbohydrates per serving: 27 g

Sodium per serving: 777 mg

Fiber per serving: 1 g

1. Bone the salmon steaks with your fingers, lifting out the center bone and taking care to get the stray bones in the tenderloin of the steak. Place the skinned, boned salmon in a food processor.

2. Add the shallot, dill, sugar, lemon juice, capers, jalapeño, and salt. Pulse to combine and blend, but don't allow to turn to mush. Form into 3 patties.

3. Dredge the burgers in the bread crumbs. Refrigerate until ready to grill.

4. Grill over medium-low (or low heat if grill is hot), basting both sides with mustard. Grill buns at the same time. Serve with lettuce leaves and Hollandaise or Wasabi Cream, if desired.

Serves 3

The New American Grill

Grilling is hot. The day when barbecue meant hamburgers, steaks, and the occasional sausage is past. America's imaginative chefs are grilling everything from shrimp to squab and accompanying dishes with sauces that would leave Grandma gasping. From barbecue Hollandaise to Spicy Plum, from Burgundy Cherry to Mustard Mousse, today's concoctions make ketchup sound about as appealing as a plastic tomato. The innovations don't stop with the food and sauces either. Where once charcoal would do, mesquite, applewood, hickory, cabernet grapevine cuttings, and cords of other woods now smoke. And all this on equipment that makes the backyard grill look about as current as a Model T. Gas and electric grills, covered models, water smokers, and fifty-five-gallon tin drums are among the grill chef's options.

SCALLOPS IN CHAMPAGNE

The delicate, sea-fresh flavor of scallops is enhanced with champagne and Pernod, a French liquor; for a more budget-conscious preparation use a Chablis and anisette.

1 pound scallops

2 tablespoons flour, instant-blending recommended

½ teaspoon salt

freshly ground pepper to taste

1 teaspoon olive oil

3 tablespoons bread crumbs

1 cup champagne or other white wine

¼ cup egg substitute

2 tablespoons nonfat sour cream

1 teaspoon Pernod or anisette

1. Dust the scallops with the flour, salt, and pepper.

Yield: 3 to 4 servings

Calories per serving: 172

Protein per serving: 19 g

Fat per serving: 2 g

Saturated fat per serving: trace

Cholesterol per serving: 31 mg

Carbohydrates per serving: 9 g

Sodium per serving: 482 mg

Fiber per serving: trace

2. Spray a 10-inch nonstick skillet with olive oil. Add the 1 teaspoon olive oil, turn heat to high, and sauté the scallops over medium-high heat for 2 minutes, shaking the pan from time to time.

3. Add 1 tablespoon of bread crumbs and continue to sauté for 3 minutes more until scallops are opaque and lightly browned.

4. Add the champagne and simmer 4 minutes over medium-high heat.

5. With a slotted spoon, transfer scallops to a broiler-safe serving dish, such as a quiche dish. Cover with a towel while completing the sauce.

6. Turn heat to high under pan juices and boil 2 minutes or until reduced to about ¾ cup.

7. Combine the pan juices with the egg substitute, sour cream, and Pernod in the bowl of a food processor. Mix at full power about 30 seconds.

8. Return sauce to the skillet and whisk over medium heat until it thickens, about 1 to 2 minutes.

9. Pour sauce over scallops, sprinkle remaining bread crumbs on top, spray with olive oil, and broil 2 minutes or until top is lightly browned.

MUSSELS IN WHITE WINE AND SAFFRON

This is not a do-ahead meal, but it is very quickly cooked. The mussels may be enjoyed as a first course, as a light dinner, or served on a bed of pasta for a heartier fare.

Yield: 4 servings

Calories per serving: 246

Protein per serving: 26 g

Fat per serving: 6 g

Saturated fat per serving: 1 g

Cholesterol per serving: 60 mg

Carbohydrates per serving: 12 g

Sodium per serving: 439 mg

Fiber per serving: trace

3 to 4 pounds mussels

1 shallot, minced

2 cloves garlic, minced

a few threads saffron

a few parsley stems

1 sprig thyme

1 bay leaf

1 cup white wine

2 teaspoons butter

1 tablespoon flour, instant-blending recommended

½ teaspoon turmeric (optional, for color)

2 tablespoons skimmed evaporated milk

1 tablespoon minced fresh parsley for garnish

1. To clean the mussels: Scrub each mussel with a brush and remove the "beard" with a sharp knife. Drop them into cold water and soak 1 to 2 hours. Some cooks add a handful of cornmeal or flour on the theory that it is ingested, thus plumping and cleansing the mussels. Lift the mussels from the soaking water and rinse again.

2. In a saucepan large enough to hold the mussels, put the shallot, garlic, saffron, parsley stems, thyme, bay leaf, and wine. Add the mussels, cover, and bring to a boil, shaking the pan frequently. When the shells open, in about 5 minutes, remove from heat. Discard any mussels that do not open.

3. Pour the mussels and cooking liquid into a strainer set over a bowl. Discard the bay leaf, parsley stems, and thyme sprig. Pour cooking liquid back

into saucepan (but not the grit at the bottom) and boil over high heat until reduced by a third.

4. Mash the butter and flour together. Whisk it into the simmering stock in two parts over medium-low heat. Stir in turmeric and milk. Whisk over medium-low heat until sauce thickens slightly.

5. To prepare the mussels for serving, discard one half of each shell. Neatly arrange the mussels on a platter. Pour the sauce over mussels and garnish with the parsley.

Saffron

The world's most expensive spice is the dried stigma of a crocus. There are only three such threads in each flower, and they must be picked by hand. Since it takes 225,000 stigmas to make a pound of saffron, small wonder it is so costly. Saffron is the signature spice of paella, a Spanish rice dish. It is also used in breads, in pilafs, and with some shellfish. It comes in powdered and dried forms.

CLAMS, MUSSELS, AND LOBSTER IN BLACK BEAN SAUCE

Any combination of shellfish would be delicious in this Asian-inspired sauce. The basic premise, however, could be applied to whatever is available—a firm-fleshed white fish or a thick fish steak, such as monkfish or shark. Fermented black beans, oddly enough a soybean product, can be found in the Asian section of your market and will last indefinitely. This dish is excellent as a first course, as part of a Chinese-style meal served with other entrees, or—my favorite—as a sauce for pasta. Easily reheated in the microwave (about 5 minutes on high, 100 percent power), it is a convenient dish for entertaining as well as a special family treat.

Yield: 6 servings

Calories per serving: 164

Protein per serving: 20 g

Fat per serving: 3 g

Saturated fat per serving: trace

Cholesterol per serving: 50 mg

Carbohydrates per serving: 12 g

Sodium per serving: 945 mg

Fiber per serving: trace

For the Fish

1½ dozen littleneck or other hard-shell clams, scrubbed

8 ounces clam broth, bottled or reconstituted

1½ dozen mussels, bearded and scrubbed

1 1½-pound lobster, cooked and cooled

For the Black Bean Sauce

1½ tablespoons Asian fermented black beans, soaked in water to cover for 1 hour, rinsed, and drained

4 tablespoons dry sherry

2 tablespoons rice wine vinegar

2 cloves garlic, chopped

⅓ cup grated fresh ginger root

1 tablespoon plus 2 teaspoons cornstarch dissolved in 3 tablespoons cold water

4 tablespoons oyster sauce

2 tablespoons reduced-sodium soy sauce

1 tablespoon minced fresh cilantro

1 tablespoon minced fresh parsley

2 scallions, green part only, chopped

¼ teaspoon Asian sesame oil

To Prepare the Fish

1. Steam the clams for 3 to 4 minutes in the clam broth. Add the mussels and continue to steam until all the shellfish have opened, about 4 to 5 minutes more. (Discard any that do not open.) Transfer shellfish with a slotted spoon to a bowl. Strain the broth through a moistened coffee filter into a 2-cup glass measuring cup or other microwave-safe container. Set aside both shellfish and broth while preparing the lobster.

2. Remove the legs from the lobster; discard the body. Cut the tail and claws into roughly 3-inch pieces, leaving the meat in the shell. Add lobster legs and meat to the bowl containing the clams and mussels. Set aside while preparing the sauce.

To Prepare the Sauce

1. Place drained beans in the bowl of a food processor with the sherry, rice wine vinegar, garlic, and ginger root. Process at high until mashed. Leave in the food processor bowl and set aside.

2. Stir the cornstarch mixture into the strained shellfish broth. Microwave at high (100 percent power) for 2 minutes or until thickened. *Alternatively, combine the broth with the dissolved cornstarch in a 1-quart saucepan. Bring to a boil over high heat, stirring constantly, until thickened, about 2 to 4 minutes.*

3. Add the thickened broth to the bean mixture in the bowl of the food processor with the oyster sauce, soy sauce, cilantro, parsley, and scallions. Process at high just until combined. Add sesame oil and blend.

To Assemble

1. Combine sauce with the seafood; stir to combine. Sauce may be chilled up to 8 hours before serving. Reheat in microwave for 5 minutes at high (100 percent power) or on the stove over medium heat. Sauce should not boil.

FILLETS OF SOLE WITH SALMON MOUSSE

A microwave oven speeds the cooking of this dish, which can be readied several hours in advance. Asparagus is the perfect accompaniment if in season, because of the Hollandaise connection, which can also be prepared ahead of time and then gently reheated.

¾ pound salmon steaks

juice of 1 lemon (about 4 tablespoons)

1 egg white

14 ounces thin white skinless fish fillets, such as sole

2 teaspoons minced fresh tarragon or 1 teaspoon dried tarragon

a few gratings fresh nutmeg or ¹⁄₁₀ teaspoon ground nutmeg

½ teaspoon salt

freshly ground pepper to taste

1 recipe Hollandaise (page 296) or Béarnaise sauce (page 298)

Yield: 4 servings

Calories per serving: 324

Protein per serving: 42 g

Fat per serving: 15 g

Saturated fat per serving: 4 g

Cholesterol per serving: 111 mg

Carbohydrates per serving: 3 g

Sodium per serving: 467 mg

Fiber per serving: 0.2 g

1. Place the salmon on a microwave-safe plate. Season with half the lemon juice (reserve the remaining juice for Step 3). Seal tightly with plastic wrap and microwave at high (100 percent power) for 1 minute. Let rest 2 minutes. Discard skin and bones. Flake fish into a food processor.

2. Pulse the fish with the egg white, tarragon, nutmeg, salt, and pepper. Set aside.

3. Spray 4 3½-inch glass or other ovenproof ramekins with olive oil. Ring the white fish fillets around the edges of the ramekins (about 2 fillets per ramekin). Spray with olive oil; season with a dash of salt and pepper. Fill centers with equal portions of salmon mousse from Step 2. Push edges of fillets over the salmon if they extend beyond the rim. Squeeze remaining lemon juice over fish.

4. Place the ramekins on a microwave-safe dish. Cover tightly with plastic wrap and cook at high (100 percent power) 4½ minutes. Let rest an additional 2 minutes; the rest time is essential.

5. To serve, drain cooking juices off, run a flexible-bladed spatula or thin knife between the fish and the ramekin, and invert on a dinner plate. Spoon a few tablespoons Hollandaise or Béarnaise over.

Serves 4

FISH IN A FLASH

Simple, delicious, and very quick. Purchase presliced vegetables for stir-fry to speed preparation even further. You may substitute either *The New Gourmet Light* Hollandaise (page 296) or Béarnaise (page 298) for the similar sauce used here.

Yield: 3 to 4 servings

Calories per serving: 223

Protein per serving: 31 g

Fat per serving: 3 g

Saturated fat per serving: 1 g

Cholesterol per serving: 58 mg

Carbohydrates per serving: 10 g

Sodium per serving: 434 mg

Fiber per serving: 3 g

For the Fish

1¼ pounds thick white fish fillets, such as scrod

juice of ½ lemon (about 1 tablespoon)

salt and freshly ground pepper to taste

1 pound, about 3 cups, mixed sliced vegetables, such as bok choy, carrots, green and red peppers, broccoli

¾ cup white wine

1 tablespoon minced fresh herb such as tarragon, basil, or thyme or 1 teaspoon dried herb (same suggestions)

For the Sauce

1 shallot, minced

½ cup white wine

½ cup egg substitute

½ teaspoon salt

freshly ground pepper to taste

To Prepare the Fish

1. Place fish, tail folded under to make thickness uniform, in the center of a microwave-safe 10- or 12-inch pie plate. Season with lemon, salt, and pepper. Surround with vegetables, without covering the fish. Pour the ¾ cup

wine over all and sprinkle with herbs. Cover with plastic wrap. Microwave at high (100 percent power) for 6 minutes.

To Prepare the Sauce

2. While the fish cooks, prepare the sauce. Combine the shallot and ½ cup wine in a 3-cup, heavy-bottomed saucepan. Boil over high heat until reduced to about ¼ cup.

3. While the wine reduces, combine the egg substitute, salt, and pepper in the bowl of a food processor (or use an immersion blender). Process 45 seconds on full power.

4. With food processor running, dribble in the hot wine. Process 30 seconds on full power.

5. Return egg-wine mixture to 3-cup saucepan. Whisk constantly over high heat about 4 minutes, adjusting heat to medium-high, if necessary, to prevent curdling. When fish is cooked, dribble in fish cooking juices and continue to whisk over medium-high heat until thickened, an additional 3 minutes. Drizzle a little sauce over fish and vegetables and pass remaining sauce at the table.

QUICK TIP

A super low-cal way to poach white fish fillets: Place in an 8-inch round or similar cake pan with the tails folded under so that the fish is uniformly thick. Pour boiling water over to just cover the fish. Cover tightly with foil or a lid. Let sit 6 to 10 minutes (no heat). Lift fish from water bath, pat dry, season with salt and pepper, and drizzle (or drench, as desired) with Hollandaise (page 296) or another compatible sauce.

FILLETS OF SOLE WITH BASIL AND TOMATO

You may prepare the sauce for this dish early in the day, or even 24 hours ahead, and finish the cooking in about 10 minutes on top of the stove. A few steamed mussels or clams in their shells would be a welcome addition to the sauce; add them the last 5 minutes of cooking. Complete the meal with a simple tossed salad and parsleyed rice.

Yield: 6 servings

Calories per serving: 177

Protein per serving: 29 g

Fat per serving: 2 g

Saturated fat per serving: trace

Cholesterol per serving: 70 mg

Carbohydrates per serving: 9 g

Sodium per serving: 481 mg

Fiber per serving: 2 g

6 tomatoes, peeled (page 52), or 3 tomatoes plus a 10½-ounce can tomatoes
or 1 16-ounce can recipe-ready tomatoes

1 shallot, minced

1 clove garlic, minced

½ teaspoon fresh thyme or ¼ teaspoon dried thyme

1 teaspoon fresh tarragon or ½ teaspoon dried tarragon

¼ teaspoon fennel seed

6 to 8 leaves fresh basil or 1 teaspoon dried basil

1 bay leaf

1 teaspoon sugar

1 teaspoon salt (½ teaspoon if using canned tomatoes)

freshly ground pepper to taste

grated zest of 1 orange

2 tablespoons orange juice (½ orange, squeezed)

2 pounds sole or other firm-fleshed white fish fillets

½ lemon

6 ounces mushrooms, sliced

a few leaves basil for garnish (optional)

1. In a 12-inch skillet, combine the tomatoes with their juice, shallot, garlic, thyme, tarragon, fennel, basil, bay leaf, sugar, salt, pepper, zest, and orange juice. Bring to a boil. Reduce to a simmer, cover, and cook for 40 to 50 minutes. (You may need to add ¼ cup red wine or chicken stock if the tomatoes boil dry.) *Alternatively, combine the ingredients in a 4-cup glass measuring*

cup or other microwave-safe container. Cover with plastic wrap and microwave at medium-high (75 percent power) for 10 minutes.

2. Meanwhile prepare the fish. Sprinkle fish with a few drops lemon juice. Roll the fillets loosely with what was the skin side facing inward. Set aside or refrigerate until ready to cook. (May be held, chilled, up to 6 hours.)

3. Remove and discard the bay leaf from the simmering sauce. Puree the tomato sauce in a food processor, if desired. Strain back into the skillet. Discard dry pulp that remains in strainer. (Straining can be omitted if you prefer the sauce chunky.)

4. Add the mushrooms to the simmering sauce. Simmer 5 minutes. Refrigerate, if desired, until you're ready to complete the dish.

5. Lay the rolled fish fillets on top of the simmering sauce. Spoon a bit of sauce over. Cover pan. Cook 5 minutes per 1-inch thickness of fish, about 12 to 15 minutes total, at medium heat. The sauce should just simmer, not boil. Spoon the hot sauce over fish once or twice. When done, remove fish with a slotted spoon to a platter. Cover with a towel. *Alternatively, place the fish fillets on the tomato sauce, then spoon some of the sauce on top. Cover with plastic wrap and microwave at high (100 percent power) for 6 minutes. Remove fish with a slotted spoon and cover to keep warm. Return sauce to the microwave and cook, uncovered, at high (100 percent power) for 3 minutes or until sauce boils and reduces somewhat. Spoon sauce over fish to serve.*

6. For stove top cooking, raise heat under tomato sauce to reduce the juices the fish gave off during cooking. When reduced to about 2 cups, pour the sauce over fish and garnish with the basil leaves, if desired.

FILLETS OF FISH MARTINI

Steaming fish helps to retain its fresh, clean flavor better than any other cooking technique. This quickly done dinner is easily accomplished with a Chinese steamer and wok, but you may fashion a steaming arrangement with a cake rack set on custard cups inside a deep electric frying pan. Look in gourmet shops for a long-handled, lipped pot for flaming liqueurs.

Yield: 4 servings

Calories per serving: 205

Protein per serving: 34 g

Fat per serving: 2 g

Saturated fat per serving: trace

Cholesterol per serving: 90 mg

Carbohydrates per serving: 10 g

Sodium per serving: 173 mg

Fiber per serving: 4 g

2 8-ounce bottles clam broth or 2 cups fish stock

¼ cup dry white vermouth

3 crushed juniper berries or 1 tablespoon gin (optional)

1 tablespoon minced fresh parsley

1¼ pounds fillets of white fish—haddock, cod, or other thick, white-fleshed fish

pepper to taste

2 cups broccoli flowerets

2 carrots, peeled and julienned

4 to 5 strips lemon peel

2 tablespoons gin

¼ cup egg substitute

1 teaspoon cornstarch

1. Combine 1⅞ cups clam broth (reserving 2 tablespoons for Step 6), the vermouth, juniper berries or 1 tablespoon gin, and half the parsley in a wok. Place a bamboo steamer over the wok. Spray the rack with olive oil. Place the fish in the center of the wok; season with pepper. Put broccoli flowerets on one side, carrots on the other side, and lemon strips on top. Cover.

2. Bring broth to a boil, then steam fish and vegetables 5 to 6 minutes.

3. Lift steamer from rack to a plate on a flame-resistant surface, such as a cutting board; set aside. Boil the broth until reduced to about 1 cup.

4. Meanwhile heat the remaining 2 tablespoons gin in a small saucepan until bubbles appear at the edge. Ignite the gin and pour over the fish in the steamer. When flames die out, cover with a towel and set aside.

5. Beat the egg substitute with an immersion blender or in a measuring cup with a fork. Dribble ¼ cup of the reduced clam broth into the egg, whisking. Add this egg-broth mixture to the remaining clam broth in the wok, whisking over low heat until the sauce becomes opaque and foamy.

6. Dissolve the cornstarch in the reserved 2 tablespoons of clam broth. Whisk this cornstarch-broth mixture into the sauce over medium-low heat until thickened. Garnish fish with remaining parsley. Serve fish right from the steamer, with the sauce passed at the table.

Lemon-Lime Fillets in Parchment Paper Hearts

Cooking in parchment paper locks in natural juices and flavors and makes serving a snap. The paper hearts may be readied up to 3 hours ahead, but no longer or the paper will become soggy. If desired, top each of the fillets with a few scallops or shrimp. Serve with Bourbon Squash Soufflé (page 137) and a salad.

Yield: 4 servings

Calories per serving: 138

Protein per serving: 22 g

Fat per serving: 4 g

Saturated fat per serving: 1 g

Cholesterol per serving: 52 mg

Carbohydrates per serving: 3 g

Sodium per serving: 199 mg

Fiber per serving: trace

1 lime and 1 lemon

1 tablespoon olive oil

2 tablespoons lemon juice

1 tablespoon lime juice

1 teaspoon grated ginger root

1¼ pounds white-fleshed fish fillets, such as sole, cod, or haddock, cut into
4 serving-size pieces

¼ teaspoon salt

freshly ground pepper to taste

1 tablespoon minced fresh parsley

1. With a vegetable peeler remove the rind of both the lime and the lemon, taking care to remove only the colored skin and none of the white, which tends to be bitter. Shred the peels in a food processor fitted with fine shredding disk.

2. Bring 2 cups water to a boil, immerse the julienned peels, and boil 2 minutes. *Alternatively, combine the peels and water in a microwave-safe container, cover, and cook at high (100 percent power) for 4 minutes. Drain.*

Cooking in Parchment Paper Hearts

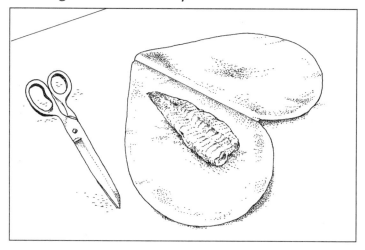

1. Lay the fish fillet, or other food, on half the paper heart, then fold the paper over it.

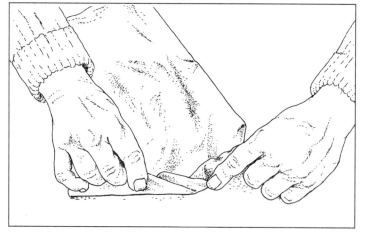

2. Pleat the paper tightly, securing the pleat with your fingertips as you move along the perimeter of the heart. Each pleat is made by making ¼-inch folds at 1½-inch intervals.

3. Mash the julienned peel with the oil, half the lemon juice, all the lime juice, and the ginger root.

4. Preheat oven to 425 degrees. Cut four parchment paper hearts and place a fish fillet on each. (You may use a double thickness of waxed paper if parchment paper is unavailable.) Season the fish with salt, pepper, and remaining lemon juice. Divide the lemon-lime mixture over it. Garnish with parsley. Fold as shown in the illustration below, pleating the edge and turning the tip under. Place on a baking sheet and bake 8 minutes. Let each diner open his or her own package and enjoy the aroma.

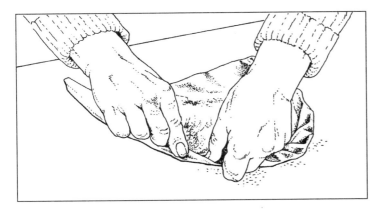

3. Continue making the pleats along the perimeter of the heart.

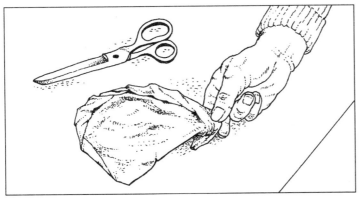

4. Secure the end by tucking the tip of paper under the package.

SCROD ON SQUASH CAKES

Fresh and fragrant. Although you'll sacrifice a little in flavor and aroma, a premixed ginger and shallot combination, available in a jar at your market's Asian section, is more convenient than grating your own. I like to plan for vegetable cake leftovers, so I make more than the recipe calls for and have some cakes to microwave the next day.

Yield: 4 servings
Calories per serving: 197
Protein per serving: 23 g
Fat per serving: 4 g
Saturated fat per serving: 1 g
Cholesterol per serving: 49 mg
Carbohydrates per serving: 16 g
Sodium per serving: 375 mg
Fiber per serving: 4 g

1 medium carrot, scrubbed

1 medium summer squash

1 medium zucchini

½ medium Spanish onion, peeled

1 tablespoon instant-blending flour

salt and pepper to taste

1 pound scrod fillets or other white-fleshed fish

¼ cup bottled clam broth or fish stock

¼ cup white wine

½ teaspoon fresh thyme leaves (stripped from about 6 sprigs)

2 tablespoons curry powder

2 teaspoons olive oil

2 teaspoons grated ginger and shallot from a jar or 1 teaspoon each grated fresh ginger root and shallot

2 teaspoons minced jalapeño (about ½ jalapeño chili)

1 tablespoon mirin (Japanese rice wine)

1. In a food processor fitted with a 6-millimeter julienne disk, or using a knife, julienne the carrot, summer squash, zucchini, and onion. Turn into a sieve placed over the sink and sprinkle with 2 teaspoons salt. Toss and let rest 10 to 15 minutes to draw out excess moisture from the squash.

2. Preheat the oven to 350 degrees. Combine the flour, salt, and pepper in a plastic bag; shake to blend. Add the fish; shake to coat evenly.

3. Spray with olive oil an 8-inch square baking dish or one just large enough

to hold the fish. Place the fish in the pan with what was the skin side down. Spray again with olive oil. Pour the broth and wine over, cover with foil, and bake 10 minutes.

4. Meanwhile, rinse the vegetable mixture thoroughly, squeezing with your hands to wash off the salt. Drain; squeeze again to remove moisture. Stir in the thyme and curry powder.

5. Spray a 10-inch skillet with olive oil spray. Add the 2 teaspoons olive oil. Sauté the ginger-shallot mixture and jalapeño 30 seconds over high heat. Add the drained vegetables and stir-fry over medium-high to high heat until the vegetables are softened. Stir in the mirin.

6. Roughly shape the vegetable mixture into 4 cakes and place one in the center of each plate. Top with the fish and pour juices over.
Serves 4

PESTO-BROILED FISH STEAKS

A perfect Monday-night dinner to atone for a calorie-taxing weekend, these broiled fish steaks may be readied in less time than it takes to empty the dishwasher if you have the Pesto tucked away in the refrigerator or freezer.

1¼ to 1½ pounds fish steaks or fillets such as cod, haddock, or halibut,
about 1-inch thick
½ teaspoon salt
freshly ground pepper to taste
juice of ½ lemon
¼ cup dry white wine
¼ cup Pesto (page 301)

Yield: 4 servings
Calories per serving: 249
Protein per serving: 50 g
Fat per serving: 3 g
Saturated fat per serving: 1 g
Cholesterol per serving: 11 mg
Carbohydrates per serving: 2 g
Sodium per serving: 455 mg
Fiber per serving: trace

1. Lay the fish in a broiling pan or roasting pan just large enough to hold it. Measure it at its thickest part. Season fish with salt and pepper. Squeeze a few drops lemon juice over fish. Spray with olive oil. Pour the wine into pan (it should just cover the bottom; add more or less, as needed). Broil 4 min-

utes, cover the top of fish with Pesto, and broil an additional 1 to 2 minutes, allowing about 5 minutes per 1-inch thickness.

Note: For juicy fish, err on the side of undercooking.

MISO-GLAZED HADDOCK IN GINGER BROTH

This light fish dish mirrors Asian tastes with its sake, miso, lemongrass, shiitakes, ginger, and cilantro, an herb even more prevalent in Thai cooking than in Mexican. If you can't locate miso or clam broth base in your own area, see Shopping Sources (page 306). Dried, ground lemongrass can be found in the Asian section of the supermarket if your store doesn't carry fresh; all the other items are supermarket-friendly. Lovely accompaniments are Stir-Fried Asian Veggies (page 144); an arugula, cilantro, and baby spinach salad with Sesame Seed Dressing (page 78); and orzo, a rice-shaped pasta, or jasmine rice or Japanese rice. If you're rushed, skip the broth altogether and simply broil the fish with the miso glaze, serve with some pea pods and rice, and enjoy.

Yield: 4 servings

Calories per serving: 257

Protein per serving: 27 g

Fat per serving: 3 g

Saturated fat per serving: trace

Cholesterol per serving: 68 mg

Carbohydrates per serving: 27 g

Sodium per serving: 1060 mg

Fiber per serving: 2 g

1 pound haddock or other white fish, skinned or not, as you prefer

4 tablespoons miso paste, yellow recommended

½ cup plus 2 tablespoons sake (or mirin)

1½ teaspoons tightly packed brown sugar

2 teaspoons fresh lemon juice

2 teaspoons clam broth base, dissolved in 1½ cups boiling water, or
*   12 ounces bottled clam broth or fish broth made from bouillon*

2 stalks fresh lemongrass, tough outer layers, tip, and bottom discarded, the
*   stalks bruised with the side of a wide knife and chopped in ¼-inch*
*   pieces, or 1 tablespoon dried ground lemongrass*

1 2-inch piece ginger root, peeled only if tough, and roughly grated

3½ ounces fresh shiitake mushrooms, stems removed and thinly sliced

a few drops Asian sesame oil

5 to 6 sprigs fresh cilantro for garnish (optional)

2 cups hot cooked orzo or rice

1. Spray an 8-by-8-inch baking dish with olive oil. Put in the fish with what was the skin side down.

2. In a small bowl mix together the miso, 2 tablespoons of the sake (reserve remaining sake for Step 3), sugar, and 1 teaspoon of the lemon juice (reserve remaining lemon juice for Step 3). Spread over fish, cover with waxed paper or plastic wrap, and refrigerate for a minimum of 20 minutes or as long as 24 hours.

3. In a 2½-quart saucepan combine the dissolved clam base in water, the reserved ½ cup sake, the lemongrass, ginger root, and reserved 1 teaspoon lemon juice. Cover and bring to a boil over high heat. Reduce heat to maintain a simmer for 15 minutes. Strain the solids from the broth, pressing the solids with the back of a spoon. Discard solids. (This step can be done several hours in advance; simply refrigerate and reheat the broth when needed.) Return broth to the pan.

4. Spray the fish with olive oil. Broil about 5 minutes per inch or until fish reaches the desired degree of doneness.

5. While the fish broils, raise the heat under the broth to high, add the shiitakes, and slow-boil 1½ minutes, covered, or until crisp-tender. Add the sesame oil. Remove from heat, and keep covered.

6. To serve, scoop a serving of orzo into the centers of 4 wide, shallow soup plates. Top each with a serving of fish. Divide the ginger broth and mushrooms around each scoop of orzo. Garnish, if desired, with cilantro.

Serves 3 to 4

SEARED GINGER TUNA WITH WASABI CREAM

This simple preparation is a compromise between my love for raw tuna and the more common preference for it cooked. Here the tuna is just seared in a very hot pan, leaving the center a hearty hue of red. Be watchful, for tuna cooks to a gray, well-done stage quite quickly. It is excellent served with rice sticks or Asian noodles and steamed pea pods with a garnish of grated carrot.

Yield: 3 to 4 servings
Calories per serving: 190
Protein per serving: 28 g
Fat per serving: 6 g
Saturated fat per serving: 1 g
Cholesterol per serving: 56 mg
Carbohydrates per serving: 5 g
Sodium per serving: 604 mg
Fiber per serving: trace

For the Tuna

1 pound tuna steaks

4 tablespoons reduced-sodium soy sauce

1 tablespoon minced fresh cilantro

2 teaspoons Asian sesame oil

1 tablespoon lemon juice

1 tablespoon grated, unpeeled ginger root

1 scallion, minced

1 clove garlic, minced

For the Wasabi Cream

2 tablespoons orange juice

2 tablespoons light mayonnaise

1 tablespoon unpeeled, grated ginger root

¼ teaspoon or to taste wasabi powder, available in the Asian section of the supermarket

1. Place the tuna in a bowl just large enough to hold it. Marinate the fish in the soy sauce, cilantro, sesame oil, lemon juice, ginger root, scallion, and garlic for at least 20 minutes or as long as 4 hours.

2. Mix together Wasabi Cream ingredients with a fork or small whisk until smooth.

3. Spray a nonstick skillet with olive oil. Heat the skillet over high heat about 30 seconds. Sear the fish about 3 minutes, basting with a bit of the marinade. Reduce heat to medium, flip fish, and cook until desired degree of doneness—about 2 minutes more will produce a rare steak. Baste with a bit more marinade.

4. Transfer fish to plate and smear each steak with a bit of Wasabi Cream. Slice the steaks on the extreme diagonal ¼-inch thick. Fan the slices to serve. Extra marinade may be spooned over steaks or mixed with rice sticks or noodles; be sure to boil it for 1 minute beforehand.

ROASTED SWORDFISH IN CORN BROTH WITH CORN SALAD

Make the broth and salad several hours ahead and rub the fish with the herbs and spices, leaving the actual mealtime cooking a snap. You may never cook swordfish any other way. You'll have a considerable amount of corn salad and broth left over; save for another meal.

Yield: 6 servings

Calories per serving: 293

Protein per serving: 37 g

Fat per serving: 8 g

Saturated fat per serving: 2 g

Cholesterol per serving: 66 mg

Carbohydrates per serving: 20 g

Sodium per serving: 659 mg

Fiber per serving: 4 g

For the Broth

4 ears corn, kernels cut from the cob and set aside in a bowl
  (reserve the cobs)

2 teaspoons clam broth base (see Shopping Sources, page 306) or
  1 8-ounce bottle clam broth

1 cup roughly chopped onion

1 large garlic clove, chopped

4 to 5 parsley stems

3 to 4 fresh thyme stems or ½ teaspoon dried thyme

salt and pepper to taste

For the Salad

the corn kernels from the four cobs

2 medium tomatoes, chopped (about 1¼ cups)

*½ cup canned, rinsed, and drained or home-cooked (see page 101) black
    beans*

½ cup (from about ½ large) red pepper, minced

2 scallions, including about 5 inches green stalk, minced (about ¼ cup)

juice of 1 lime (2 tablespoons)

1 tablespoon minced fresh basil or 1 teaspoon dried basil

1 teaspoon ground cumin

1 teaspoon each sugar and salt

*½ teaspoon fresh or from a jar minced jalapeño pepper (this is mild; use
    more for "hot")*

For the Fish

*2 pounds 1-inch-thick fish steaks, such as swordfish, halibut, bass, or
    salmon*

1 tablespoon fresh thyme leaves or ¾ teaspoon dried thyme

¾ teaspoon fennel seed

½ teaspoon ground cumin

about 2 teaspoons lemon juice

For the Garnish (optional)

10 to 12 scrubbed littleneck clams

fresh whole basil leaves

To Prepare the Broth

1. Chop the corn cobs into thirds or fourths and place in a 12-inch skillet
with the clam broth base and 3 cups water (or the clam broth and 2 cups
water), onion, garlic, parsley, thyme, and salt and pepper. Cover, bring to a
boil, and reduce heat to low to maintain a bare simmer. Simmer 35 to 40
minutes. Strain and discard solids, pressing to release liquid. Set corn broth
aside.

To Prepare the Salad

1. In a medium bowl combine the corn kernels, tomatoes, beans, red pepper, scallions, lime juice, basil, cumin, sugar, salt, and jalapeño. Stir. Cover with plastic wrap and set aside at room temperature for up to 6 hours.

To Prepare the Fish

1. Up to 2 hours before serving or as long as 24 hours, rub the fish with thyme, fennel, and cumin; sprinkle with lemon juice (one side only). Rewrap and refrigerate.

To Prepare and Serve

1. Preheat the oven to 400 degrees. Spray both sides of the fish with olive oil. Spray an ovenproof skillet with olive oil. Sear the fish over high heat on both sides just until browned, about 1 minute on each side. Place in the oven with the clams, if using, for 8 minutes. Adjust timing according to thickness of fish. Remove the pan from the oven, flip the fish to show the browner side, and slice into the fish with a thin knife. If the fish looks underdone, cover and let rest off heat for a few minutes. If done, leave uncovered. While the fish cooks, reheat the broth.

2. Spoon the corn salad into the bottom of a wide, shallow soup bowl. Top with a serving of fish and, if using, a few clams per diner. Ladle about ¼ cup broth over each serving. Garnish, if desired, with basil leaves.

Serves 6 with leftover corn salad and broth

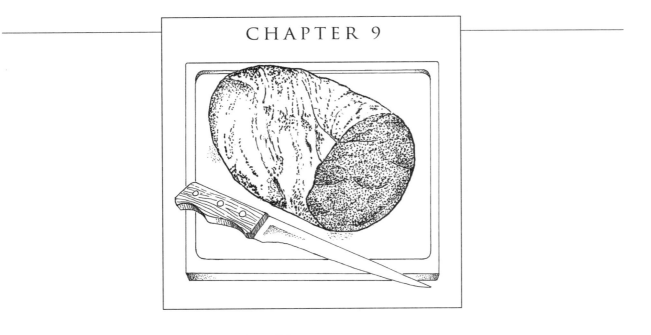

MEATS

THE RECIPES

MEATS

America produces more meat than any other country, and we eat almost all of it. Beef is still the national favorite; it's estimated that every man, woman, and child will consume 120 pounds in a single year. This is good news/bad news.

The good news, of course, is that meat is nutrient-dense. An excellent source of protein, as well as minerals such as iron, phosphorus, and copper, it contributes B vitamins too. And because it takes a little longer to digest, you won't get hungry as soon as you might after just a green salad. But with the good comes the bad, in the form of fat, including a high percentage of the worst kind—saturated—and dietary cholesterol. *The fat you see isn't all the fat you get either.* Consider this: A well-trimmed T-bone steak with no visible fat still holds about 40 percent of its calories as fat. A 6-ounce steak, completely trimmed, would still have 13 grams of fat, contributing about 120 of the 310 calories.

But you don't need to eschew meat for tofu. You can enjoy America's signature food by choosing the leanest types and cuts and controlling portion size. A 3-ounce portion of most meats—minuscule really, by our standards—supplies a whopping 23 grams of protein, about half the daily requirement for someone 120 pounds, about a third the daily value for a 200-pound male. It's been estimated that Americans probably eat two to three times the amount of protein they need. Our bodies store this excess protein and convert it to fat. Remember too that although the USDA suggests consuming two (for smaller people) to three (for larger ones) servings from the protein group of meat, poultry, fish, eggs, and so on, they call a serving *as little as 2 ounces* and no more than 3 ounces. Most of us eat at least 4 to 6 ounces of meat at a single meal, to say nothing of protein eaten in other forms, such as milk. If the serving size of meat in a recipe seems inadequate, add vegetables, fruits, and other skinny carbs to fill out the meal, not more meat.

Food Values for Common Meats*

	Total Fat	Total Cholesterol	Total Calories
Veal	5 g	88 mg	143
Lamb	8 g	78 mg	175
Pork	4 g	67 mg	139
Flank Steak	9 g	67 mg	175
Lean Ground Beef	15 g	76 mg	231

* The totals listed here are based on 3-ounce portions.
  Because a 3-ounce serving looks so small to us, most of the recipes in this necessarily lean chapter make the most of a little, mixing meat with fruits, vegetables, grains, and the like to bolster the total quantity of food.

POT ROAST

No 1990s names, no recipe title that reads like an ingredients' list for this old-fashioned favorite. Plan ahead for this one, but don't be put off by the 8 to 14 hours' (!) cooking time. That's in a slow cooker, while you're hard at work or, if lucky, play. Your prep time is really about 15 minutes, and you can shorten that by substituting a large (28-ounce) jar of your favorite spaghetti sauce for the tomatoes, herbs, and broth. There are instructions for microwaving too. Serve on wide noodles with salad or a green veggie.

Yield: 12 servings

Calories per serving: 216

Protein per serving: 27 g

Fat per serving: 7 g

Saturated fat per serving: 2 g

Cholesterol per serving: 67 mg

Carbohydrates per serving: 11 g

Sodium per serving: 588 mg

Fiber per serving: 3 g

3 pounds top or bottom round beef roast, trimmed completely

3 medium onions, chopped

2 carrots, chopped

2 cloves garlic, minced

1 13¾-ounce can beef broth

½ cup red wine (optional)

1 28-ounce can ground peeled tomatoes

4 tablespoons tomato paste

1 tablespoon dried basil

2 teaspoons salt

freshly ground pepper to taste

1 teaspoon dried oregano

1 teaspoon sugar

1 bay leaf

1. Place all ingredients in a 4-quart or larger Crock-Pot or other slow cooker. Cover and simmer at the slow setting for 10 hours. Stir from time to time. The beef can cook as long as 14 hours if you like fork-tender meat. If cooking for just 8 hours, cook for 2 hours at the high setting, then reduce heat to low. Remove bay leaf before serving.

2. To microwave, pierce the meat 10 to 12 times from both the top and the bottom with a carving fork. Place in a 4-quart microwave-safe dish. Add the remaining ingredients. Microwave at high (100 percent power) for 10 min-

utes. Microwave at medium (50 percent power) for 2½ hours. Stir from time to time. Let rest 15 minutes before serving. Remove bay leaf before serving. *Note:* If you line the cooking container with a cooking bag, you'll have virtually no dishes to clean up!

LONDON BROIL ON WHITE BEAN AND ARUGULA SALAD WITH GREMOLATA

While cooking beans from scratch requires some planning, it really isn't particularly taxing. Soak the beans in the evening after the dishes are done. Next morning, rinse the beans, then microwave them (100 percent power) about 45 to 50 minutes while you're getting ready for work. Drain, rinse, pop in the fridge, and they're ready for dinner at 6:00. Make a double batch and use in the Penne with Broccoli Rabe, White Beans, and Ham (page 164). A canned substitute (although a poor one) is cannelini beans; I find them mealy, mushy, and too big. One recipe of Balsamic–Walnut Oil vinaigrette (page 75) will dress both the beans and enough arugula and cilantro to make a delicious salad for 3 that complements the dish if served as an entree. You'll probably have gremolata—the mixture of lemon zest, parsley, and garlic—left over; it's very versatile and keeps up to 1 week.

Yield: 5 servings

Calories per serving: 320

Protein per serving: 34 g

Fat per serving: 9 g

Saturated fat per serving: 2 g

Cholesterol per serving: 74 mg

Carbohydrates per serving: 26 g

Sodium per serving: 441 mg

Fiber per serving: 6 g

2 cups cooked white (navy) beans, from half a 10-ounce cellophane package (cooking instructions follow), or canned, drained, small white beans

1 cup arugula, rinsed and shredded

1 tomato, diced

4 tablespoons minced red onion

2 medium carrots, julienned or diced

3 ½ ounces of red pepper from a jar or 1 red pepper, peeled and julienned (see Quick Tip, page 44)

¾ teaspoon salt

¼ teaspoon diced jarred or fresh jalapeño

5 tablespoons Balsamic–Walnut Oil vinaigrette (page 75) heated until steaming

1 pound grilled London broil, rubbed with Cajun seasoning or some other
   spicy beef rub sliced thinly
1 recipe gremolata (page 172) made with basil instead of parsley
1 recipe Béarnaise sauce (page 298) (optional)

1. To prepare the beans, cover the contents of half a cellophane package by 3 inches of water in a bowl. Soak 8 to 24 hours. Change the water once if the spirit moves. Drain and rinse. To cook, place the beans in a microwave-safe bowl, cover again with 3 inches of fresh cold water, and microwave at high (100 percent power), covered, for 40 to 50 minutes (drain the beans after 25 minutes, cover with fresh water if desired, and continue cooking) or until a bean is tender but "toothsome" and not mushy when bit. (If you change the cooking water, it will take the longer time to cook the beans but they will be unlikely to be so gassy.) Drain, rinse, and refrigerate until ready to use (within 48 hours), or freeze. If continuing with the recipe immediately, set the drained beans aside, covered, to keep warm.

2. In a medium bowl combine the still warm beans (reheat in the microwave or on the stovetop with ½ cup beef broth, if needed), arugula, tomato, onion, carrots, red pepper, salt, jalapeño, and dressing. Taste and correct seasoning. Set aside.

3. To serve, mound some beans on the center of a plate. Fan a few slices of meat around the mound. Garnish the beans with gremolata, sprinkling some unevenly over the whole plate rim. Dribble Béarnaise sauce, if desired, over the meat.

   Serves 4 to 5 as an entree, up to 6 or more as a small plate

Nutrabyte

Of the three food types—carbohydrates, fats, and proteins—which should you eat least of? According to nutritionists, protein should account for 10 to 15 percent of your daily calories; fats, no more than 30 percent, and no more than 10 percent of that saturated; and carbohydrates, the remaining 60 to 65 percent.

SIRLOIN TIPS IN ORANGE-SAGE SAUCE

This looks and tastes like a shiny, syrupy reduction sauce but requires none of the effort or time needed for that classic. The quick sauce starts as a marinade and is then boiled down, transforming itself to a delicious, shimmery veil for any beef dish. Keep a jar of dried, small hot chilies on hand if you don't stock your veggie tray with fresh chilies regularly. Serve this dish with roasted sweet and white potato slices.

1 cup orange juice

4 tablespoons reduced-sodium soy sauce

2 tablespoons fruit-only apricot preserves or orange marmalade

juice of 1 lime

2 tablespoons minced fresh sage leaves or 1 teaspoon dried crumbled sage

1 tablespoon grated horseradish (fresh is best, of course)

1 small hot red chili, dried, or ½ fresh jalapeño pepper, minced, or ¼ teaspoon jarred minced jalapeño

1 beef bouillon cube or 1 teaspoon beef broth concentrate (see Shopping Sources, page 306)

1 pound lean sirloin tips

1. Combine and blend all ingredients, except meat, in a medium, non-corrosive bowl. Marinate meat in this mixture for at least 1 hour. Remove meat and skewer it.

2. Discard the dried chili. Grill or broil the beef.

3. Meanwhile bring marinade to a boil. Boil at least 10 minutes or until marinade is reduced to about ½ cup and is syrupy. Brush over grilling meat a few times. Serve remaining sauce at the table.

Serves 4

Yield: 4 servings

Calories per serving: 247

Protein per serving: 29 g

Fat per serving: 7 g

Saturated fat per serving: 2 g

Cholesterol per serving: 79 mg

Carbohydrates per serving: 16 g

Sodium per serving: 792 mg

Fiber per serving: 1 g

QUICK TIP

Adding a teaspoon of molasses to a cup of soy sauce adds a nice flavor for marinades.

Two-Sesame Beef and Two-Pepper Stir-Fry

A fast and savory stir-fry, this needs nothing other than rice. Hoisin sauce is akin to Chinese BBQ sauce; an opened jar, like so many other Asian ingredients, seems to keep indefinitely in the fridge. Try it instead of mayonnaise on your next chicken sandwich. Japanese short-grain rice (follow the cooking instructions on the box) furthers the Asian theme and makes a lovely presentation. For a pretty presentation press the cooked rice into a cereal bowl, pack down with the back of a spoon, and invert the bowl over a plate. Lift off bowl. Sprinkle the compact dome with a few black sesame seeds. Don't forget the chopsticks!

Yield: 4 servings

Calories per serving: 313

Protein per serving: 22 g

Fat per serving: 13 g

Saturated fat per serving: 4 g

Cholesterol per serving: 51 mg

Carbohydrates per serving: 26 g

Sodium per serving: 438 mg

Fiber per serving: 5 g

2 tablespoons dry sherry

2 tablespoons reduced-sodium soy sauce

2 tablespoons hoisin sauce

2 teaspoons cornstarch

1 teaspoon sugar

2 tablespoons fresh minced basil

1 scallion, green part included, minced

1 clove garlic, minced

2 teaspoons grated fresh ginger root (about 1½-inch-long piece, unpeeled)

2 teaspoons oil, such as walnut, olive, or canola

¾ pound top round steak, partially frozen, thinly sliced

8 ounces canned, drained, sliced water chestnuts

2 carrots, thinly sliced, preferably with a 4-millimeter slicing disk

1 each red and green pepper, seeded, thinly sliced with a 4-millimeter slicing disk

½ Spanish onion (about 5 ounces), thinly sliced with a 4-millimeter slicing disk

2 to 3 ounces pea pods

1 tablespoon toasted sesame seeds, black or white (see page 38)

1 teaspoon Asian sesame oil

a few drops Asian hot oil

a few leaves basil for garnish (optional)

1. In a small bowl combine the sherry, soy sauce, hoisin, cornstarch, and sugar. Set aside near the cooking surface.

2. Spray a wok with olive oil. Add basil, scallion, garlic, ginger, and 1 teaspoon of the oil (reserve remaining teaspoon for Step 4). Stir-fry, over high heat, 1 minute. Push to rim of wok.

3. Add the meat, stir-fry. In about 2 minutes add the water chestnuts. Time for 1 minute more and scrape all into a bowl.

4. Add to the wok the remaining teaspoon of oil and the carrots. Add the juices from the bottom of the meat bowl to the carrots as they cook. Stir-fry 2 to 3 minutes (carrots should be very crisp when bitten.) Scrape the carrots into the meat bowl.

5. Add the peppers and onion to the wok, spraying with olive oil, if needed. Stir-fry 2 to 3 minutes, then scrape into the carrot-meat bowl.

6. Add the pea pods to the wok, spraying with olive oil, if needed. Stir-fry 1 minute.

7. Scrape the meat and the other vegetables into the wok. Toss. Add the reserved soy mixture and sesame seeds. Stir-fry 1 minute. Season with sesame oil and hot oil. Garnish, if desired, with basil.

Serves 4

QUICK TIP

For an all-purpose cooking spray, add ½ teaspoon lemon extract to the canister of a vacuum-pump sprayer such as a Misto (see Shopping Sources, page 306). Lemon juice won't emulsify the way the extract does with the oil. Use a high-quality olive oil.

BLACK BEAN AND BEEF CHILI

This hearty dish is perfect fare after a few hours' activity in the frosty out-doors. Make it ahead and take it to the ski house or serve after sledding at home. A meal in itself, this chili calls for just some rice, maybe tossed with a little fresh cilantro. It will keep frozen, without flavor loss, for up to 2 months.

Yield: 10 servings

Calories per serving: 289

Protein per serving: 26 g

Fat per serving: 5 g

Saturated fat per serving: 2 g

Cholesterol per serving: 40 mg

Carbohydrates per serving: 35 g

Sodium per serving: 581 mg

Fiber per serving: 6 g

9 plum tomatoes

1 jalapeño pepper or 1 teaspoon from a jar of minced jalapeño

3 medium onions, chopped

4 cloves garlic, chopped

½ cup red wine or beef broth

1½ pounds lean red beef, such as top or bottom round, partially frozen and well trimmed

3 tablespoons minced fresh cilantro

1 tablespoon ground cumin

2 teaspoons dried oregano

2 tablespoons chili powder

1 teaspoon salt

6 cups black beans, cooked (see page 101), or 4 1-pound cans black beans, drained and rinsed

4 teaspoons beef broth base (see Shopping Sources, page 306) or 4 beef bouillon cubes

3 tablespoons cornmeal

1. Blacken the tomatoes and jalapeño pepper in a 10-inch skillet over high heat for 15 minutes, shaking the pan from time to time to blacken evenly. Reduce heat to medium-high as tomatoes become blackened. Remove tomatoes and pepper from pan to cool.

2. Meanwhile combine the onions and garlic with the red wine or beef broth in a 4-cup glass measuring cup or other microwave-safe container. Cover with plastic wrap and microwave at high (100 percent power) for 4

minutes or until the onions are softened. Place onions and cooking broth in a 1.3-gallon microwave-safe container.

3. Thinly slice the partially frozen meat either by hand or using a food processor. Add meat to onions.

4. When tomatoes are cool enough to handle, peel, core, and chop them roughly. Add to the onion-meat mixture.

5. Wearing rubber gloves, peel, stem, and seed the jalapeño. Mince. Using the whole pepper will produce a medium-hot chili; using a level tablespoon of minced jalapeño produces a mildly spicy dish. Add as much as you like to the tomato-onion-meat mixture.

6. Stir in the cilantro, cumin, oregano, chili powder, salt, and beans. Dissolve the bouillon cubes or beef broth concentrate in 2 cups boiling water. Add to the tomato-onion-meat mixture.

7. Cover and microwave at high (100 percent power) for 15 minutes. Stir. Cover and microwave again at medium-high heat (75 percent power) for an additional 40 minutes. Stir in cornmeal, if needed, for thickening. Microwave at high (100 percent power) for an additional 5 minutes to thicken. (If the chili is being reheated, it will thicken during chilling and may not need the cornmeal.)

Nutrabyte

Realistically assess your exercise schedule. Try to add 15 extra minutes a day or 1½ hours a week, split up any way you like. The benefits are many: Your heart health will benefit, your stress will decrease, your color will improve, and you'll burn calories.

CILANTRO AND LIME PORK KABOBS WITH HOT CHILI CHUTNEY

This easily prepared dish, festive enough for guests, pairs the cool tang of yogurt-cilantro marinated pork with a chili-tinged apple-based chutney, a modern variation on the traditional combination of pork and apples. While tenderloin is called for, another pork cut, well trimmed, would be fine. Make the chutney a day ahead, if you like, when you marinate the meat. Serve with rice flecked with a bit of tomato and chilies to further the southwestern theme and Zucchini Sauté (page 131). Leftover chutney is excellent with grilled poultry and will last, chilled, up to 1 month.

Yield of meat with chutney:
  4 servings
Calories per serving: 211
Protein per serving: 30 g
Fat per serving: 5 g
Saturated fat per serving: 2 g
Cholesterol per serving: 85 mg
Carbohydrates per serving: 11 g
Sodium per serving: 372 mg
Fiber per serving: 1 g

1 pound pork tenderloin, trimmed of all fat and cut into 2-inch chunks

1 cup plain nonfat yogurt

¼ cup lime juice

3 tablespoons minced fresh cilantro

½ teaspoon salt

1 Spanish or other sweet onion, cut into 2-inch chunks

1. Combine the pork and yogurt, lime juice, cilantro, and salt in a plastic bag. Tie the bag and knead with your hands to mix seasonings. Marinate in the refrigerator for 4 to 24 hours.

2. Thread 4 skewers with the meat and onion. Grill the kabobs over a medium-hot fire for approximately 20 minutes, basting often with the remaining marinade. Serve with heated chutney.

Hot Chili Chutney

2 Granny Smith apples, peeled, cored, and diced
½ cup diced dried mixed fruits, such as prunes, apricots, and peaches
1 tablespoon chopped canned chilies
1 tablespoon minced fresh cilantro
2 teaspoons balsamic vinegar
1 teaspoon sugar
1 teaspoon ground cinnamon
½ teaspoon salt
¼ teaspoon ground cloves

Yield: 4 servings (4 tablespoons each)
Calories per serving: 41
Protein per serving: trace
Fat per serving: trace
Saturated fat per serving: trace
Cholesterol per serving: none
Carbohydrates per serving: 11 g
Sodium per serving: 153 mg
Fiber per serving: 1 g

1. Combine the ingredients in a 1-quart, heavy-bottomed saucepan. Cover. Bring to a boil over high heat, reduce to medium-low, and simmer, stirring occasionally, for 30 minutes. Chutney may be prepared several days in advance.

2. If the chutney has been refrigerated for more than 2 hours, mix with 3 tablespoons liquid, such as water, cider, or white wine. Microwave at high power (100 percent) for 4 minutes, or simmer on the stove-top, covered, about 5 minutes, stirring occasionally. Serve chutney hot with the kabobs.

Yogurt

Yogurt is a fermented milk product that has long been used in the Middle East but has been used here only since the 1940s. Widely regarded as a health food, it supplies, it should be noted, no more nutrients than a glass of partially skimmed milk, although it does aid in digestion. Yogurt, like its roly-poly cousin sour cream, must be cooked at low temperatures or it will curdle. Fruit-flavored yogurts are comparatively high in calories, 1 cup supplying about 260 to 300 calories.

PORK CUTLET IN CIDER CREAM SAUCE

Here's a quick and delicious meal for midweek dining when time is of the essence. Pork cutlets are lean, boneless cuts taken from the loin, and they cook with little waste. After an initial searing, the pork must be slowly cooked to avoid toughening.

1 pound boneless pork cutlets, trimmed of all fat

¾ cup cider (hard or nonalcoholic sparkling cider recommended)

4 small apples, such as McIntosh, peeled, cored, and thinly sliced

¼ teaspoon salt

freshly ground pepper to taste

2 teaspoons (or to taste) stone-ground mustard (the kind made with horse-radish is excellent)

½ cup nonfat sour cream

1. Spray a 10-inch heavy-bottomed nonstick skillet with olive oil. Pat the cutlets dry. Sear the cutlets for about 1 minute on each side or until well browned.

2. Reduce the heat, add the cider and apples, season with salt and pepper, and half-cover the pan. Stirring the apples occasionally, simmer for 8 minutes, or until the pork is cooked through and the apples are tender but not mushy.

3. Remove the cutlets from the pan to a serving plate; cover with a towel to keep them warm. Boil pan juices, if necessary, to reduce to ¼ cup.

4. Stir the mustard into the sour cream. Whisk the mixture into the cider. Pour the sauce and apples over the pork cutlets.

Yield: 4 servings

Calories per serving: 282

Protein per serving: 27 g

Fat per serving: 7 g

Saturated fat per serving: 2 g

Cholesterol per serving: 63 mg

Carbohydrates per serving: 29 g

Sodium per serving: 235 mg

Fiber per serving: 3 g

Pacific Rim Pork Tenderloin with Grilled Pineapple Salsa

Also excellent on the grill, this taste of the tropics can be marinated early in the day or the night before. Mix the salsa up to 6 hours before dinner. Serve with sticky Japanese short-grain rice and Stir-Fried Asian Veggies (page 144) or Rice Noodle Salad *without* the Sesame Shrimp (page 170).

Yield: 6 servings

Calories per serving: 266

Protein per serving: 33 g

Fat per serving: 6 g

Saturated fat per serving: 2 g

Cholesterol per serving: 89 mg

Carbohydrates per serving: 19 g

Sodium per serving: 413 mg

Fiber per serving: 2 g

For the Marinade

1 cup reduced-sodium soy sauce

3 tablespoons rum

2 tablespoons molasses

2 large or 3 small cloves garlic, minced

2 tablespoons grated, unpeeled ginger root

a few drops hot (spicy) oil (see Shopping Sources, page 306)

2 pork tenderloins (about 1¾ pounds), trimmed of any fat

For the Salsa

1 large pineapple, peeled, cored, and sliced ½- to ¾-inch thick (reserve juice)

¼ cup minced red onion

2 tablespoons chopped cilantro

¼ cup orange juice

1 tablespoon Grand Marnier or other orange-flavored liqueur (optional)

2 tablespoons minced basil

1 teaspoon minced fresh mint (optional)

¼ teaspoon or to taste minced fresh jalapeño or from a jar

To Marinate the Meat

1. In a medium bowl combine the soy sauce, rum, molasses, garlic, ginger, and oil. Marinate the meat for at least 6 hours or as long as 48 in the fridge. If time allows, bring to room temperature before cooking.

To Prepare the Salsa

1. Grill the pineapple, brushing each side with a tablespoon or two of the meat marinade. *Alternatively, spray a skillet with olive oil and sauté the pineapple until lightly browned on both sides over medium-high heat.* While the pineapple cooks, mix together the onion, cilantro, orange juice, liqueur, basil, mint, and jalapeño in a medium bowl. Cube the grilled pineapple and add, with any juices, to the bowl. Cover with plastic wrap and set aside at room temperature up to 6 hours. If chilled before serving, bring to room temperature.

To Cook the Meat

1. Preheat the oven to 500 degrees. Line an 8-inch square roasting pan with foil and spray with olive oil. Add meat. Roast in the upper third of the oven for 8 minutes. Check the internal temperature with an instant-reading meat thermometer (see Glossary). The meat will have a whisper of pink at 130–135 degrees (the internal temperature will drop slightly as the meat rests). Plan accordingly, roasting another 2 to 4 minutes, as needed. If temperature (test in several spots) is 140 degrees immediately out of the oven, or even 145 degrees, it will probably be fine; if less than 130 degrees, it must cook a few minutes longer. Let the meat rest at least 5 minutes or as long as 15 minutes before cutting on the extreme diagonal. To serve, mound salsa in the center of a serving platter and fan the meat in a ring around it.

Serves 6

Nutrabyte

A paper clip weighs about 1 gram

5 grams = 1 teaspoon

14 grams = 3 teaspoons =
1 tablespoon

1 ounce = 2 tablespoons =
28 grams

(information is rounded, so there
is a small discrepancy)

OVEN-BRAISED PORK TENDERLOIN WITH SPICED FRUITS

An easily-put-together recipe (about 20 minutes), this Caribbean-inspired braise does require a substantial 90 minutes in the oven, nice for a weekend meal. While tenderloin is specified for its lean stats, pork loin would work equally well. Tenderloins are generally packaged in 1¾- to 2-pound cellophane packs, which is more meat than four people need, but the leftovers freeze beautifully so it seems easier to cook the whole lot. Any mix of trail fruits or even a single dried fruit will do; a mixture of dried prunes, plums, apricots, pears, and mangoes is delightful. Look for these sold in the bulk section of the market. Mashed baked sweet potatoes (microwave, peel, and mash) are the perfect accompaniment, seconded by couscous or orzo. Add a green or a salad, or both, and you have a terrific cold-weather meal.

Yield: 6 servings

Calories per serving: 267

Protein per serving: 29 g

Fat per serving: 5 g

Saturated fat per serving: 2 g

Cholesterol per serving: 76 mg

Carbohydrates per serving: 23 g

Sodium per serving: 492 mg

Fiber per serving: 3 g

3 to 4 ounces mixed dried fruits, such as dried prunes, plums, apricots,
pears, and mangoes
¾ cup wine (red or white; it doesn't matter)
½ teaspoon ground cloves
¼ to ½ teaspoon ground cinnamon (more if you love it, less otherwise)
¼ teaspoon freshly grated nutmeg or ⅛ teaspoon ground nutmeg
2 tablespoons instant-blending flour
½ teaspoon salt
ground pepper to taste
1½ to 1¾ pounds pork tenderloin, cubed into pieces about 1½-by-1-inches
½ Spanish or large white sweet onion, chopped (about 1 cup loosely packed)
1 cup (6 ounces) green grapes
1 medium green apple, such as Granny Smith, peeled, cored, and chunked
the leaves from 10 to 12 sprigs fresh thyme or 1 teaspoon dried thyme
1 tablespoon grainy mustard, such as Pommery
1½ teaspoons beef broth concentrate (see Shopping Sources, page 306)
dissolved in 1 cup boiling water or strong beef stock or beef broth

1. Combine the dried fruits with ½ cup wine (reserve the remaining ¼ cup for Step 4) in a glass measure or other microwave-safe container and microwave at high (100 percent power) for 2 minutes until softened. *Alternatively bring the fruit and wine to a boil in a small saucepan and simmer for 2 minutes. Set aside for 10 to 20 minutes.*

2. Preheat the oven to 350 degrees. In a 2-quart plastic bag, combine the cloves, cinnamon, nutmeg, flour, salt, and pepper. Shake to blend. Add the meat, seal the bag, and knead to blend the spices. Empty meat into a medium bowl.

3. Add the onion, grapes, apple, and thyme leaves to the meat. Chop the softened wine-fruit mixture in a food processor or by hand. Add to the meat.

4. Stir the mustard into the beef broth and remaining wine. Add to the meat and stir well to blend.

5. Spray a 9-by-9-inch ovenproof dish with olive oil. Add the meat and fruit. Cover tightly with foil and bake in the upper third of the oven about 90 minutes, or until the fruits lose distinction and the meat is fork-tender. Stir every 20 minutes. Remove foil the last 20 minutes (the dish can be held up to 30 minutes, covered, before serving).

Serves 6

Nutrabyte

If you choose well, what you eat is more important than how much you eat.

CURRIED BEEF AND MUSHROOMS ON COUSCOUS WITH GREMOLATA

This is one of those chameleon recipes that adapts to your larder. You may substitute ¼ teaspoon of Marmite, a widely available beef extract, for the demi-glace (see Shopping Sources, page 306) or enhance the dish with ½ ounce of soaked, drained porcini. Or add peas to the finished dish and serve on rice, polenta, or noodles instead of couscous. Regardless, the protein portion here adheres to the USDA guideline of a 2- to 3-ounce serving. Such a little piece of meat looks mighty paltry to our American tastes, but stretched out with mushrooms, the finished plate looks—and is—bountiful.

Note: The meat slices beautifully if frozen solid then thawed about 1½ hours at room temperature. Slice with the medium disk of a Cuisinart. This recipe is ample for 4, but the whole package of couscous serves 5.

Yield: 4 servings

Calories per serving: 509

Protein per serving: 33 g

Fat per serving: 8 g

Saturated fat per serving: 3 g

Cholesterol per serving: 46 mg

Carbohydrates per serving: 74 g

Sodium per serving: 775 mg

Fiber per serving: 5 g

For the Beef

¾ pound flank steak, partially frozen, thinly sliced

1 tablespoon instant-blending flour mixed with 1 tablespoon curry powder

For the Mushrooms

1/2 Spanish or sweet white onion, chopped (about 1 cup or 5 ounces)

5 cloves roasted garlic (see page 305) or 2 cloves raw garlic, minced

1 tablespoon beef base concentrate (see Shopping Sources, page 306),
*   dissolved in 2 cups hot water, or 2 cups rich beef broth*

10 ounces mushrooms, thinly sliced

3 to 4 ounces shiitakes, stemmed and thinly sliced

1 large portabella mushroom cap, thinly sliced

4 tablespoons nonfat sour cream

2 teaspoons cornstarch (use 3 teaspoons if omitting demi-glace), dissolved
*   in 2 tablespoons dry sherry*

2 teaspoons demi-glace (see Shopping Sources, page 306) or ¼ teaspoon
*   Marmite (available in most supermarkets near the gravies or spices)*

the leaves from about 10 sprigs fresh thyme (about 1 teaspoon) or
*   ½ teaspoon ground thyme*

freshly ground pepper to taste

10-ounce package couscous, cooked (follow package instructions for
making with beef broth but omit butter)

For the Gremolata

mix together in a food processor or by hand

2 tablespoons finely grated lemon zest (from 2 to 3 lemons)

2 tablespoons finely minced parsley

2 cloves garlic, minced

1. Mix together the meat, flour, and curry. Set aside.

2. Spray a 10-inch or larger skillet with olive oil. Over high heat stir together the onion and garlic in 2 tablespoons of the beef broth for about 2 to 3 minutes or until the onions are softened somewhat. Adjust heat to prevent burning.

3. Add all three kinds of mushrooms and cook, stirring frequently, over high heat until softened, about 6 to 8 minutes. Remove to a bowl.

4. Spray the same skillet with olive oil. Add the meat and stir-fry over high heat until no longer pink, about 3 minutes. Spray with olive oil again, to prevent sticking, if need be. Add cooked meat to the mushrooms.

5. Add the remaining broth to the now empty skillet. Stir vigorously with a wooden spoon to dislodge bits of stuck meat. Bring the broth to a boil, then reduce heat so broth simmers.

6. Stir in the sour cream, dissolved cornstarch, demi-glace, and thyme, and season with pepper. Simmer sauce until blended, about 2 minutes.

7. Return meat and mushrooms to the skillet. Simmer as long as 15 minutes or hold, refrigerated, up to 24 hours. Serve with couscous flavored after cooking with 1 tablespoon gremolata, and the beef and mushrooms garnished with 1 or so tablespoons gremolata.

Serves 4

Nutrabyte

Veal has more cholesterol than some cuts of beef because cholesterol, a fatlike substance, is concentrated not in the fat but in the muscle, the meaty portion, of the animal. Calves, with a higher muscle-fat ratio because of their tender age, thus have higher concentrations of cholesterol.

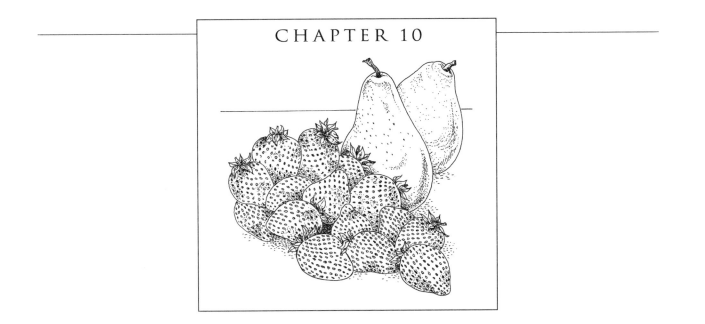

SWEETS
AND TREATS

THE RECIPES

Cakes

Muffins

Fruits

Specialty Desserts

SWEETS AND TREATS
ON MAKING DESSERTS SKINNY

These desserts range from a simple but intense Chocolate Cake to a showy, elegant Raspberry Crepes Soufflé. The baked goods rely in part on fat replacers to reduce calories. One kind of fat replacer is based on a prune puree; jamlike, it is nearly black and is best in batters that are flavored with cinnamon and other spices. The other widely available fat replacer is a honey-colored fluid based on apples and is best in yellow and white types of cakes. A third type of fat replacer, Oatrim (see Shopping Sources, page 306), is available, at this writing, only by mail order, so I haven't included recipes for it here, although you might like to experiment with it. The apple-based fat replacer is used in a one-to-one ratio: If ½ cup of shortening is used in the original recipe, use ½ cup of the apple puree. The prune fat replacer is used in a one-to-two ratio: Use ¼ cup of the prune product if ½ cup of shortening is called for. Therefore, in my recipes, while I generally recommend which fat replacer produces superior results, I specify not an amount of fat replacer, but, rather, how much shortening needs to be replaced. Some recipes also call for a tablespoon of butter or margarine, because this prevents the texture from becoming rubbery. Real eggs also help keep the texture pleasantly crumbly, so egg whites are used instead of egg substitutes. Sugar has occasionally been reduced, when possible, but none of these desserts is really diet food; instead, they are healthier alternatives that more than satisfy the pang for something sweet.

ALMOND ANGEL FOOD CAKE

This quickly made cake pairs the lightness of beaten egg whites with the crunch of almonds. Baked in a ring mold, it can be served with a mound of fresh sliced fruit in the center, and the whole napped with Almond Cream (page 271). It would also make a nice addition to a fruit fondue tray, and it is very tempting all by itself.

Yield: 8 servings

Calories per serving: 100

Protein per serving: 4 g

Fat per serving: 2 g

Saturated fat per serving: trace

Cholesterol per serving: 0

Carbohydrates per serving: 17 g

Sodium per serving: 59 mg

Fiber per serving: 1 g

1 ounce slivered or sliced almonds

½ cup sugar

6 tablespoons cake flour

½ cup egg whites (about 5 to 6)

a pinch salt

½ teaspoon cream of tartar

1 teaspoon vanilla extract

½ teaspoon almond extract

1. Spray a 4-cup ring mold with cooking spray or butter and flour. Preheat oven to 300 degrees.

2. Pulverize the almonds in a food processor or blender. Do not allow them to get mushy. Set aside in a bowl.

3. Sift together the sugar and flour; mix with the almonds.

4. Beat the egg whites until foamy, add salt, and continue to beat until soft peaks form. Add the cream of tartar and continue to beat until stiff but not dry.

5. Fold the flour-sugar-nut mixture into the egg whites along with the extracts. Do not overbeat. Spoon into the prepared ring mold and place in the bottom third of the oven. Turn heat off after 30 minutes but leave the cake in oven for an additional 10 minutes. Then cool, inverted on a rack, for 30 minutes. Run a flexible-bladed spatula around the rim and center of the mold to release the cake. If it doesn't come free, let it cool a while longer.

CARROT CAKELETTES

Bake this old favorite in a cake pan, rather than a muffin tin, if desired. For best results use a fat replacer made from prune puree and 2 tablespoons butter. While you may omit the butter altogether, increasing the fat replacer to equal ¾ cup shortening, a bit of butter tenderizes the cake texture.

Yield: 14 servings
Calories per serving: 138
Protein per serving: 3 g
Fat per serving: 2 g
Saturated fat per serving: 1 g
Cholesterol per serving: 5 mg
Carbohydrates per serving: 27 g
Sodium per serving: 200 mg
Fiber per serving: 2 g

1½ cups flour (6 ounces, by weight)
1 teaspoon baking soda
2 teaspoons ground cinnamon
½ teaspoon salt
2 carrots, grated (about 1 cup)
¾ cup sugar
½ cup crushed pineapple, undrained
fat replacer to equal ¾ cup oil (¼ cup fat replacer made from prune puree
*   recommended and 2 tablespoons butter)*
1 teaspoon grated ginger root (no need to peel)
3 egg whites
1 tablespoon pine nuts or walnuts

1. Line 14 3-inch muffin cups with paper liners. Preheat the oven to 350 degrees.

2. Sift together the flour, baking soda, cinnamon, and salt.

3. Beat together in a food processor or bowl the carrots, sugar, pineapple, fat replacer and butter, and ginger root until light. Beat in the egg whites.

4. Sift the flour mixture into the wet ingredients in three batches, just pulsing or stirring lightly after each addition, to prevent the cake's texture from becoming coarse and tough. Beat in the nuts.

5. Bake 18 minutes or until a skewer inserted slightly off center comes out clean.
    Makes 14 cakelettes

CHOCOLATE CAKE

When I was a kid, it was my job to make the cookies and cakes we always had on hand to satisfy Daddy's sweet tooth. And although our kitchen was by no means a gourmet operation, these were always made from scratch. As the baker, I often made this cake, although in a fattier version, because it was just so quick and easy and I wouldn't have to walk to the store for anything. Almost as fast as a mix, it's surprisingly chocolatey and very moist. Imagine my chagrin, then, when I recently opened a package of flour only to find "my" treasured family recipe on the back. So much for "ownership"! My eighteen-year-old, who doesn't love everything in this book, branded these cupcakes "Excellent!" Be sure to buy unsweetened baking cocoa, not hot chocolate drink mix.

Yield: 46 servings

Calories per serving: 35

Protein per serving: trace

Fat per serving: trace

Saturated fat per serving: trace

Cholesterol per serving: none

Carbohydrates per serving: 8 g

Sodium per serving: 49 mg

Fiber per serving: trace

1½ cups cake or all-purpose flour, not self-rising (6 ounces in weight)

1 cup sugar

5 tablespoons unsweetened cocoa

1 teaspoon baking soda

½ teaspoon salt

1 cup cold water or ½ cup cold coffee and ½ cup water

fat replacement equivalent to 5 tablespoons oil (for best results use the liquid type based on apple puree)

1 tablespoon regular white vinegar

1 tablespoon Kahlúa or other coffee liqueur (optional)

1 teaspoon vanilla extract

confectioners' sugar (optional)

1. Preheat the oven to 350 degrees. Spray a 7-by-7-inch baking dish or 4 12-cup mini muffin pans with cooking spray; for faster cleanup use mini cupcake liners.

2. Sift together 3 times into a medium-size bowl the flour, sugar, cocoa, baking soda, and salt.

3. In a 2-cup measure, mix together the water, fat replacement, vinegar, Kahlúa, and vanilla.

4. Pour three-fourths of the liquid ingredients into the dry ingredients. Mix with a spatula until small lumps remain but the liquid is incorporated. Add remaining liquid, mixing just to combine; don't overmix, or the cake will be tough. Pour into the pan or divide among 46 mini muffin cups.

5. Bake in the upper third of the oven 25 to 30 minutes for the cake, 15 to 17 minutes for cupcakes, or until a toothpick inserted slightly off center comes out clean. Serve sprinkled with confectioners' sugar.

Makes 46 2-inch cupcakes or a 7-by-7-inch cake

CHEESECAKE

This creamy rich cheesecake will require planning, for you'll need to make yogurt cheese, a simple process of draining yogurt 8 hours or overnight. The cake is best about 2 days after baking, but you can serve it within 4 hours of removing it from the oven. Topped with the berry of the season or served plain, it's (nearly) fat-free bliss!

Yield: 12 servings

Calories per serving: 126

Protein per serving: 11 g

Fat per serving: 1 g

Saturated fat per serving: trace

Cholesterol per serving: 27 mg

Carbohydrates per serving: 18 g

Sodium per serving: 319 mg

Fiber per serving: none

16 ounces plain or vanilla yogurt

1½ pounds (3 8-ounce packages) fat-free cream cheese

1 whole egg plus 2 additional egg whites

⅔ cup sugar

½ cup nonfat sour cream

1 tablespoon cornstarch

1 teaspoon vanilla extract

⅛ teaspoon salt

zest of 1 lemon

few drops lemon extract (optional)

few gratings fresh nutmeg (optional)

1 pint fresh strawberries, thinly sliced if large, for garnish (optional)

4 tablespoons "fruit-only" strawberry preserves, melted, for garnish
    (optional)

cinnamon sugar (optional)

1. The day before assembling the cheesecake, line a sieve with a double layer of cheesecloth and place it over a bowl. Pour in the yogurt, tie the ends of the cheesecloth securely over the yogurt, and refrigerate for 8 hours or overnight. Discard the liquid that will drain from the resulting cheese, pressing the yogurt once or twice to extract more water.

2. Preheat the oven to 325 degrees. In a food processor, beat together for 4 minutes the yogurt cheese, cream cheese, egg and egg whites, sugar, sour cream, cornstarch, vanilla, salt, lemon zest, and, if desired, lemon extract and nutmeg.

3. Meanwhile spray a 9-inch springform pan with cooking spray. Sprinkle with cinnamon sugar, if desired. Place pan on a cookie sheet for stability. Pour the cheesecake batter into the pan and bake in the upper third of the oven for 50 to 55 minutes or until a skewer inserted slightly off center comes out sticky but not wet. Check the cake after 40 minutes and reduce temperature to 300 degrees if the edges are browning.

4. Chill the cake at least 4 hours before serving. If desired, garnish with sliced strawberries and brush with melted preserves.

    Makes 8 to 12 slices

Nutrabyte

There are several fat replacements on the market. At least two are based on fruit concentrates and available in supermarkets, usually near the oils or baking products section. One is a measure-for-measure replacement; the other uses a 1-to-2 ratio. Both supply about the same number of calories. Of course, the 1-to-2 ratio will have half the calories, but it's not a significant amount. Another fat replacer, Oatrim, can be mail-ordered. (See the Glossary or Shopping Sources for more on this product.)

Cinnamon-Apple Cake Vienna

The original recipe for this cake came from my friend Marylee, a neighbor of ours when we lived on the edge of the Vienna Woods. Marylee is an excellent baker, and this was one of my favorites that she made. I've reduced the calories somewhat in several ways, such as by adding apples, but remember, no cake is exactly diet food. For this cake the apple puree fat replacer by Smucker's gives the most satisfying results. (See page 257 for more information on fat replacers.) Keep walnut oil in the fridge to prevent it from becoming rancid. Consult the Index for other uses for tiny (of course!) amounts of this excellent oil.

Yield: 15 servings

Calories per serving: 203

Protein per serving: 4 g

Fat per serving: 2 g

Saturated fat per serving: trace

Cholesterol per serving: 1 mg

Carbohydrates per serving: 43 g

Sodium per serving: 303 mg

Fiber per serving: 2 g

2 baking apples, such as McIntosh, peeled, cored, and diced (about 2 cups)

1 cup brown sugar, packed

2½ cups (10 ounces by weight) plus 1 tablespoon flour

2 tablespoons finely chopped walnuts

1 teaspoon baking soda

1 teaspoon baking powder

1 teaspoon cinnamon

1 teaspoon salt

2 egg whites

1 tablespoon walnut oil or canola or similar oil

fat replacer to equal 11 tablespoons (⅔ cup plus 1 tablespoon) oil, liquid
*   type based on apple puree recommended*

1 cup buttermilk

1 teaspoon vanilla extract

1. Preheat the oven to 325 degrees. Spray a 9-by-9-inch cake pan with cooking spray and line, if desired, with waxed or parchment paper. Set aside.

2. Combine the apples in a 2-cup glass measure or other microwave-safe bowl with 2 tablespoons of the brown sugar. Stir. Cover with plastic wrap and microwave on high (100 percent power) for 1 minute. Set aside.

3. Combine the single tablespoon flour, 2 more tablespoons of the brown sugar, and the walnuts. Toss well to combine, and set aside.

4. Sift together twice the 2½ cups flour, baking soda, baking powder, cinnamon, and salt.

5. Beat together in a food processor or with a hand-held mixer the egg whites, oil, fat replacer, buttermilk, and vanilla.

6. Sift the dry ingredients into the wet ingredients in three batches, beating after each addition, just until the dry ingredients are incorporated; overbeating will toughen the cake.

7. Stir in the apples. Pour batter into the pan. Sprinkle flour-sugar-nut mixture from Step 3 over the top, pressing lightly with your hand to anchor the nuts.

8. Bake in the upper third of the oven 40 minutes or until a skewer inserted slightly off center comes out clean.

Makes 12 good-size pieces, 15 smaller ones

Nutrabyte

A cup of flour weighs 4 ounces. Your cakes and other baked goods will be much lighter if you weigh the flour rather than rely on measuring alone.

CRADLE CAKE

Meringue lines a loaf pan, creating a "frosting" for a light yellow cake. Delicious. Be sure to use baker's cocoa, not hot chocolate mix. For additional information on fat replacers, see page 257.

Yield: 8 servings

Calories per serving: 202

Protein per serving: 4 g

Fat per serving: 3 g

Saturated fat per serving: 1 g

Cholesterol per serving: 32 mg

Carbohydrates per serving: 41 g

Sodium per serving: 278 mg

Fiber per serving: 1 g

2 egg whites plus 1 egg (or 2 additional egg whites)

1 cup sugar

3 tablespoons cocoa powder

1 cup flour (4 ounces by weight)

1½ teaspoons baking powder

1½ teaspoon salt

1 tablespoon butter or margarine, softened

fat replacer to equal 3 tablespoons butter (use a fat replacer based on apple puree for this cake, not a prune puree)

5 tablespoons skim milk

1 teaspoon vanilla extract

1. Spray with cooking spray a 1½-quart (preferably glass) loaf pan that measures 8½-by-2½ inches. Line with waxed or parchment paper. Set aside. Preheat the oven to 325 degrees.

2. Beat the 2 egg whites until stiff peaks form. Gradually beat in ½ cup of the sugar. Beat in the cocoa. Spread the resulting meringue as evenly as possible on the bottom and three-quarters up the sides of the loaf pan. Concentrate the meringue on the bottom and sides, not the corners. Set aside while preparing the batter.

3. Sift together three times the flour, baking powder, and salt.

4. Cream together in a bowl or food processor the butter, fat replacer, and remaining ½ cup sugar. Beat in the egg (or 2 egg whites).

5. Mix together the milk and vanilla in a medium-sized bowl. Sift the dry ingredients into the fat replacer in three batches, alternating with the milk-

vanilla mixture. Pulse just to combine; do not overbeat or the cake will be tough.

6. Spread the batter in the meringue-lined pan. If the meringue is higher than the batter, press it down, lightly, onto the batter. Bake in the upper third of the oven for 45 minutes or until a skewer inserted slightly off center comes out clean.

Makes 8 generous slices

PEAR AND ALMOND CRUMB CAKE

Delicious served warm. If you can't eat it right out of the oven, undercook it by about 4 minutes and then reheat it at medium (50 percent power) in a microwave. If your cholesterol count isn't in a crisis state, real eggs produce a lighter product than egg substitute. For best results choose a fat replacer based on prune puree (see page 257 for more information).

Yield: 8 servings

Calories per serving: 266

Protein per serving: 5 g

Fat per serving: 5 g

Saturated fat per serving: 2 g

Cholesterol per serving: 33 mg

Carbohydrates per serving: 52 g

Sodium per serving: 318 mg

Fiber per serving: 3 g

For the Topping

2 tablespoons brown sugar

2 tablespoons oatmeal

1 tablespoon flour

1 ounce slivered almonds

1 teaspoon lemon zest

1 teaspoon butter

For the Cake

2 Bosc pears, peeled with a vegetable peeler, cut in half lengthwise, and
    cored

fat replacer to equal ½ cup shortening (prune puree base recommended);
    follow label instructions for amount

1 tablespoon butter, softened

⅔ cup sugar

½ teaspoon almond extract, or ¼ teaspoon almond extract plus 1 tablespoon
    almond liqueur, such as amaretto or Frangelica

1 egg plus 2 additional egg whites (or egg substitute to equal 2 eggs)

1 cup flour (4 ounces by weight)

1 teaspoon baking powder

¾ teaspoon salt

½ teaspoon ground ginger

To Prepare the Topping

1. Combine the brown sugar, oatmeal, flour, almonds, and lemon zest in a small bowl. Cut in the butter with your fingers and set aside.

To Prepare the Cake

2. Slice the pears lengthwise as thinly as possible. Set aside. Spray an 8½- or 9-inch round baking dish with cooking spray. Line with waxed paper or parchment paper. Preheat the oven to 350 degrees.

3. In a food processor or bowl, cream together the fat replacer, butter, sugar, and almond extract. Beat in the egg and egg whites.

4. Sift together twice the flour, baking powder, salt, and ginger. Sift these dry ingredients a third time directly into the food processor in two batches, just pulsing the machine to incorporate after each batch; overprocessing will make the cake porous and tough.

5. Pour the batter into the prepared pan. Ring the pear slices, like spokes on a wheel, over the batter, overlapping just to accommodate all the pears, covering any open surface with fruit. Sprinkle the topping over and bake in the upper third of the oven for 55 minutes or until a thin skewer inserted slightly off center comes out clean. Serve warm.

Makes 8 generous wedges.

SPICED OATMEAL MUFFINS

Basic, quick (once the oats have soaked), and good. Rolled oats are not to be confused with instant oatmeal—they are a precursor to that convenience and need an hour's soak before continuing with the recipe (they can soak overnight, in the fridge). Look for rolled oats near the regular oatmeal or in bulk in the "natural foods" section of many megamarkets. See the Index for additional ways to use leftover buttermilk.

Yield:10 servings

Calories per serving: 122

Protein per serving: 4 g

Fat per serving: 3 g

Saturated fat per serving: 1 g

Cholesterol per serving: 1 mg

Carbohydrates per serving: 19 g

Sodium per serving: 344 mg

Fiber per serving: 1 g

1 cup rolled oats

1 cup buttermilk

2 tablespoons soft margarine or butter

2 tablespoons brown sugar

1 egg or 2 egg whites

1 cup all-purpose flour (4 ounces by weight) or ½ cup all-purpose flour and
*   ½ cup whole wheat flour*

1 teaspoon baking powder

¾ teaspoon salt

½ teaspoon baking soda

½ teaspoon cinnamon

dash (about 1/16 teaspoon) of both ground cloves and nutmeg

cinnamon sugar for topping (optional)

1. Stir together the oats and buttermilk and let rest for at least 1 hour (at room temperature) or as long as 10 hours in the fridge.

2. Preheat the oven to 400 degrees. Line 10 3-inch muffin cups with paper liners.

3. In a bowl or food processor, beat together the margarine, brown sugar, and egg until frothy. Stir in the oats-buttermilk mixture.

4. Sift together the flour, baking powder, salt, baking soda, cinnamon, cloves, and nutmeg.

5. Sift the dry ingredients in three batches into the wet ingredients in the food processor, just pulsing after each addition; overprocessing will make the muffins tough.

6. Using an ice cream scoop, divide the batter among the muffin cups, filling each about three-quarters full. Sprinkle tops with cinnamon sugar, if desired.

7. Bake 20 minutes or until a thin skewer comes out clean when inserted slightly off center into one muffin.

Makes 10 medium muffins

MARY'S BLUEBERRY CRUNCH MUFFINS

The original, fattier version of this classic came from a family friend who bred smooth-haired terriers in rural Connecticut. As a teenage houseguest and eager kennel hand, I awoke to the smell of these muffins mingling with the grassy smell of dewy meadows. Mary's recipe is now yellowed, spattered, and torn, but my memories spring alive when these lower-fat versions come from the oven. They freeze beautifully. For the Nutrabyte on fat replacers, see page 262.

For the Topping

2 tablespoons sugar

1 tablespoon flour

½ teaspoon cinnamon

1 teaspoon lemon zest

1 teaspoon butter

Yield: 8 servings

Calories per serving: 142

Protein per serving: 3 g

Fat per serving: 1 g

Saturated fat per serving: trace

Cholesterol per serving: 1 mg

Carbohydrates per serving: 31 g

Sodium per serving: 227 mg

Fiber per serving: 1 g

For the Muffins

apple fat replacer to equal 2 tablespoons butter

6 tablespoons sugar

2 egg whites

¼ cup skim milk

zest of 1 lemon

1 cup flour

1 teaspoon baking powder

½ teaspoon salt

1 cup blueberries, frozen or fresh

To Prepare the Topping

1. Preheat the oven to 350 degrees. Line 8 3-inch muffin tins with paper liners. In a small bowl combine the sugar, flour, cinnamon, and lemon zest; cut in the butter with your fingers. Set aside.

To Prepare the Muffins

2. In a food processor or medium-size bowl, beat together the fat replacer, sugar, egg whites, milk, and lemon zest.

3. Sift together twice the flour, baking powder, and salt. Sift the dry ingredients again, in two batches, into the wet ingredients in the food processor, just pulsing after each addition.

4. Stir in the blueberries, and divide the mixture among the muffin cups. Sprinkle the Topping over the muffins.

5. Bake in the upper third of the oven for 15 minutes or until a skewer inserted slightly off center comes out clean.

    Makes 8 muffins

BERRIES AND ALMOND CREAM

Fresh strawberries, blueberries, or raspberries smothered in cream—sweet heaven that can be yours given *The New Gourmet Light* touch. This custard sauce, with the texture of clotted cream and the fragrance of almond, is wonderful over fresh, ripe fruits or as a dipping sauce for a fruit fondue, all for a meager 55 calories and 1 gram of fat. It is also delightful spooned over slices of Almond Angel Food Cake, page 258. Perhaps the best endorsement is from a friend, who mused, "Mmmmmmmmm, it tastes fattening!"

Yield: 6 servings

Calories per serving: 104

Protein per serving: 6 g

Fat per serving: 1 g

Saturated fat per serving: trace

Cholesterol per serving: 37 mg

Carbohydrates per serving: 18 g

Sodium per serving: 71 mg

Fiber per serving: 3 g

For the Almond Cream

1½ cups skim milk

3 egg whites

1 egg

3 tablespoons sugar

1 teaspoon almond extract

a few gratings fresh nutmeg

For the Berries

1 quart fresh strawberries or other berries, stemmed and rinsed

1 tablespoon sugar

1. Scald the milk in a heavy-bottom 1-quart saucepan. *Alternatively, in a microwave oven at high (100 percent power), heat the milk in a 4-cup measuring cup or other microwave-safe container for 5 minutes or until scalded.*

2. While the milk heats, process the egg whites and egg in the bowl of a food processor on high for 1 minute.

3. With the food processor on high, dribble the scalded milk into the eggs. Add the sugar. Continue to process for an additional 2 to 3 minutes.

4. Pour the egg-milk mixture into a heavy-bottom 2½-quart saucepan. Place over medium-high heat, stirring constantly in a figure-eight pattern with a

wooden spoon. As mixture begins to emit steam wisps, lower heat to medium. Continue to stir until custard doubles in volume and begins to thicken. Reduce heat if sauce nears the boiling point. The custard will condense, thicken to the consistency of melted ice cream, and coat a metal spoon. This happens when the sauce reaches about 175 degrees, in a total cooking time of about 6 minutes.

5. Strain the sauce into a bowl. Stir in the extract and nutmeg. The sauce can be served warm, at room temperature, or chilled.

6. Clean the berries. Cut strawberries in half, if desired. Toss with the tablespoon sugar. Divide berries among serving dishes and spoon on Almond Cream.

Note: Some chefs like to toss fresh strawberries with just a touch of black pepper, on the premise that it heightens their flavor.

BURGUNDY POACHED PEARS WITH CREME ANGLAISE

For this variation on a classic dessert, poached pears perched atop a puddle of custard sauce are gently broiled until lightly browned. The components of the dish may be readied a day before, then assembled up to 4 hours before serving. The poaching liquid may be frozen and reused over and over again.

Yield: 4 servings

Calories per serving: 185

Protein per serving: 6 g

Fat per serving: 1 g

Saturated fat per serving: trace

Cholesterol per serving: 1 mg

Carbohydrates per serving: 41 g

Sodium per serving: 226 mg

Fiber per serving: 4 g

4 pears, peeled, halved, and cored

2 tablespoons lemon juice

For the Poaching Liquid

1 liter burgundy wine

½ cup sugar

1 vanilla bean

juice of ½ lemon

1 cinnamon stick

3 whole cloves

For the Crème Anglaise

¾ cup egg substitute

3 tablespoons sugar

¼ teaspoon salt

1 cup skim milk, scalded

1 teaspoon vanilla extract

To Prepare the Pears

1. As you peel the pears, slip them into a bowl of water with the lemon juice to keep them from turning brown.

2. Bring the poaching ingredients to a boil in a 4-quart saucepan. Reduce to a simmer, immerse the pears, cover, and poach until a skewer easily pierces the fruit. Turn the pears during cooking, as they will not be completely covered. Do not cook until mushy. The cooking time will depend entirely on the ripeness of the fruit, anywhere from 10 to 25 minutes or even longer.

3. Drain the pears when tender on a rack over a sheet of waxed paper (to collect drippings). Freeze liquid for future poachings (you can leave the spices in the wine).

To Prepare the Crème Anglaise

1. In a heavy 2½-quart saucepan, beat together the egg substitute, sugar, and salt. Do not ribbon the mixture (do not overbeat).

2. Slowly add the scalded milk, whisking all the while.

3. Insert a thermometer at the side of the pan if you like. Stirring with a wooden spoon over medium heat, notice the changes that occur. At 140 degrees steam rises from the custard. At 155 degrees the foam starts getting lighter, and at 165 degrees the surface is smooth and the custard is ready. You may heat the custard to 180 degrees, but not higher, or the eggs will curdle. Without a thermometer, stir the custard over medium heat until it is thick enough to coat a metal spoon, about 3 to 4 minutes.

4. Strain the custard into a bowl and stir in vanilla extract.

To Finish the Dessert

1. Preheat broiler. Spread the custard sauce on an ovenproof serving dish, such as a quiche dish, or on 4 ovenproof serving dishes, such as baking shells.

2. Place the poached pear half, flat side down, on a cutting surface. Cut into 5 to 6 segments, but leave stem end uncut so the pear becomes "fanned." Repeat with remaining pears. Place the pear fan on the custard sauce and broil until heated through.

Note: A few drops of red food coloring added to the poaching liquid will heighten the color of the poached pears.

Making a Pear Fan

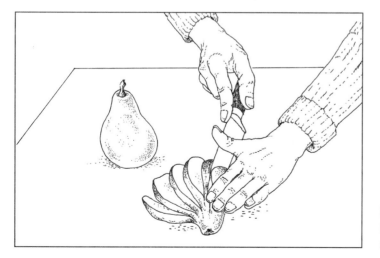

Place a poached pear half, flat side down, on a flat surface. Cut it on the diagonal into five or six segments, leaving them attached at the stem end.

CANDIED ORANGES WITH MELBA SAUCE

The simplicity of this classic dessert I find very appealing—juicy seedless oranges enhanced with a sugar syrup and drizzled with ruby-red raspberry sauce. It may be prepared a day in advance.

8 small navel oranges

¾ cup sugar

1½ cups water

juice of ½ lemon

2 kiwis

2 tablespoons orange-flavored liqueur, such as Triple Sec or Grand Marnier

1 10-ounce package frozen raspberries, thawed

Yield: 8 servings

Calories per serving: 178

Protein per serving: 1 g

Fat per serving: trace

Saturated fat per serving: trace

Cholesterol per serving: none

Carbohydrates per serving: 44 g

Sodium per serving: 3 mg

Fiber per serving: 4 g

1. With a vegetable peeler remove the zest (no white) from 2 of the oranges. Julienne the rind and set aside.

2. In a heavy 2½-quart saucepan, dissolve the sugar in ½ cup of the water over very low heat. The solution must not boil until the sugar is thoroughly dissolved or it will crystallize. Do not stir the sugar as it dissolves, but swirl the pan by its handle.

3. When all the sugar is dissolved, add the remaining cup of water, the lemon juice, and the julienned orange peel. Bring to a boil for 30 seconds, then lower the heat so solution simmers. Cover and simmer 1 hour.

4. Meanwhile peel the oranges over a bowl to catch the juices. Peel the kiwis. Slice both the oranges and the kiwis thinly horizontally. Reshape the oranges into their original form, interspersing the kiwi slices between the orange slices. Hold together with toothpicks. Pile into a deep glass bowl and chill until serving time.

5. Remove the sugar syrup from heat. Stir in the orange-flavored liqueur. Pour it over the oranges.

6. Place the berries in a food processor or blender and puree. Force the puree through a strainer. Discard the seeds. Stir in the orange juice from peeling the oranges in Step 4. Drizzle half the sauce over oranges and pass remaining sauce at the table.

Note: The oranges may be sauced with the sugar syrup and held at room temperature up to 6 hours before serving.

HOT APPLE TART

This thin apple tart, with its crust of phyllo and icing of Almond Cream (page 271), is best served hot. All components may be readied up to 4 hours in advance, then assembled and baked just prior to serving time. Poached pears may be used in addition to or instead of the apples. Leftovers may be gently reheated in a 300-degree oven for 10 minutes.

Yield: 4 servings

Calories per serving: 159

Protein per serving: 4 g

Fat per serving: 6 g

Saturated fat per serving: 2 g

Cholesterol per serving: 22 mg

Carbohydrates per serving: 23 g

Sodium per serving: 126 mg

Fiber per serving: 1 g

½ ounce sliced or slivered almonds

2 tablespoons dried bread crumbs

1 tablespoon sugar

dash cinnamon

2 sheets phyllo dough

1 tablespoon butter, melted

1 apple, Granny Smith or Golden Delicious recommended

1 tablespoon brown sugar

4 tablespoons Almond Cream (page 271) or softened vanilla ice milk

1. Spray a 7½-inch, removable-bottom tart ring with cooking spray. You may use a slightly larger pan, but results won't be as pleasing.

2. In a food processor or blender, combine the almonds, bread crumbs, sugar, and cinnamon. Pulverize until they're fine crumbs. Set aside.

3. Lay a sheet of phyllo into the tart ring, vertically, overlapping it in the middle as you would a sheet of tissue paper in a box. Butter sparingly with a pastry brush dipped in the melted butter. Sprinkle with half the nut-crumb mixture.

4. Now lay another sheet in the pan, horizontally, also overlapping in the center. Butter very slightly and sprinkle with the remaining crumbs.

5. Fold the overhang inside the rim of the pan.

6. Slice the apple in half lengthwise, then into quarters. Core it. Slice the quarters very thinly. Arrange the apple slices over the tart ring in circles, with pieces of the apple resting on the phyllo dough rim. Brush all with the remaining butter. Sprinkle brown sugar over the apples. Set aside, if you wish.

7. When you're ready to complete the tart, preheat the oven to 425 degrees.

8. Place the tart in the lower third of the preheated oven for 20 minutes or until the apples are softened.

9. Spread Almond Cream over the apple tart and broil for 4 to 5 minutes or until the Almond Cream is bubbly and golden (or omit cream and serve with softened ice milk). Let the tart rest 5 minutes and serve. It can also be held up to 1 hour on a serving tray.

Nutrabyte

If you're trying to wean yourself from cream and/or sugar in coffee, try adding a 3-inch piece of vanilla bean or a cinnamon stick to the grounds when you make it. The added flavor will help.

GRAND MARNIER MOUSSE

This cool, cloudlike mousse literally melts in your mouth. It needs at least 2 hours' chilling time to set before serving; yet it should be served within 24 hours, as the egg whites break down with time.

1 envelope unflavored gelatin

¾ cup cold water

½ cup plus 2 tablespoons sugar

½ cup cold water

4 eggs

¼ teaspoon salt

⅔ cup freshly squeezed orange juice

zest of 1 orange

3 tablespoons orange-flavored liqueur, such as Grand Marnier or Triple Sec

2 tablespoons rum

Yield: 8 servings

Calories per serving: 128

Protein per serving: 4 g

Fat per serving: 3 g

Saturated fat per serving: 1 g

Cholesterol per serving: 106 mg

Carbohydrates per serving: 19 g

Sodium per serving: 101 mg

Fiber per serving: trace

1. Soften the gelatin in ¼ cup of the water in a glass measuring cup for about 2 minutes. Place the cup in a small saucepan one-third full of water and warm over medium heat, stirring occasionally, until gelatin is dissolved and clear, about 3 minutes. Set aside.

2. Meanwhile combine ½ cup of the sugar with the remaining ½ cup of water in a 1-quart saucepan. Dissolve the sugar over very low heat, swirling the pan by the handle. Do not stir with a spoon. When the solution is clear, turn the heat to high and boil 1 minute. Do not let sugar syrup begin to brown. Set it aside.

3. Separate the eggs. Break the egg yolks into the top part of a double boiler, the whites into a glass, ceramic, or copper bowl. Set the bottom of the double boiler with 1 inch of water over high heat. Insert the top half of double boiler. Beat the yolks over the simmering water until thickened and very pale in color, about 2 minutes. Regulating heat so the water just simmers, continue beating while dribbling in the hot sugar syrup from Step 2. Beat

until the mixture doubles in volume, thickens, and feels warm to the touch, about 6–8 minutes. Remove from heat and continue beating until mixture ribbons (falls from beaters in a wide band that lies on top of the mass for a moment before sinking in).

4. Stir the dissolved gelatin, salt, orange juice, zest, orange liqueur, and rum into the yolks.

5. Wash the beaters thoroughly and beat the egg whites until stiff. Gradually beat in the remaining 2 tablespoons sugar.

6. Fold the whites into the gelatin-yolk mixture.

7. Pour the mousse into individual glasses or a 6-cup mold sprayed with cooking spray. Chill at least 2 hours to set. Unmold if desired.

CREPES SUZETTE

Fussy and old-fashioned, but a low-calorie, low-fat dessert of the first order. The crepes and sauce may be readied early in the day, then assembled and flamed before serving to appreciative guests.

For the Crepes

⅓ cup egg substitute
¾ cup skim milk
6 tablespoons flour
pinch salt

For the Sauce

2 teaspoons butter
2 tablespoons sugar
2 tablespoons orange marmalade
1 tablespoon each orange and lemon zest
juice and pulp of 3 fresh oranges (reserve 2 tablespoons for dissolving cornstarch)

Yield: 4 servings

Calories per serving: 193

Protein per serving: 5 g

Fat per serving: 3 g

Saturated fat per serving: 1 g

Cholesterol per serving: 6 mg

Carbohydrates per serving: 34 g

Sodium per serving: 112 mg

Fiber per serving: 1 g

2 teaspoons cornstarch

1 tablespoon orange-flavored liqueur, such as Grand Marnier, curaçao, or
    Triple Sec

1 tablespoon kirsch (or use 2 tablespoons orange liqueur)

To Prepare the Crepes

1. Beat the egg substitute and milk together, add the flour sifted with the salt, and stir just to combine. Chill 2 hours.

2. Spray a nonstick 8-inch skillet with butter-flavored cooking spray. Ladle just enough batter into the pan to film bottom. Pour excess batter back into bowl when bottom sets. Cook a crepe over medium-high heat until browned on one side. Flip, cooking on underside just to firm (this will be the inside, unseen part), and slide onto a plate. Continue cooking, spraying with cooking spray as necessary and placing a sheet of waxed paper between the crepes. Crepes may now be used or chilled up to 12 hours or frozen until needed. The recipe makes 10 to 12 12-inch crepes.

To Prepare the Sauce

1. Combine butter, sugar, marmalade, orange and lemon zest, and juice and pulp of oranges in a 1-quart saucepan over medium heat until heated through.

2. Dissolve the cornstarch in the reserved juice. Stir into the hot orange sauce and cook over medium heat, stirring, until thickened, about 4 minutes.

To Assemble the Crepes and Serve

1. Fold the crepes in triangle shapes with the unbrowned side facing in, by folding first into halves and then into quarters. Arrange on a flameproof serving dish with sides, such as a quiche dish or a chafing dish. Overlap the crepes by ½ inch. If preparing early in the day, cover with aluminum foil. Before serving, sprinkle very lightly with water and heat in a 350-degree

Vanilla

Vanilla beans come from a variety of orchid. When fresh, the pods are green and oddly odorless, but when dried, they become incredibly fragrant. To make your own vanilla extract, split a vanilla bean in half and make a slit along its length to expose the minute tiny beans inside. Place the beans in a 2-ounce jar (an old vanilla extract bottle is perfect), fill it with vodka, cap the jar tightly, and let it rest 1 month in a cool, dark place. The resulting extract is wonderful in many desserts. Add 2 drops to the coffee beans in your next pot for a delicious cup of coffee.

oven for about 15 minutes, covered, until warmed through.

2. Pour the warmed sauce over the heated crepes. Keep them warm in the oven or over hot water in a chafing dish while preparing the liqueur for flaming.

3. Heat the liqueurs in a long-handled butter warmer; one with a lip is preferred. When bubbles appear at the pan's edge, remove from the heat. Place dish of warmed crepes on the table. Ignite liqueur with a fireplace match or other long taper. Pour the flaming liqueur over the crepes. Use a spoon to lift sauces as it flames. Serve when flames die out.

Flaming

Recipes frequently call for igniting liquor, sometimes for effect, sometimes to mellow the sharp alcohol taste. For success with flaming liquors, remember the following tips:

* The liquor must be heated just to the point where small bubbles appear at the edges of the pan.

* If it boils longer than about 10 to 20 seconds, add more liquor.

* Add a pinch of sugar to ensure long burning.

* Select a long-handled, small pot, preferably with a spout, to heat the liquor. Butter warmers are ideal.

MIMOSA SHERBET

Celebrate your success with this champagne-based sherbet. While it may be made without an ice cream freezer simply by hardening in a conventional freezer, it will have a smoother texture if processed in an ice cream freezer.

1 scant cup sugar
⅞ cup water
juice of 1 orange
1 cup brut champagne
1 tablespoon orange-flavored liqueur, such as Triple Sec or Grand Marnier
2 egg whites
mint leaves (optional)

1. Combine sugar and water in a 2½-quart saucepan. Swirl the pan by the handle over very low heat until the sugar is dissolved. Do not stir. When the solution is perfectly clear and the sugar is dissolved, raise heat to high and boil without stirring for 7 minutes.

2. Remove the sugar water from heat, pour it into a bowl, and place in the freezer for 15 minutes.

3. Remove from freezer and stir in orange juice, champagne, and orange liqueur.

4. Beat egg whites until stiff, then fold them into champagne mixture. Freeze in an ice cream freezer according to the manufacturer's instructions. Sherbet will be soft after processing. Place in freezer to harden. Garnish with mint leaves, if desired.

Yield: 6 servings
Calories per serving: 158
Protein per serving: 1 g
Fat per serving: trace
Saturated fat per serving: trace
Cholesterol per serving: none
Carbohydrates per serving: 32 g
Sodium per serving: 22 mg
Fiber per serving: trace

Nutrabyte

Other words for sugar on labels:

fructose
fruit juice concentrate
glucose (dextrose)
high-fructose corn syrup
lactose
maltose

RASPBERRY CREPES SOUFFLÉ

This showy dessert—a raspberry meringue folded inside a thin crepe, which in turn is doused with more raspberry—waits for no one. It needs to be served immediately from the oven, or a slumped collection of crepes will be all you will have to show for your efforts. The crepes and the meringue soufflé mixture, however, may be readied and assembled days in advance, frozen, and baked without thawing, making a light and lovely dessert that takes just 20 minutes from freezer to table.

Yield: 6 to 8 servings

Calories per serving: 107

Protein per serving: 4 g

Fat per serving: 1 g

Saturated fat per serving: trace

Cholesterol per serving: 28 mg

Carbohydrates per serving: 21 g

Sodium per serving: 64 mg

Fiber per serving: 1 g

For the Crepes

1 egg, beaten, or ¼ cup egg substitute

½ cup nonfat milk

¼ cup flour

pinch salt

1 tablespoon sugar

1 tablespoon orange zest

For the Soufflé

1 10-ounce package frozen unsweetened raspberries, thawed (fresh, of
*   course, would be wonderful)*

4 egg whites

½ teaspoon cream of tartar

4 tablespoons sugar (slightly more for fresh berries)

1 teaspoon cornstarch or arrowroot

1 tablespoon orange-flavored liqueur, such as Grand Marnier or Triple Sec

To Prepare the Crepes

1. Beat the egg and milk together, add the flour (sifted with the pinch of salt) and remaining ingredients, and stir just to combine. Chill for 2 hours.

2. Spray a nonstick 8-inch skillet with nonstick cooking spray. Place skillet

over high heat. Ladle just enough batter into the pan to film bottom. Pour excess batter back into bowl after bottom has set. Cook crepe over medium-high heat until browned on one side. Flip, cook on underside just to firm (this will be the inside, unseen part of the crepe), and slide onto a plate. Continue cooking, spraying skillet as necessary. Place a sheet of waxed paper between the cooked crepes. Crepes may now be used or chilled or frozen until needed. The recipe makes 6 to 8 6-inch crepes.

To Prepare the Soufflé

1. Preheat the oven to 350 degrees. Spray an ovenproof serving dish large enough to hold 8 folded crepes with cooking spray.

2. Puree the raspberries in a food processor or blender. Strain and discard the seeds.

3. Measure ⅓ cup raspberry puree and set it aside.

4. Beat egg whites until foamy. Add cream of tartar, gradually beat in sugar, and beat until just shy of stiff peaks.

5. Fold the ⅓ cup raspberry puree into the beaten egg whites. Divide soufflé mixture among the crepes, placing about 3 heaping tablespoons on the unbrowned side of each crepe. (Discard or cook separately any leftover soufflé.) Fold crepe ends to middle. Place crepes seam-side down in prepared ovenproof dish. Crepes can now be frozen, or they must be baked immediately. Bake unfrozen crepes soufflés 12 to 15 minutes (bake frozen crepes soufflés 15 to 20 minutes) or until puffed and golden. Serve with confectioners' sugar sifted on top or the following sauce.

6. Combine the remaining raspberry puree with cornstarch dissolved in the orange liqueur. Cook, whisking over medium-low heat, until slightly thickened, about 2 minutes. Film serving plates with thickened raspberry puree, place puffed crepe soufflé on top, or drizzle raspberry puree over the crepe soufflé.

CHAPTER 11

STOCKS
AND SAUCES

THE RECIPES

Stocks

Sauces

Other

THE FOUNDATIONS

In the Primer we covered the fundamentals that can help you lose weight or maintain weight loss without depriving yourself of the enjoyment of good food. The following are the foundations upon which this cooking style is built: the stocks, or enriched commercial products; reduced-calorie sauces, such as Hollandaise and Béarnaise; and more.

TAKING STOCK

Because stocks and broths are used extensively in *The New Gourmet Light* cooking, you might like to make your own. The microwave makes this otherwise time-consuming process infinitely quicker. If you do make stock on the stovetop, I'd suggest doing it in large quantities and freezing the stock in various-size containers. Canned broths may be used or enriched with additional bones and/or vegetables if added flavor or thickness is desired. Commercially prepared consommé is an excellent alternative, because the added gelatin nicely equates the natural thickness of a homemade stock.

BEEF STOCK

8 pounds uncooked beef bones, marrow bones highly recommended

3 carrots, sliced (no need to peel)

3 small to medium onions, sliced (no need to peel; the skins add color)

3 celery stalks, sliced

7 quarts water

1 cup red wine (optional)

a small handful fresh parsley stems, chopped

freshly ground pepper to taste

1 bay leaf

1 clove garlic, halved

Yield: 4 quarts

Calories per cup: 17

Protein per cup: 2 g

Fat per cup: 1 g

Saturated fat per cup: trace

Cholesterol per cup: 4 mg

Carbohydrates per cup: 1 g

Sodium per cup: 18 mg

Fiber per cup: trace

1. Put the bones and vegetables in a 12-quart stockpot, cover with the water, add the wine, and bring to a full boil.

2. Reduce heat to a simmer and, with a slotted spoon, scrape the scum that rises to the surface. Repeat scrapings two or three times until most of the scum is removed.

3. Add parsley, pepper, bay leaf, and garlic. Half-cover the pan and simmer about 8 hours, adding more water if the volume falls more than a quart below the original.

4. Wring out an old kitchen towel or a piece of cheesecloth in cold water and line a strainer with it. Pour or ladle the stock through the strainer.

5. If using the stock immediately, pour what you need into a degreaser to complete the defatting, or refrigerate the stock. A pancake of fat will form that is easily scraped off. Freeze stock in plastic containers of various sizes.

Meat Glaze (Demi-Glace)

Like an expensive perfume, meat glaze is used sparingly—a little goes a long way. One-half to 1 teaspoon's worth in a sauce boosts the flavor exponentially. It is truly a chef's secret.

To make it, boil down homemade broth until you have an iridescent, deep brown syrup, thick enough to coat a metal spoon. Watch the glaze carefully at the end, for it can burn easily. Meat glaze will keep in the refrigerator in a sterile glass jar for about 2 weeks.

Demi-glace can also be purchased from a mail-order source such as More Than Gourmet. (See Shopping Sources, page 306.)

Microwave Beef Stock

The microwave makes quick work of homemade stock. Stock may be frozen with no flavor loss up to 6 months.

Yield: 4 cups

Calories per cup: 9

Protein per cup: trace

Fat per cup: trace

Saturated fat per cup: trace

Cholesterol per cup: none

Carbohydrates per cup: 2 g

Sodium per cup: 125 mg

Fiber per cup: none

8 cups water

5 to 6 pounds beef marrow bones

1 cup red wine (optional)

3 carrots, roughly chopped

2 stalks celery, roughly chopped

2 cloves garlic, halved, unpeeled

1 teaspoon fresh thyme leaves or ½ teaspoon dried thyme

1 teaspoon liquid beef bouillon

4 to 5 parsley sprigs

1. Combine all ingredients in a 1-gallon, microwave-safe container. Cover and microwave at high (100 percent power) for 90 minutes.

2. Strain into a bowl. Discard bones. Press vegetables with the back of a spoon to extract juices. Discard contents of strainer.

3. Refrigerate stock until fat coagulates on the surface, about 6 hours.

4. Discard fat. If desired, strain stock through a double thickness of moistened cheesecloth or a moistened coffee filter. You may find it necessary to heat the last cup or so of stock to facilitate straining, because it will be so thick from the naturally occurring gelatin. Stirring the stock as it strains will also speed the process.

CHICKEN STOCK

5 to 6 pounds uncooked chicken bones (saved from boning breasts, or buy
wings and backs and discard skin)
2 to 3 carrots, sliced (no need to peel)
2 medium onions, sliced
2 celery stalks, sliced
4 quarts water
1 cup dry white wine (optional)
a small handful fresh parsley stems, chopped
freshly ground pepper to taste
1 bay leaf
1 clove garlic, halved

Yield: 3 quarts
Calories per cup: 6
Protein per cup: 1 g
Fat per cup: trace
Saturated fat per cup: trace
Cholesterol per cup: 3 mg
Carbohydrates per cup: none
Sodium per cup: 9 mg
Fiber per cup: none

1. Place bones and vegetables in a 12-quart stockpot, cover with the water, and add the wine. Bring to a boil.

2. Reduce heat to a simmer and, with a slotted spoon, scrape the scum that rises to the surface. Repeat scrapings two or three times until most of the scum is removed.

3. Add the parsley, pepper, bay leaf, and garlic. Half-cover the pan and simmer about 4 hours, adding more water if the volume falls more than a quart below the original.

4. Wring out an old kitchen towel or a piece of cheesecloth in water and line a strainer with it. Pour or ladle the stock through the strainer.

5. If using the stock immediately, pour what you need into a degreaser to complete the defatting, or refrigerate until a pancake of fat forms. Scrape off the fat and freeze the stock in plastic containers of varying sizes.

Microwave Chicken Stock

The microwave makes quick work of homemade chicken stock. Freeze the stock without flavor loss for up to 6 months. There's no need to peel the onion, as the skins lend color.

2 pounds uncooked chicken bones (or wings and backs, skin discarded)

10 cups water

3 stalks celery, roughly chopped

2 or 3 carrots, roughly chopped

1 small yellow onion, unpeeled and quartered

1 clove garlic, unpeeled and halved

a few sprigs fresh thyme or ½ teaspoon dried thyme

3 to 4 sprigs fresh parsley

½ teaspoon salt

1. Combine all ingredients in a 1-gallon, microwave-safe container. Cover and microwave at high (100 percent power) for 90 minutes.

2. Strain into a bowl. Discard bones. Press vegetables with the back of a spoon to extract juices. Discard contents of strainer.

3. Refrigerate stock until fat coagulates on the surface, about 6 hours.

4. Discard fat. If desired, strain stock through a double thickness of moistened cheesecloth or a moistened coffee filter. You may find it necessary to heat the last cup or so of stock to facilitate straining, because it will be so thick from the naturally occurring gelatin. Stirring the stock as it strains will also speed the process.

Yield: **2 quarts**

Calories per cup: 6

Protein per cup: trace

Fat per cup: trace

Saturated fat per cup: trace

Cholesterol per cup: none

Carbohydrates per cup: 1 g

Sodium per cup: 148 mg

Fiber per cup: trace

QUICK TIP

To quickly defat chicken or beef broth, pour it into a degreaser (looks like a measuring cup with the spout coming off the bottom) and place in the freezer until cool. The fat-free broth will pour from the bottom, leaving the grease behind.

ENRICHED QUICK COMMERCIAL BEEF OR CHICKEN BROTH

½ pound uncooked beef or chicken bones

3 unpeeled carrots, sliced

1 onion, chopped

1 quart canned beef or chicken broth

½ cup red or white wine (optional)

1 bay leaf

1 clove garlic, halved

freshly ground pepper to taste

a small handful fresh parsley stems, chopped

Yield: 3½ cups

Calories per cup: 23

Protein per cup: 4 g

Fat per cup: 1 g

Saturated fat per cup: trace

Cholesterol per cup: 4 mg

Carbohydrates per cup: none

Sodium per cup: 104 mg

Fiber per cup: none

1. Put all ingredients in a 2½-quart saucepan, half-cover, and simmer 30 minutes.

2. Broth may be used immediately after straining and discarding bones, vegetables, and herbs.

Ice Cube Stock

Freeze homemade stock in ice cube trays and pop the frozen cubes into a plastic bag. Use when a few tablespoons of broth are called for to "sauté" an ingredient.

VEGETABLE STOCK

Any other vegetable parings or bits and pieces you happen to have—such as mushroom stems; celeriac trimmings; a fennel bulb; a leek, including the green tops; or a half a green pepper—are fine here. The recipe doubles and freezes well too.

7 cups water

1 cup wine (or water if preferred)

1 onion, peeled and roughly chopped

3 medium carrots, roughly chopped

3 celery ribs, roughly chopped

1 potato, scrubbed but unpeeled and roughly chopped

3 cloves garlic, halved but not peeled

½ bunch parsley, roughly chopped

2 bay leaves

1 teaspoon fresh thyme leaves or ½ teaspoon dried thyme

6 to 7 peppercorns

Yield: 6 cups

Calories per cup: 10

Protein per cup: 1 g

Fat per cup: trace

Saturated fat per cup: none

Cholesterol per cup: none

Carbohydrates per cup: 2 g

Sodium per cup: 4 mg

Fiber per cup: none

1. Combine all ingredients in a 4-quart stockpot. Cover and bring to a boil over high heat. Remove cover and simmer 1 hour.

2. Strain. Press solids with the back of a spoon to release juices. Refrigerate stock for up to one week; bring to a boil before using.

   Makes 6 cups

Nutrabyte

The number one killer of women? Not breast cancer, but heart disease. Eat to protect your health.

FISH STOCK

This delicate stock must be frozen if not used within 24 hours.

1 fish rack (skeleton), weighing about 1½ pounds, from a white-fleshed,
*   nonoily fish such as haddock or cod, innards removed and rack rinsed*
6 cups water
2 cups dry white wine (optional)
1 small onion, chopped
1 small carrot, chopped
1 bay leaf

Yield: 1 quart
Calories per cup: 9
Protein per cup: 1 g
Fat per cup: trace
Saturated fat per cup: trace
Cholesterol per cup: 3 mg
Carbohydrates per cup: trace
Sodium per cup: 12 mg
Fiber per cup: trace

1. Put the fish rack (don't shy away from using the head, as it contains lots of collagen, which melts into gelatin) in a heavy pot, preferably nonaluminum if using the wine, and add the water and wine.

2. Bring to a boil, reduce heat so liquid just simmers, and scrape the scum away with a slotted spoon. When most of the scum is removed, add the remaining ingredients and half-cover pot. Simmer 40 minutes.

3. Rinse out an old kitchen towel or a piece of cheesecloth in water, line a strainer with it, and pour or ladle stock through. Refrigerate or freeze stock.

Note: Bottled clam juice is a very acceptable substitute in recipes calling for fish stock. Dilute the bottled product with ¼ cup dry white wine or vermouth to 8 ounces clam juice and omit salt from the recipe—or use concentrated clam broth base (see Shopping Sources, page 306).

QUICK TIP

Concentrated broth bases—with a thick, pastelike consistency—are superior to bouillon cubes and offer more flavor than canned broths. A teaspoon or less stirred into a lackluster sauce adds flavor and color or stir a little into the water used to cook rice, pasta, or vegetables. Watch added salt in the recipe, however, as these broth bases tend to be very salty. They come in beef, chicken, mushroom, clam, and lobster flavors. See Shopping Sources (page 306) for one brand.

THE TRADEMARKS OF CLASSIC COOKING—SAUCES

The cynosures of fine cooking are frequently the sauces: lemony Hollandaise ribboning asparagus, rich and pungent Béarnaise complementing a flavorfully steamed fish. *The New Gourmet Light* cooking doesn't deny the lover of good food the pleasures of the table. Here are the reduced-calorie and reduced-fat versions of such classic recipes.

Egg-Based Sauces

Egg-based sauces owe their creamy richness to the emulsion that forms when egg yolks poach in butter and an acid such as lemon juice (Hollandaise), vinegar (Béarnaise), or wine. You'll find my thin versions of these sauces packed with flavor that belies their lightness. These sauces may be prepared ahead and gently reheated, with little danger of curdling or separating.

The New Gourmet Light version of the classic Hollandaise is much less fattening (8 calories per tablespoon and .5 fat gram, compared with 67 calories and 7 fat grams for the traditional recipe), tastes lighter, holds better than the traditional sauce, and may even be gently reheated.

QUICK TIP

Always store lemons—tomatoes too—at room temperature, out of direct sunlight, for maximum juiciness and flavor.

HOLLANDAISE SAUCE

The directions look forbidding, but this recipe is easily done. The explicitness is an attempt to control the variables that could sabotage the sauce. This is delicious on poached eggs (the American Heart Association says you can have three eggs a week), broccoli, asparagus, and delicate white fish fillets. It's just fine served at room temperature, so make it up to an hour in advance and gently reheat on very low heat, whisking constantly. Leftovers (unlikely) are excellent mixed with a little mustard and used as a sandwich, pretzel, or raw vegetable dip. Lacking an immersion blender, the sauce will take a bit longer to thicken.

Note: The sauce thickens as it sits—don't overcook or it will curdle.

Yield: 1 cup
Calories per 2 tbsp serving: 16
Protein per 2 tbsp serving: 1 g
Fat per 2 tbsp serving: 1 g
Saturated fat per 2 tbsp serving: 1 g
Cholesterol per 2 tbsp serving: 3 mg
Carbohydrates per 2 tbsp serving: 1 g
Sodium per 2 tbsp serving: 23 mg
Fiber per 2 tbsp serving: none

> *¾ cup rich chicken broth*
> *4 tablespoons lemon juice (the juice of 1 lemon)*
> *⅓ cup plus 2 tablespoons egg substitute*
> *1 tablespoon whipped butter (or other spread of choice, but not light butter)*
> *salt and pepper to taste*

1. Bring the broth and lemon juice to a rolling boil in a 1-quart or smaller heavy-bottomed saucepan. (Although the reduction will happen faster in a larger pan, you're likely to end up with a spattered stove during Step 3.) When a boil is reached, set a timer for 5 minutes and continue to boil until the liquid reduces to about ½ cup.

2. Meanwhile, in a glass measure whisk the egg substitute with an immersion blender (use the chopping attachment, *not* the whisk) for about 1 minute or until the egg quadruples in volume to the 1-cup mark.

3. When broth is reduced, add the butter; boil just until it is melted. For ease pour the broth into a measure with a good pouring lip, such as a fat separator. Slowly drizzle broth into the egg while whisking at slow speed (remember to reduce the setting after the first whisking or you'll be covered in egg splatter!).

4. When the glass measure can hold no more, pour the mixture into the now empty saucepan and place over medium-low heat, whisking constantly in both directions, for 30 seconds or until thickened. Remove from heat and continue to whisk, to cool somewhat to prevent curdling, for 30 seconds more. Season with salt and pepper.

Makes 1 cup plus 2 tablespoons

Variations

1. Make a maltaise sauce (yummy on asparagus) by substituting orange juice for the lemon juice and adding 1 teaspoon lemon juice and the zest of 1 orange. If you have leftover gremolata (page 172), add a pinch for garnish.

2. If you have yogurt cheese (page 305) on hand, combine 1 part yogurt cheese with 2 parts Hollandaise in a small bowl and microwave briefly to meld. Delicious with fish or chicken. Garnish with a pinch of minced herbs.

Troubleshooting

The sauce overcooked and curdled: Process with a little lemon juice in a blender or food processor.

The sauce didn't thicken, even after sitting at room temperature for 10 minutes: Next time be sure to measure the lemon juice, as the full 4 tablespoons is needed to set the emulsion. Also be sure to reduce the liquid to the required amount. For now whisk 1 or 2 more tablespoons of egg substitute into the sauce over medium heat, whisking with an immersion blender until sauce is the consistency of melted ice cream. It will thicken on standing.

BÉARNAISE SAUCE

Much less finicky than a traditional Béarnaise sauce, this recipe may well become a staple at your house as it has at mine. It can be gently reheated in a microwave oven at medium (50 percent power) for about 30 seconds. It is excellent with fish, chicken, beef, or vegetables. Cold Béarnaise makes an excellent dip for crudités.

4 tablespoons red wine vinegar

1 tablespoon minced shallot

1 tablespoon minced fresh tarragon or 1 teaspoon dried tarragon

½ cup egg substitute

¼ cup chicken broth

1 tablespoon butter (not light butter)

salt and pepper to taste

1. Combine the vinegar, shallot, and tarragon in a 3-cup, heavy-bottomed saucepan. Boil over high heat until reduced by half to about 2 tablespoons liquid.

2. Meanwhile process the egg substitute in a food processor (or use an immersion blender) for about 30 seconds on full power.

3. Add the chicken broth and butter to the vinegar mixture. Heat over high heat until the butter is melted.

4. Dribble the vinegar-broth mixture into the egg substitute with the food processor (or immersion blender) on high.

5. Return mixture to the saucepan. Whisk continually over high heat, reducing, if necessary, to prevent mixture from curdling. Sauce will thicken in about 4 minutes (less with an immersion blender) and continue to thicken as it cools. It may be made ahead and gently reheated on the stovetop or in the microwave. It keeps, chilled, up to 1 week.

Yield: ½ cup

Calories per tablespoon: 25

Protein per tablespoon: 2 g

Fat per tablespoon: 2 g

Saturated fat per tablespoon: 1 g

Cholesterol per tablespoon: 4 mg

Carbohydrates per tablespoon: 1 g

Sodium per tablespoon: 41 mg

Fiber per tablespoon: none

Variations

1. Add 1 tablespoon tomato paste to the finished Béarnaise to make Sauce Robert. This is an excellent sauce with meats.

2. Horseradish Béarnaise is delicious as a spread for cold roast beef. Add 2 teaspoons prepared or freshly grated horseradish to the finished Béarnaise.

Mayonnaise Variations

To 1¼ cups fat-free mayonnaise, add any of the following:

2 tablespoons chopped fresh dill for use with fish salads.

2 tablespoons chopped fresh basil for use with tomatoes (or use 1 teaspoon dried basil).

1 tablespoon chopped dill pickles, 1 tablespoon capers, 1 tablespoon fresh tarragon (or 1 teaspoon dried tarragon), and 1 tablespoon chopped chives for a gribiche sauce for steamed or poached fish.

1 tablespoon horseradish and 1 tablespoon minced fresh parsley for use with cold roast beef.

3 tablespoons tomato paste, 3 tablespoons minced green pepper, and 1 teaspoon snipped chives for use with ground chicken or turkey burgers or as a dip for raw vegetables.

¼ cup either Pesto (page 301) or Red Pepper Butter (page 124).

LEMON-HERB SPREAD

A chameleon of a spread, this lively blend of herbs spiked with flavors of raspberry and lemon becomes whatever you make of it. Smear it on thickly sliced tomatoes, top with a smattering of Parmesan-Reggiano cheese, and broil until heated through. Toss with pasta for a hearty lunch or a light dinner. Spread it on grilling chicken or a thick fish steak such as halibut for instant pizzazz. As is, it's a delightful dip for crudités. Don't feel a slave to the proportions here, as they are really just a guideline; taste and correct the seasoning to complement the spread's purpose. Leftovers will keep about 5 days, refrigerated.

Yield: ⅔ cup

Calories per tablespoon: 20

Protein per tablespoon: trace

Fat per tablespoon: 1 g

Saturated fat per tablespoon: trace

Cholesterol per tablespoon: none

Carbohydrates per tablespoon: 2 g

Sodium per tablespoon: 137 mg

Fiber per tablespoon: trace

½ cup each tightly packed parsley and watercress leaves

3 tablespoons dried bread crumbs

juice of ½ lemon (about 2 tablespoons)

2 tablespoons consommé or chicken broth

1 tablespoon raspberry vinegar or other fruity vinegar

1 tablespoon low-fat mayonnaise

2 teaspoons lemon oil (see Shopping Sources, page 306)

2 cloves roasted garlic (page 305) or 1 clove raw garlic

1 teaspoon capers, drained

½ teaspoon salt

pepper to taste

1. Rinse the parsley and watercress well. Squeeze out excess moisture in a towel. Mince in a food processor.

2. Add all remaining ingredients to the food processor and puree. Taste for seasoning.

Makes ⅔ cup

Pesto

The New Gourmet Light version has one-fourth the calories of a traditional pesto sauce. Its uses go far beyond a simple and delicious toss with pasta (a wonderful hot-weather dinner). Brush it on grilling chicken or fish during the last few minutes of cooking, dab it on sun-warmed tomatoes, or stir it into a cool bowl of fresh Chilled Tomato Soup (page 50).

Yield: ¾ cup

Calories per tablespoon: 11

Protein per tablespoon: 1 g

Fat per tablespoon: 1 g

Saturated fat per tablespoon: trace

Cholesterol per tablespoon: 1 mg

Carbohydrates per tablespoon: 1 g

Sodium per tablespoon: 17 mg

Fiber per tablespoon: trace

> *½ cup fresh parsley, snipped and loosely packed*
>
> *½ cup fresh basil, snipped and loosely packed*
>
> *1 tablespoon balsamic or malt vinegar*
>
> *2 tablespoons grated Parmesan-Reggiano cheese*
>
> *1 teaspoon sugar*
>
> *2 tablespoons chicken broth, more if a thinner sauce is desired*
>
> *1 clove garlic, minced*
>
> *1 tablespoon finely chopped walnuts*
>
> *freshly ground pepper to taste*

1. Combine and process all ingredients in a food processor or blender. Use as described above.

Variations

For Basil-Walnut Cream, combine in a food processor or blender until smooth equal amounts of Pesto and nonfat cream cheese, nonfat sour cream, or yogurt cheese (page 305).

For a delicious dip for asparagus or Sweet 100s (or other excellent cherry tomatoes), add ½ cup nonfat ricotta, a couple cloves of roasted garlic, and a squirt of lemon juice to Pesto recipe.

LEMON BUTTER SAUCE

When you've eaten all the dry green beans you can, try this. Simple and delicious.

1 tablespoon butter

2 to 3 tablespoons freshly squeezed lemon juice

½ teaspoon salt

freshly ground pepper to taste

1 clove garlic or 1 clove roasted garlic (see page 305), minced

1 teaspoon minced fresh parsley

½ teaspoon minced shallot or scallion

1. Combine all ingredients in a small skillet or saucepan and heat until butter melts. Pour over cooked, drained vegetables.

Yield: 4 servings

Calories per tablespoon: 30

Protein per tablespoon: trace

Fat per tablespoon: 3 g

Saturated fat per tablespoon: 2 g

Cholesterol per tablespoon: 8 mg

Carbohydrates per tablespoon: 1 g

Sodium per tablespoon: 297 mg

Fiber per tablespoon: trace

Nutrabyte

Good fats:

* canola
* olive
* sunflower
* soybean
* corn

TOMATO SAUCE

Tomato-based sauces are used extensively in *The New Gourmet Light* cooking, for they score high on flavor and low in calorie tally. Although many will opt to purchase tomato sauce to make the sauce recipes called for in this book, here is a homemade version for those with gardens and/or the inclination to prepare their own.

Yield: approximately 3 cups

Calories per tablespoon: 6

Protein per tablespoon: trace

Fat per tablespoon: trace

Saturated fat per tablespoon: trace

Cholesterol per tablespoon: trace

Carbohydrates per tablespoon: 1 g

Sodium per tablespoon: 110 mg

Fiber per tablespoon: trace

2 pounds tomatoes, roughly chopped, or 44 ounces canned tomatoes (2
*   large cans)*

1 small onion, chopped

1 clove garlic, minced

1 tablespoon tomato paste

2 cups chicken stock (1 cup if using canned tomatoes)

4 leaves fresh basil, snipped, or 1 teaspoon dried basil

⅔ teaspoon sugar

½ teaspoon salt if using fresh tomatoes (omit if using canned)

1. Combine all ingredients in a medium-size saucepan and boil, uncovered, until reduced by half.

2. Puree the mixture in a food processor or blender and, if desired, strain to remove the seeds and skins.

Discolored Sauces

Although aluminum is one of the fastest conductors of heat, an unlined aluminum pot may discolor a sauce if there is acid present, such as tomato, wine, vinegar, or lemon juice. The discoloration is caused by a reaction of the acid with the pot. Unlined aluminum pans become stained when washed with a high-alkali cleanser or used for cooking high-alkali foods such as potatoes. The acid in the sauce removes some of that stain, transferring it to the sauce, causing a grayish tint that is unappetizing but, fortunately, not a health hazard.

BLACKENED TOMATO SALSA

The simple process of blackening the plum tomatoes and the fresh chili lends a rich, smoky flavor to the salsa, which will keep up to 2 weeks chilled. Serve it with simple grilled chicken breasts or grilled fish. Use it to enhance green beans, as a dip for raw vegetables and no-oil taco chips, or to flavor an egg white omelet. The recipe-ready tomatoes called for are available at most major markets in the canned tomato section. Be sure to select those that are not processed with oil.

Yield: 3½ cups
Calories per tablespoon: 5
Protein per tablespoon: trace
Fat per tablespoon: trace
Saturated fat per tablespoon: trace
Cholesterol per tablespoon: none
Carbohydrates per tablespoon: 1 g
Sodium per tablespoon: 43 mg
Fiber per tablespoon: trace

4 plum tomatoes
1 fresh jalapeño pepper
1 14½-ounce can recipe-ready tomatoes
1 cup diced red onion
2 cloves garlic
2 tablespoons minced fresh parsley
⅓ cup minced fresh cilantro, stemmed
1 teaspoon dried oregano
1 teaspoon salt
minced parsley or cilantro for garnish (optional)

1. Place the plum tomatoes and jalapeño in a small skillet over high heat. Add no oil or liquid. Shake the skillet from time to time until tomato and jalapeño skins are blistered and blackened, about 12 to 15 minutes. Remove from skillet and cool.

2. When cool enough to handle, quarter the tomatoes (no need to discard the skin) and place in the bowl of a food processor. Wearing rubber gloves, hold the jalapeños under running cool water and peel and discard the blackened skin. Split in half and discard seeds and stem. Add flesh to food processor.

3. Process a few seconds to chop tomatoes. Add all remaining ingredients. Salsa will keep in the refrigerator up to 2 weeks.

ROASTED GARLIC

Roasted garlic imparts a smooth, mild, but rich flavor. Substitute about 2 cloves of roasted garlic for a single raw clove almost anytime. The roasted garlic can be refrigerated in the foil used to cook it in, or you can take the time to squeeze the heads into a small glass jar, mashing them to a paste worth its weight in gold. Spritz the top with olive oil. Store foil-wrapped roasted garlic in the fridge for about 3 weeks; it's good longer but might dry out. I cook about 3 heads at a time, because that's what I'll use in 3 weeks' time. Adjust amounts to meet your needs.

Yield: 12 servings
Calories per ¼ head: 16
Protein per serving: 1 g
Fat per serving: trace
Saturated fat per serving: trace
Cholesterol per serving: none
Carbohydrates per serving: 4 g
Sodium per serving: 4 mg
Fiber per serving: trace

3 heads garlic, unpeeled, a thin slice cut off from the pointy end

1. Preheat oven to 350 degrees. Hold the garlic under a running faucet about 15 seconds to wet. Place in a foil-lined baking dish. Add about 1 tablespoon of water per head, with the foil cupped around the garlic. Spritz with olive oil, if desired. Wrap in foil tightly and roast 1 to 1¼ hours.

YOGURT CHEESE

Recipes for yogurt cheese have appeared in several books over these last few fat-restricted years. You'll find it a useful and remarkably easy basic to prepare. Simply turn a quart container of nonfat plain yogurt into a double thickness of cheesecloth. Gather the cloth into a ball and suspend, tied to the faucet, over the kitchen sink. Drain overnight. Refrigerate the resulting cheese (about 1¾ cups) for up to 5 days. The cheese may be frozen; although the texture will be grainy, it will be fine when cooked. Stir spoonfuls of the cheese into dips or sauces that need thickening and/or added pizzazz.

Yield: 1¾ cups
Calories per ¼ cup serving: 56
Protein per ¼ cup serving: 3 g
Fat per ¼ cup serving: trace
Saturated fat per ¼ cup serving: trace
Cholesterol per ¼ cup serving: 2 mg
Carbohydrates per ¼ cup serving: 6 g
Sodium per ¼ cup serving: 17 mg
Fiber per ¼ cup serving: none

Shopping Sources

Oils

Flavored oils, such as Lemon and Smoke: The California Oil Corp.: (508) 745–7840; Web site: http://www.olive-oil.com.

Olive Oil Sprayer

Olive oil sprayer: A stainless steel canister to be half-filled with your best-quality oil, flavored or plain. Pump the can to pressurize and spray without chemicals. Widely available in home stores, cooking shops, and culinary catalogs and by mail order. Culinary Parts Unlimited: (800) 543–7549.

Broths and Stocks and Reduction Bases

The Better than Bouillon Company: Jars of pastelike broth base that keep indefinitely. Reconstitute in water, allowing the cooking to intensify the flavor. Comes in eight flavors: chicken, beef, vegetable, ham, mushroom, chili, clam, and lobster. The Better than Bouillon Company: (800) 429–3663.

More Than Gourmet: This company sells a wide range of reductions of meat, chicken, and vegetables stocks. This book makes use of their **Demi-Glace Gold**. Stir tiny bits into soups and sauces for a rich, fat-free flavor. Keeps indefinitely. Available from several sources or directly from the manufacturer. More than Gourmet: (800) 860–9385: e-mail: demi-glace@worldnet.att.net.

Fat Replacer

Oatrim: A fat replacer that resembles very fine Cream of Wheat (see Glossary). Bob's Red Mill, Milwaukie, Oregon: (503) 654–3215.

Asian Ingredients

Rice paper rounds, all Asian ingredients, and all manner of culinary exotica, including Demi-Glace Gold. Adriana's Caravan: (800) 316–0820; e-mail: Adricara@aol.com.

Seeds and Sprouters

Broccoli sprouts seeds and sprouter (see Nutrabyte, page 107): Sheperd's Garden Seeds (860) 482–3638; Park Seed Co. (800) 845–3369; Johnny's Selected Seeds (207) 437–4301.

GLOSSARY

Because *The New Gourmet Light* borrows many flavors and ingredients from other cultures, some may be unknown. See Shopping Sources (page 306) for mail-order information.

arugula A pungent green, eaten raw and used in salads. The younger leaves are far better than the overgrown large leaves, which can be bitter.

cèpes A dried mushroom, similar to the Italian porcini, earthy. Expensive, but a few go a long way. Consider buying in bulk if you use them often. Available at specialty food shops, at megasupermarkets, and by mail order.

chèvre Goat cheese, sold flavored or plain. Among the lower-fat cheeses.

chili paste Available in the Asian section of many markets. Spicy, hot, sometimes sold with garlic. Keeps forever.

cilantro Leaves of coriander used in Mexican, Thai, and Asian recipes. People seem to polarize around cilantro; simply omit if you hate it. I like it so much that I use it like watercress or arugula in salads. Coriander seed has a similar flavor. Cilantro in a jar has little flavor after opening. Like coffee beans, it's terrific when just opened but fades quickly.

couscous An "instant" grain, widely available.

deglaze To add a small amount of liquid, usually wine or liquor, to a hot pan after removing whatever was sautéed. Stir to dislodge bits on the pan's bottom. Often can be accomplished with no added heat. Finished when a tablespoon or so of liquid remains.

fermented black beans A salty soybean sold in jars. Soak 1 hour or overnight before using. Available by mail order.

fish sauce A little lighter than soy sauce, salty, made with anchovies. Use as a seasoning as you would soy sauce. Widely available in stores or by mail order.

gremolata Mix of lemon zest, garlic, and parsley. Wonderful on meats, grains, and pastas. Experiment with other citrus zests and herbs. Keeps in the refrigerator for a few days.

hoisin sauce A Japanese barbecue-type sauce. Very sweet; thick. Keeps forever and is widely available.

hot oil A spicy oil; use a very few drops only. Widely available in the Asian section of markets.

instant-reading meat thermometer You gotta have one. Indispensable for checking the internal temperatures of meat and poultry (the temperature varies with where the thermometer is poked).

jicama A round, hard vegetable used in Mexican cooking. Faintly sweet; very moist. Good in salads, raw.

julienne To slice in thin, matchlike strips. Time-consuming by hand but quick with appropriate food processor disk.

lemongrass Sold fresh, in a jar, and dried. Fresh is by far the best. Strip the outer tough leaves and dice the stalk. A wonderful perfume and light lemony flavor.

mirin A sweet Asian wine. Excellent to keep on hand. Many uses in sauces and salad dressings. Keeps forever and is widely available.

miso A soybean product, pastelike and salty. Lends a wonderful flavor and body to broths, sauces, and salad dressings. Available in specialty food stores or by mail order. Keeps forever. Comes in different colors: white and red. The white is a good all-purpose one to buy.

Oatrim A fat replacer, available as of this writing by mail order (see Shopping Sources, page 306). Claims to reduce cholesterol as well as reduce fat calories.

porcini A dried Italian mushroom. See **cèpes**. Available at specialty food shops, at megasupermarkets, and by mail order.

rice noodles and rice sticks An Asian, ultrathin noodle. Available in specialty food stores and by mail order.

rice roll wrappers, spring roll skins, or rice paper rounds Ultrathin, translucent wrappers, low-calorie and easy to use. Available by mail order.

scrod A mild-flavored white fish indigenous to Northeastern waters.

sesame oil Wonderful all-purpose condiment oil made from toasted sesame seeds, not to be confused with plain sesame oil. Buy in a small quantity, as you use only a little and it goes bad. Keep refrigerated. Use just before serving food, as heat diminishes the flavor. Referred to here as Asian sesame oil.

shiitake mushrooms Slightly bitter flavor; always snap off stems. Widely available.

tamarind Used in Thai and some Chinese cooking. Sweet, citrus flavor. If you purchase a block soak until a paste forms and discard the residue. Tamarind is added to curries and marinades. Or purchase tamarind concentrate (available by mail order) and skip the soaking process. Available in specialty food stores.

tomatillos Look like unripe cherry tomatoes with a papery wrapping; remove the wrapping. Used in green sauces in Mexican cooking.

wasabi powder Not a true wasabi, which is prohibitively expensive, but an adequate powder, pungent and sharp. Traditionally used to form a paste served with sushi. Used here in a few sauces for bite.

INDEX